The Ark the Ephod and the "Tent of Meeting"

The Ark the Ephod and the "Tent of Meeting"

By JULIAN MORGENSTERN

WIPF & STOCK · Eugene, Oregon

Wipf and Stock Publishers
199 W 8th Ave, Suite 3
Eugene, OR 97401

The Ark the Ephod and the "Tent of Meeting"
By Morgenstern, Julian
Softcover ISBN-13: 978-1-7252-9310-6
Hardcover ISBN-13: 978-1-7252-9309-0
eBook ISBN-13: 978-1-7252-9311-3
Publication date 11/13/2020
Previously published by The Hebrew Union College Press, 1945

This edition is a scanned facsimile of the original edition published in 1945.

TO

BILLY AND JUNI

IN THE HOPE THAT SOME DAY
EACH OF THEM MAY READ THIS BOOK AND THAT
IT MAY NOT ONLY SPEAK TO THEM OF
THEIR GRANDPARENTS' LOVE FOR AND FAITH IN THEM,
BUT MAY ALSO STIMULATE THEM TO LIVE
THOUGHTFULLY, USEFULLY AND CREATIVELY

Preface

THIS STUDY appeared originally in the *Hebrew Union College Annual.* Its length forbade its being printed as a unit in one volume. Accordingly it was published in two successive volumes, XVII (1942–1943) and XVIII (1944). Inasmuch as it deals with and endeavors to solve an important problem of the history of the religion of Israel in its earliest period, and should therefore have considerable interest for biblical scholars, it was felt that it would become more accessible and usable if republished as a unit in book form. Therefore this volume.

In order to facilitate reference to either of the two printed forms of the study the pagination in the two volumes of the *Annual* is recorded upon the inner margin of each page of the book. It should be understood that the page references in the notes are necessarily to this inner margin pagination.

J. M.

Table of Contents

I.	Introduction	1
II.	The *'Oṭfe*	5
III.	The *Maḥmal*	41
IV.	The *Ḳubbe*	55
V.	Historical Forerunners of the *Ḳubbe*	71
VI.	The Ark	77
VII.	The Ephod	115
VIII.	The "Tent of Meeting"	131
IX.	Historical Survey	161

THE ARK THE EPHOD AND THE "TENT OF MEETING"*

i. Introduction

IN a study published in 1928[1] I discussed in considerable detail the important question of the origin and history of the so-called "ark of the covenant." Among other matters I endeavored to show that the ark had certain very positive relations to the *maḥmal*, the sacred, tent-like structure which, empty and borne upon the back of the sacred camel, is carried in the *ḥaǧ*, or annual

*For convenience previous publications of the author, which are cited frequently in this work, are here listed:

"Two Ancient Israelite Agricultural Festivals," *JQR* (n. s.), VIII (1917), 31–54.

"The Tent of Meeting," *JAOS*, XXXVIII (1918), 125–139.

"Kedesh-Naphtali and Ta'anach," *JQR* (n. s.), IX (1919), 359–369.

"The Sources of the Creation Story — Genesis 1.1–2.4," *AJSL*, XXXVI (1920), 169–212.

"The Three Calendars of Ancient Israel," *HUCA*, I (1924), 13–78.

"The Oldest Document of the Hexateuch," *HUCA*, IV (1927), 1–138.

"The Book of the Covenant, I," *HUCA*, V (1928), 1–151.

"*Beena* Marriage (Matriarchat) in Ancient Israel and Its Historical Implications," *ZAW*, (n. F.), VI (1929), 91–110.

"Supplementary Studies in the Calendars of Ancient Israel," *HUCA*, X (1935), 1–148.

"Amos Studies, I," *HUCA*, XI (1936), 19–140.

"A Chapter in the History of the High-Priesthood," *AJSL*, LV (1938), 1–24, 183–197, 360–377.

"Amos Studies, III; The Historical Antecedents of Amos," *HUCA*, XV (1940), 59–304.

"Psalm 48," *HUCA*, XVI (1941), 1–95.

[1] "The Book of the Covenant, I."

pilgrimage of the Moslem faithful to Meccah, and likewise to [154] the *'oṭfe*, the somewhat similar, tent-like structure which serves as the palladium of a number of Bedouin tribes, and particularly of the truer and more primitive camel-Bedouin tribes, such as the Ruwala. The points of similarity and of evident relationship between the ark, on the one hand, and the *maḥmal* and *'oṭfe*, on the other hand, are striking and significant.

I discussed various functions which these three sacred objects served, such as going into battle in company with the tribe and assuring it of victory over its enemies, selecting the road which the tribe or the pilgrim caravan must travel through the desert, that it might reach its goal safely, imparting oracular decisions, and the like, and then drew the general conclusion that all three sacred objects must have been regarded originally as the abode or container of the tribal deity or deities. From this, and coupling this evidence and conclusion with the further tradition of the two tablets of the Decalogue stored in the ark, I drew a second inference, viz., that these two tablets of the Decalogue[2] represent a development in tradition growing out of the actual, historical fact that in the ark there were originally two sacred stones, two betyls, in which the deity or deities were thought to dwell.

Furthermore, I concluded that the ark, with its two sacred stones, must have been originally the tribal cult-object and palladium of Ephraim; then it must have come to be regarded as the inter-tribal palladium of that close federation of northern tribes of Israel which had united their forces for joint resistance to the common Canaanite enemy at the decisive Battle of Ta'anach,[3] and which likewise offered joint resistance to the later and more dangerous common enemy, the Philistines, at the even more decisive but quite futile second Battle of Eben Haezer;[4] from there, after an interval of approximately three quarters of a century, during which it was stationed, apparently half-forgotten, at Kiryat Yearim, the ark was brought by David to Jerusalem and there deposited in his tent-sanctuary, the new national

[2] "Amos Studies, III," 121 f.

[3] Cf. Jud. 5 and "Kedesh-Naphtali and Ta'anach."

[4] I Sam. 4–6.

[155] shrine. This event marked the end of the first, the primitive, period in the history of the ark.

I then endeavored to trace the history of the ark and of the various traditions concerning it, recorded in the Bible, in the second period of its existence, the period extending from its installation in the national sanctuary at Jerusalem until the Deuteronomic Reformation in 621 B.C., or perhaps even until the destruction of the Temple at Jerusalem by the Babylonians in 586 B.C. I sought to show in particular that it was during this period, and beginning quite early therein, under the influence of evolving national religion and of prophetic doctrine, with its uncompromising antagonism to idols and related cult-objects, that the two former sacred stones or betyls of the ark came rather speedily to be reinterpreted as two stones still sacred, but sacred now only because of a newly arisen tradition, viz., that upon them were written the ten "words" of divine revelation.[5] During this entire period the ark was manifestly regarded primarily as the container of the two stone tablets of the Decalogue.

Thereupon I endeavored to determine the history of the ark in the third period of its existence, in post-exilic times. The conclusion was reached that actually there was no ark at all in the post-exilic Temple and that the authors of the Priestly Code had only a vague tradition of the ark and of its actual contents and nature. Therefore they could coin the fiction of an ark in the tabernacle in the wilderness, and so impliedly in the post-exilic Temple, which was only secondarily, and in the most uncertain and obscure way imaginable, the container of the two tablets of the Decalogue, or rather of the "tablets of testimony," as the the P authors termed them; primarily the ark was the throne upon which Yahweh sat as divine King in majestic solitude in the holy and holies, and into whose august presence no mortal might enter except the high-priest, and even that only once in the year, upon the annual New-Year's Day-Day of Atonement, and as the culminating rite in the peculiar ceremonies of this great day. Influenced chiefly by this principle of the transcendence and the consequent inaccessibility by mortal beings to this

[5] Cf. also "Amos Studies, III," 118 ff.

august deity and its obvious relationship to the inaccessibilty by ordinary mortals to the presence of the Persian king, recorded at least in persistent tradition, I drew the inference that this picture of Yahweh enthroned upon the ark and the attendant reinterpretation of the ark, no longer primarily as a container of the two sacred stones, but now primarily as the throne of Yahweh, were evolved under Persian cultural influence, so potent in Judaism in the post-exilic period.[6] The entire tradition of the ark in the post-exilic period and in the second Temple, as well as in the tabernacle in the wilderness of the Priestly Code, is theoretical and doctrinal, and has little foundation in historic reality. [156]

Shortly after the appearance of the article my attention was called by Professor Albright to a very important study by Père Lammens entitled "Le culte des bétyles et les processions religieuses chez les arabes préislamites,"[7] the significance of very much of the material contained in which for the subject which I had under consideration was unmistakable. With the help of this new material, drawn entirely from the pre-islamic period of Arabic culture and religious practice, the close relationship, and in fact the relative identity, of which with much of the culture and religious belief and institutions of the pre-Canaanite, desert, nomadic or semi-nomadic Israelite tribes, and also with

[6] Subsequently, in "Amos Studies, III," I established that the real source of this concept was a persistent and lively reminiscence of a golden image of Yahweh in human form, seated upon a throne and with feet resting upon a footstool, which stood in the *d^ebir*, or inner shrine, of the Temple from its erection by Solomon until the reformation of Asa in 899 B.C. It was indubitably the figure of the august and inaccessible, enthroned Persian "king of kings" which revived this reminiscence of the ancient enthroned Yahweh and gave form and content to the picture of Yahweh, enthroned upon, or above, the ark, in the august and, to mortals, inaccessible solitude of the "holy of holies" of the tabernacle in the wilderness of the Priestly code.

[7] First published in the *Bulletin de l'Institut français d'archéologie oriental,* XVII (1919) and then reprinted in the volume of studies by the same author, *L'Arabie occidentale avant l'Hégire,* (1928), 101–179. The importance of this authoritative and well-documented study for the history of Semitic religions cannot be overemphasized. The article as first published was quite inaccessible to me; the reprint appeared only in the same year in which my own study was published.

[157] much of the culture and religious belief and institutions of the present-day Bedouins, especially of the true, nomadic, camel-Bedouins, are beyond question, it has become possible not only to establish with complete certainty the large majority of the conclusions to which I had come with regard to the origin and history of the ark, but also to carry these conclusions further, and, as the result thereof, to solve other related and equally significant problems, those connected with the so-called "tent of meeting," and also with the much discussed and still quite perplexing ephod; and with this to get a better knowledge of the most primitive concept of Yahweh and of the nature and manner of His earliest worship.

Moreover, since the publication of my study in 1928 quite a mass of material bearing upon the *'oṭfe* has appeared, or at least has become known to me, material which, while perhaps not greatly expanding our knowledge of this strange object, none the less confirms most, if not all, of the conclusions with regard to it there reached and sets forth their significance for our particular study so much more clearly and convincingly, that it is eminently worth while to consider anew the question of the *'oṭfe*, its nature and origin, and its relation, on the one hand, to the *ḳubbe* of the pre-islamic Arabs and, on the other hand, to the ark of ancient Israel. In so doing some repetition of material presented in my original article is almost unavoidable.

ii. The *'Oṭfe*

The starting-point in the study of the *'oṭfe* is the earliest account of this object given by Musil.[8] "The Ruwala have a structure made out of thin wooden boards, decorated with ostrich feathers, which is fastened upon the baggage-saddle of a camel. It is called *abu ẓhûr al-markab*. Only the Ruwala possess this. No other tribe has anything like it. As they believe, the *abu ẓhûr* comes from Ruweil (the eponymous ancestor of the Ruwala) and is called

[8] *Die Kultur*, XI (1910), 8 f.; quoted from Hartmann, "Zelt und Lade," *ZAW*, 37 (1917–1918), 220 f.

abu ẓhûr (*pater aeterni saeculi*) because it is passed on from generation to generation through the ages. *Abu ẓhûr* is the visible focus . . . . of all the tribes of the *zana*-Moslems. Whoever has it in his possession is prince of all these tribes, and they are obligated to follow him in battle. Every year a white camel is sacrificed before it, with the words, 'This is thy sacrifice, O Abu Ẓhûr!,' and its blood is sprinkled upon the corner posts of the structure. In this *abu ẓhûr* Allah takes pleasure in abiding and imparts directions to the tribes through external signs. Ofttimes the ostrich-feathers are supposed to tremble, although there may be no wind. Ofttimes the structure is believed to bow itself unceasingly to the right. This signifies *ḳudrat min allâh*, 'the power of God.' . . . . If the camel bearing the *abu ẓhûr* begins to move, the entire tribe follows it; where the *abu ẓhûr* lets itself down, there the camp is set up. Whenever the Ruwala are threatened by a powerful enemy and fear defeat (but only then), they bring the *abu ẓhûr*, and with it at their head they attack the enemy." [158]

Upon this description of the *'oṭfe* I commented as follows: The points of similarity and manifest relationship between this strange object and the various Biblical traditions about the ark are almost startling. It too has the power of selecting the road it wishes to take, by driving the camel which bears it irresistibly onwards. It too leads its people through the desert and determines their nightly camping-places by causing the camel bearing it to kneel, implying thereby that there it desires to stop and remain for the night. It too imparts oracles and, in the interest of its tribe, declares future events. It too goes into battle with its people, especially decisive battle, when the very existence of the people is threatened, and gives them victory over their enemies . . . . Most significant of all these points of contact with the ark, Allah is thought to reside in the *abu ẓhûr*, if not permanently, then upon occasions when the tribe has need of him and his presence with them; . . . . and every year a sacrifice . . . . is offered to the *abu ẓhûr*, or to the deity associated with it, and the blood thereof is sprinkled upon the corner-posts of the peculiar object, with the significant words, "This is thy sacrifice, O Abu Ẓhûr."

159] This parallelism becomes still more significant when we realize that Musil did not at the moment grasp the full significance of this peculiar object and its role in the life of the tribe, and particularly in its warfare, having been misled somewhat by the popular but incorrect interpretation of the name *abu ẓhûr*. This was more clearly recognized by Hartmann[9] and Torczyner.[10] The latter scholar quotes a verse, recorded by Curtiss,[11] communicated to him by a Ruwala-tribesman,

> Abu ed-Duhûr will come unfailingly
> To help those who put on their equipment for war;
> And through him their horses become fear-inspiring.

As Curtiss has pointed out, *abu ẓhûr*, according to these verses, plays exactly the role of a tribal deity, and particularly a deity who gives his tribesmen victory in war. Not improbably *abu ẓhûr* was originally the actual name of the tribal deity of the Ruwala, which has, however, under the influence of official Islam, superficial though it be with the Bedouin tribesmen, been half forgotten with the passage of time, and lingers on chiefly, if not entirely, in its association with this peculiar tribal cult- or war-object.

In one other respect Musil's description of this object, based upon the information then given to him, was somewhat inexact, in that it was claimed that this was the only object of its kind, and that no other people possessed anything like it. The full name of this object was communicated to Musil as *abu ẓhûr al-markab*. The consideration given by him to the very important first half of the name has tended to detract somewhat from the consideration which the second half likewise merits.

Markab connotes in Arabic a vehicle of any kind used for transportation, whether wagon, boat or beast of burden. Burckhardt[12] is our authority for the fact that the Bedouin tribes of

[9] *Op. cit.*

[10] "Die Bundeslade und die Anfänge der Religion Israels," *Festschrift zum 50-jährigen Bestehen der Hochschule für die Wissenschaft des Judentums*, 265.

[11] *Ursemitische Religion im Volksleben des heutigen Orients*, XV; cf. also "The Book of the Covenant, I," note 114.

[12] *Notes on the Bedouins and Wahábys*, 82 f.

the North Arabian desert actually possess several such objects, [160]
or at least did so a century ago. He says, "Some of the Aeneze chiefs use, in time of war, what may perhaps be styled the 'battle banner'; for it is never displayed but in decisive and important actions, where the fall or the loss of it is regarded as a signal of defeat. The standard is of two sorts, one called *merkeb* (مركب or the 'ship'), consisting in two stands of wood, about six or seven feet high . . . . These are placed one opposite to the other on a camel's back, so that above there is not more than a span's distance between them; but below they are sufficiently separated for a person to sit in the midst on a saddle, and guide the camel: the upper part of this standard is covered with black ostrich feathers.

"The other sort of banner is called *'oṭfe* (عطفة); this consists of two side pieces of board, of an oblong square form, about five feet high, ornamented like the other with ostrich feathers. Such is now used by the *Teyar*, the chief of *Would Aly* . . . . *En Ibsmeyr* and *Ibn Fadhel* have each a *merkeb* . . . . All the horsemen assemble around it; and the principal efforts of both parties are directed against the respective *merkeb* or *'oṭfe* of the enemy. A captured banner is borne in triumph to the tent of the victorious sheikh."

Likewise Wetzstein's description of the *'oṭfe*[13] is of sufficient importance for this study to warrant its repetition. "Should it develop that they become convinced that victory can not be won except by extreme measures, they have still in the 'Oṭfa a final, and in fact a very drastic means of inflaming the battle-spirit. The 'Oṭfa is a lattice-work object, made of strong wood, four-cornered, of greater length than width, and almost oval in shape, which is fastened upon the back of a strong, decorated camel. The older the 'Oṭfa is, the more it possesses the qualifications for serving as the palladium of its people; that of the Ruwala . . . . is said to be hundreds of years old. Before the beginning of the battle an especially handsome and reputable woman or maiden, if possible the one of highest rank within the tribe, adorned as a bride, unveiled, and, what has a peculiarly disturbing effect upon

[13] *Verhandlungen der Berliner Gesellschaft für Anthropologie,* X (1878), 389; quoted from Hartmann, "Zelt und Lade," 219 f.

[161] the Arabs, with hair flying loose and neck laid bare, mounts the 'Oṭfa, rides in front of the first battle-line and halts before the elite of the army, the youth of the tribe, in order to direct toward them the Intichâ, i. e., the solemn charge either to win the victory or to die . . . . Thereupon the 'Oṭfa advances upon the enemy and the battle begins. The greatest slaughter naturally takes place in the neighborhood of the 'Oṭfa, towards the capture and defense of which the main efforts of both sides are directed. During the combat the occupant of the 'Oṭfa, standing erect and turning now here, now there, spurs her fellow-tribesmen on with glance and gesture, with loud challenge and calling individual warriors by name, with praise and blame and the trilling sounds of the Zaġrûta (the customary cries of joy of the attendants of the bride at weddings). Not infrequently the entire body of male youth has fallen beside the 'Oṭfa. Likewise it is often captured, a fact which is remembered as a lasting humiliation for many generations. However, the beautiful woman, captured with the 'Oṭfa, is always treated honorably and is released for a ransom, but one of very great amount. The 'Otfa remains as the trophy of the victor, if it is not recaptured by an attack upon the enemy's camp."

Particularly significant for our study in this account of Wetzstein is the fact that this object, which Musil heard designated by the descriptive title *al-markab*, Wetzstein must have heard called *'oṭfe*. This indicates that the two names are apparently used interchangeably, without the distinction between them which Burckhardt recorded.

No less significant, however, is the procedure, here encountered for the first time, but which we will meet again and again, though almost always in slightly varying form, of the woman in the *'oṭfe* when it goes into battle, into the very thickest of the melee, encouraging by word and gesture the warriors to fight on courageously, even to death. Here she is either a woman or a maiden of the very highest rank within the tribe, especially handsome and reputable, adorned as a bride, but unveiled, with hair flying loose and neck or, as we will see is really the case, with bosom, laid bare, manifestly a form of dress which ordinarily would be looked upon decidedly askance.

I shall not repeat here the description of the *'oṭfe* given by Lady Anne Blunt,[14] but merely the significant inferences which I have drawn from it, first the fact that she describes the *'oṭfe* simply as "a gigantic camel-howdah," and second that, when the Ruwala are about to migrate, the *'oṭfe* is the very last object which is loaded upon camel-back. Apparently this act serves as the signal for the tribe to set out upon its journey. [162]

The account of the *'oṭfe* given by Rogers,[15] however, merits repetition here. "The sheikhs of the 'Anazy tribes say that in ancient times every tribe had its 'Atfah, which was regarded as the repository of its valour and honour, and was only made use of on occasions of unusually serious importance. When a tribe went to war with a powerful opponent, the 'Atfah was placed on a strong and handsome camel, and was gaily and gorgeously decorated with ostrich-feathers, carpets, and embroidery work, and was surrounded by a band of warriors selected from among the bravest men of the tribe. In some tribes it was customary for a virgin, the daughter of one of the sheikhs, to take her seat under the canopy, and, by her singing, to incite the men to acts of bravery. Every effort was made and every precaution taken to prevent its falling into the hands of the enemy; and, if the men engaged in fighting in another part of the field, or told off for the protection of the flocks or of the tents, perceived that the 'Atfah was in danger, they would leave their occupation, abandoning everything to rally round the mysterious emblem for its protection; for, if lost, the tribe was disgraced, and a new 'Atfah could not be made until after a victory over the enemy who had possessed himself of the original and the recovery of a remnant — be it ever so small a portion — of the old wooden framework. The captured 'Atfah could not be used by the victorious tribe, and it was therefore generally destroyed after capture. This custom accounts for the fact that of all the numerous tribes in the Syrian desert only two now possess an 'Atfah."

Upon this description of the *'oṭfe* I commented as follows: This account is of extreme importance. In the first place it gives

[14] *The Bedouins of the Euphrates*, 351.

[15] In *The Academy* of March 31, 1883, 221 f., writing from Cairo.

[163] further confirmation to the conclusion that the customary, though by no means invariable, occupant of the *'oṭfe* was a maiden. And in the second place it too records that at one time the institution of the *'oṭfe* was quite common among Bedouin tribes . . . . A new *'oṭfe* could not be made indiscriminately to replace an old one, which had been captured or destroyed in battle. The capture of an *'oṭfe* was regarded as such a supreme calamity that the tribe did not shrink from the most extreme efforts and sacrifices to protect it. The tribe whose *'oṭfe* had been captured in battle was regarded as, and felt itself, disgraced and humiliated. Not until it had regained its old *'oṭfe* through victory in battle, could it hold its head high once more. A new *'oṭfe* could be made only with at least a remnant of the old *'oṭfe* as its nucleus. A captured *'oṭfe* could not be used by its captors. Therefore, in order to forestall all possibility of its former tribe regaining it, or at least a portion of it, from which a new *'oṭfe* might be made, symbolic of the restored power of the now conquered tribe, a captured *'oṭfe* was usually destroyed. The inevitable result of such a practice must have been the gradual disappearance of the *'oṭfe* from among the Bedouin tribes . . . .

But the question arises here; Why, if the old *'oṭfe* were captured, could not a new one be made to replace it, unless at least a fragment of the old *'oṭfe* was used as the nucleus for it? An answer altogether natural and of deep significance suggests itself. We have seen that, according to Musil's direct account, Allah was believed to reside in the *'oṭfe,* if not permanently, at least occasionally. Moreover, other important evidence links this particular *'oṭfe* of the Ruwala with Abu Ẓhûr, apparently the ancient, half-forgotten deity of this tribe. It is altogether probable that every *'oṭfe* had similar associations, that it was regarded, in earlier and more primitive stages of its development, as the symbol, or even as the actual container, of the tribal deity. In such case its capture in battle would mean nothing other than this deity's capture by his enemies. It would imply, on the one hand, his own weakness and impotence in comparison with the enemy tribe and its deity; and, on the other hand, it would imply that his old tribe was now without divine protection, was therefore in truth divinely forsaken, weak and humiliated. We can

well understand, on the basis of this hypothesis, why a tribe [164]
would spare no effort and sacrifice to prevent the capture of its *'oṭfe*, and would even leave its cattle and its tents, of course with the women and children in them, unguarded and at the mercy of the enemy, in order to protect its *'oṭfe* against capture.

Above all, on the basis of this assumption of an original association of *'oṭfe* and tribal deity, we can understand why a new *'oṭfe* could be made only with a portion, no matter how small, of the old one serving as a nucleus. For the old *'oṭfe* must have been charged in its every part with the spirit or indwelling of a deity, in other words, with *mana*. And this *mana* could be communicated to the new *'oṭfe* only by contact with the old one, and particularly if a portion of the old *'oṭfe*, charged with this divine essence, were built into the new one. From this nucleus this *mana* spread, until it completely permeated the new *'oṭfe* and endowed it with a divinity and power equal to, and in fact identical with, that of the old *'oṭfe*. Accordingly the complete destruction of an *'oṭfe* by its captors made it absolutely impossible for its old owners to replace it. It must have meant to them and to their neighbors that they were a tribe entirely without divine protection, that they were therefore weak and impotent, held in light esteem by the surrounding tribes, and themselves dispirited and humiliated. It goes almost without saying too, just as Rogers states, that a captured *'oṭfe* could not be used by its captors. For, on the one hand, it had been the tribal deity of their enemies, and therefore could not be expected to bestow its divine help and blessing upon its former foes; and, on the other hand, of what value would its help and blessing be to its captors, since in comparison with their own tribal deity it had proved of inferior strength and powerless to protect even itself from capture? To its captors it was of no avail whatever; but it might, despite its unquestionably divine nature, be destroyed by them with impunity. From such an impotent deity they had naught to fear.

There is no need to repeat here the accounts of the *'oṭfe* given by Leachman[16] and Seabrook,[17] except to note that the latter,

[16] "A Journey in North-Eastern Arabia," *Geographical Journal*, 37 (1911), 267.

[17] *Adventures in Arabia*, 85 ff.

[165] although not actually using the name, *'oṭfe*, records the fact that various tribes employed this object when they went into battle, and that he gives a detailed account of the *'oṭfe* of the Sirdieh, a small tribe dwelling east of the Djebel Druse, in which not one, but four, of the most beautiful, marriageable virgins of the tribe, dressed in crimson silks and adorned with all their jewels, occupied the *'oṭfe* during the course of the battle. However, inasmuch as Seabrooke had his information from a secondary source, there may well be some inaccuracy in his statement that four maidens instead of the customary one, occupied the *'oṭfe*, and this all the more so since his actual narrative tells of the conduct of only one maiden within the *'oṭfe*. The other three were probably maidens who, as we shall see, quite often attended upon the girl in the *'oṭfe*, but upon camels of their own. It is to be noted, however, that here too these were marriageable maidens, virgins, and of the best tribal families, and clad in their dearest finery, as if for their own marriage.

Thus far the material bearing upon the *'oṭfe* and its use contained in my first study of this interesting object and its related objects and institutions. However, since the publication of that study in 1928 I have gathered quite a bit of additional material bearing upon the *'oṭfe*, most of it corroborating fully and clarifying materially the information already gathered and adding quite a number of new details of much significance.

And first a record of the *'oṭfe* of the Ruwala by Oliphant,[18] made in 1881. "One of the most interesting tribes on the Syrian border is the Roala . . . . They alone still retain the famous war-cradle which all the tribes once possessed. It is a sort of car, called 'uttfa', composed of ostrich feathers; and before the tribe goes to war, the most lovely girl in it is selected, and placed, in the lightest possible attire, in the cradle, which is then put on the back of a camel. The silken string by which the camel is led is then placed in her hand, and the warriors of the tribe pass before her. Whoever she selects as the leader of the camel becomes the leader of the host, which she accompanies, and is a prominent figure in the battles. If, in the war which follows, the tribe is

[18] *The Land of Gilead*, 122 f.

beaten and the war-cradle captured, it is deprived forever after [166]
of the privilege of possessing one. The Roala are the only tribe who still retain this singular distinction; but one or two Arabs whom I afterward spoke to on this subject told me they were not likely ever to lose it, as they now never perform the ceremony, or risk the capture of the cradle in battle."

This account should not be pressed too strongly since Oliphant too had his information not at first hand. There is some minor confusion in his narrative, and some of the details which he gives do not agree completely with later and much more authentic information about this particular *ʿoṭfe*, some of which has already been considered and other of which is still to be presented. These facts, however, are to be noted in this description of this object, that Oliphant's source heard this particular object, which we know from Musil as *abu ẓuhûr* and *al markab*, called by what was obviously the more generic and inclusive term, *ʿoṭfe*; that it speaks of the maiden in the *ʿoṭfe* as being lightly clad, manifestly with reference to the fact that in the course of her functioning during the battle, as we shall later see more clearly, she lays bare her neck and breasts; and finally, that she selects from among the warriors who defile before her the one who is to lead in the battle. Actually, as we shall see, there is only a half-measure of truth in this statement; yet it must recall to us the role of Deborah at the Battle of Taʿanach, playing the role of the battle-maiden, as we have endeavored to show,[19] and selecting Barak as the actual leader in the battle.[20]

Of fuller detail and greater significance is the account of this same object given by Jaussen.[21] "Every tribe has its standard and its war-cry. The Eben Šaʿalān[22] have preserved the *merkab*, which is kept in the tent of the sheikh. . . . Furthermore, the Eben Šaʿalān employ the *merkab* in a triumphal march, in which a large portion of the tribe participates, or in war. In this latter case the *merkab*, brought forth from the tent of the sheikh, is

[19] *Op. cit.*, 112 f.

[20] Jud. 4.6 ff.; cf. 5.12.

[21] *Coutumes des Arabes au pays de Moab*, 173 f.

[22] Actually he means the Ruwala, of whom the Eben Šaʿalān are the ruling family.

[167] carefully decorated with ostrich plumes and all manner of shells; it is then placed upon a strong *ḏeloul* richly caparisoned. The sheikh himself leads forth his own daughter, adorned as a bride; her long hair falls in heavy tresses upon her shoulders; she has put on her most beautiful dress; many necklaces are suspended about her neck; on her arms silver bracelets gleam; about her head ostrich plumes seem a veritable aureole.

"Lightly she mounts the *merkab* and seats herself upon the triumphal throne. In her hand she takes the bridle so that she herself may guide the *ḏeloul* and in some manner direct the affair. All about her the braves of the tribe arrange themselves in order to serve her as escort, determined to die rather than abandon the *'oṭfah*, that is the *merkab* made ready and mounted for the battle. The battle begins; the efforts of the enemy concentrate about it (the *'oṭfe*); to capture it would constitute a complete victory and at the same time the forfeiture (of the *'oṭfe*) by the conquered tribe, which would lose permanently the right to employ a new one. But the defence is vigorous. Should the enemies succeed in pressing too near to the *'oṭfah*, its defenders with a stroke of the sword would hamstring the camel which carries it so that it would fall. Then, the combat having become desperate, the struggle goes on hand to hand under the eyes of the young heroine, who, standing at full length within the *merkab*, by her words, her cries and motions animates and stirs up the combatants.

"Every year a camel is sacrificed by the chief on behalf of the *merkab*, the various parts of which ought to be anointed with the blood of the victim. The sheikh speaks the following words; 'O Allah! here is the camel for the *merkab*; may Abou'ẓ-Ẓohor regard it with favor.' "

Jaussen too himself never actually saw this *merkab* but had all his information indirectly. But inasmuch as his informer was a member of the clan of Eben Ša'alān, and Jaussen himself an experienced and authoritative investigator of Bedouin life and institutions, his account of this object may be accepted without the slightest hesitation. Significant in it is first the fact that he designates it by both names *merkab* and *'oṭfe*, and that he likewise heard the name of Abu Ẓhûr associated with it; moreover, Abu Ẓhûr, as Jaussen heard it used in connection with the *'oṭfe*, was manifestly not the name of the object itself, but rather of the deity or divine presence thought to dwell in it or to be associated with it in some way. Annually a camel is sacrificed to Abu Ẓhûr on behalf of the *'oṭfe.* Jaussen too emphasizes the fact that the maiden within the *'oṭfe* is clothed and adorned as a bride. Finally, as we shall see in due time, his reference to the role which the *markab* or *'oṭfe* plays in triumphal marches or processions, in which the major portion of the tribe participates, is of great significance, while no less is the import of the statement that normally the *'oṭfe* was kept in the tent of the sheikh. [168]

Curtiss too speaks[23] of the *merkab*, "a canopy resting upon four uprights and adorned with ostrich feathers, placed upon the back of a camel, beneath which the daughter or sister of the emîr rides into battle, surrounded by at least five hundred chosen warriors. Should she be captured, the tribe could never bring another into battle." Actually Curtiss spent only two days among the Ruwala and obviously learned of the *merkab* only by hearsay and not at all by personal observation or actual experience. Otherwise he could not have described the *merkab* as being covered with a canopy, for, as will soon be established with absolute certainty, just this piece of equipment the *merkab* of the Ruwala, in contradistinction to the *'oṭfe*'s of other tribes, did not possess. Furthermore, Curtiss seems to have confused the *merkab* itself with the maiden in it, for, as has already been amply attested, it was the capture of the *merkab*, rather than of the maiden in it, which would have forbidden the tribe ever to substitute another for it.[24] Unquestionably Curtiss' confusion resulted from the fact that both the *merkab* and the maiden within it were called by the same name, *'oṭfe*, though whether he had himself heard this latter name applied to either the *merkab* or to the maiden, Curtiss gives no indication whatever. Elsewhere[25] he relates that "at the outbreak of a war the Ruwala offer a sacrifice to their ancestor, Abu

[23] *Ursemitische Religion im Volksleben des heutigen Orients*, 34 (not in the English original).

[24] Geyer ("Die arabischen Frauen in der Schlacht," *Mitteilungen der anthropologischen Gesellschaft in Wien*, XXXIX [1909], 148–155) follows Curtiss in this same confusion of terms and ideas.

[25] *Op. cit.*, XV f. (likewise not in the English original).

[169] ed-Duhûr, so that he might aid them in gaining the victory over their enemies. With the blood of the sacrifice they anoint the *merkab*, borne by a camel, in which the daughter or sister of the sheikh is carried into battle. She has clad herself magnificently, darkened her lashes with antimony, greased her hair and bared her bosom, so that, as the ideal of Arab femininity, she might incite the warriors to heroic deeds." Of major significance in this account is that it completely substantiates the statement of Jaussen and of Oliphant that when going into battle the *merkab* is inhabited by a maiden, the noblest of the entire tribe, magnificently clad and with bosom bared.

An account by Canaan[26] gives certain additional details of importance. "The custom of *el-'uṭfeh* still exists among some Bedouin tribes. In raids the noblest and most courageous girl of the tribe mounts a camel and takes a central position in the camp. The young men and warriors, all fully armed, pass and ask her to lead the raid. She remains motionless and silent until the most valiant group of the tribe arrives, which group she chooses as her protector (*ḥaiyâlet el-'uṭfeh*). The camel is allowed to rise and the girl rides on, stimulating her party by fiery songs and speeches. As soon as the place of battle is reached the camel sits on the ground; the rider upon its back continuing to excite her people. Should her division retreat, she reproaches them with cowardliness and blames them with scorching words for leaving her to fall a captive in the hands of the enemy. A tribe whose *'uṭfeh* is once captured has no longer the right to replace her. At present only the Rwala, a Bedouin tribe of Syria, has an *'uṭfeh*." To this account Canaan adds the note; "Such a girl is called *'uṭfet el-hōdadj*, since the camel on which she mounts has a domed litter. The Liâṯneh Bedouin assured me that some Bedouin tribes of Transjordania still have an *'uṭfeh*."

This account contains some confusion and one or two inaccuracies, due no doubt to the fact that in all likelihood Canaan himself had never actually seen an *'oṭfe*, and that all his information about it came from secondary sources. Unquestionably he

[26] "Unwritten Laws Affecting the Arab Women of Palestine," *JPOS*, XI (1931), 197.

is mistaken in his statement that the *'oṭfeh* was or is employed by the tribes in their raids or *ghazû*'s, for the procedure when such a raid is undertaken is not at all that which he describes, nor as a rule do such a considerable number of warriors participate in a raid. Actually what he has in mind are important or decisive battles, in which the very existence of the tribe is at stake. Evidence of this has been presented already, and more, and that even more conclusive, will follow soon. Likewise his account confuses the *'oṭfe* itself and the maiden within it, a confusion natural however, since, as we have seen, the same name, *'oṭfe*, is actually applied to both. Of extreme significance, however, are the two facts recorded in his footnote, that the girl is called *'uṭfet el-hōdadj*, and that the camel which she mounts bears a domed litter. Here, for the first time, we have the word, *howdaǧ*, the tent-like and curtained camel saddle in which women customarily ride, specifically linked with the *'oṭfe*;[27] and in addition thereto we have the explicit statement that the *'oṭfe*, as Canaan heard about it, had the appearance of a domed litter. The deep import of this will be developed later. But this much is already clear, that in his description Canaan did not have at all the *'oṭfe* of the Ruwala in mind, even though he says that they are the only tribe which at present possesses one, for, as has been suggested already, and as will become clear very shortly, the *'oṭfe* or *markab* of the Ruwala had an altogether different shape and appearance than the *'oṭfe* which he describes. But this very fact renders his statement all the more significant for our study. It recalls the statement of Burckhardt that there were actually two varieties or forms of this object,[28] one called *merkeb* and the other *'oṭfe*. We will see that the designation of these two types of this object by these two distinguishing names is by no means so constant and absolute as Burckhardt seems to imply. In fact we have already learned that the two names seem to be used more or less synonymously, and that in particular both are applied indiscriminately to the sacred standard of the Ruwala. None the less this much is certain, that the *markab* or *'oṭfe* appears [170]

[27] Though, as we have seen, Blunt described the *'oṭfe* as a "gigantic camel-howdah."

[28] Above, p. 8.

[171] in what seem to be two distinct and rather dissimilar forms. And unquestionably the *'oṭfe* which Canaan described is of the type which Burckhardt has designated as *merkab.*

Just as at first our fullest and obviously most authentic account of the *'oṭfe* was that of Musil, quoted at the beginning of this section, so now our most complete and illuminating account comes from the same scholar in his most recent work.[29] It is interesting to note that Musil's acquaintance with the *'oṭfe* seems to have developed only gradually, for in his earliest work on the manners and customs of the Bedouin he manifested no knowledge of the *'oṭfe* whatever, except that implied in the single and, in the light of our present knowledge of the object, somewhat obscure statement, "The Ṣḫûr lost their banner, el-bêraḳ, in an unsuccessful battle with Ibn Ša'lân. It was borne by the 'Aṭfa'. 'Aṭfa' means a fully matured maiden who, adorned with her best ornaments, sits upon a good riding-camel, swings the banner and with words and lashes drives the animal into the midst of the enemy. She is surrounded by the chosen men of her tribe, who must defend her; for should she be captured the battle is lost and the tribe may never again carry with them either 'Aṭfa' or banner."[30] From this account it is clear that in 1908 Musil had only a vague and inaccurate knowledge of what the *'oṭfe* really was, and that in this account he too has confused the maiden with the *'oṭfe* proper, since the name, *'oṭfe*, was, as we have seen, likewise applied to her. By 1910 Musil's knowledge of the true nature of the *'oṭfe*, or at least of the *merkab* of the Ruwala, was much more complete and authentic. In his latest work his information about both *'oṭfe* and *merkab* has expanded greatly. And first of all, his account of various *'oṭfe*'s other than that of the Ruwala.

Describing the procedure in important and decisive battles, he says,[31] "The fight called *manâḫ*, as distinguished from the *ɣazw* or raid for booty, is very different. When a stronger tribe wants to possess itself of the territory of a weaker or to increase its fame . . . . , it moves with all its herds and tents into the terri-

[29] *The Manners and Customs of the Rwala Bedouins*, New York, 1928.

[30] *Arabia Petraea*, III, 377.

[31] *The Manners and Customs of the Rwala Bedouins*, 540 f.

tory occupied by the latter, ... and finally encamps near the main camp of the enemy. The tents form as a rule two long rows . . . . ; in front of them, within rifle shot, stands the tent of the leader and a few others belonging to his retinue . . . . Before the attack, the men on foot sometimes hide by the war tents. The cavalry attempts to drive the enemy to them and within rifle shot . . . .[32] These warriors are accompanied by the prettiest women and girls of the camp, who, with their bosoms bared and hair loosened, keep shouting: "He who runs away today shall never receive anything from us; *illi ješred al-jowm mâ leh 'endana ḥaḳḳ.*"[33] Their inspiring high-pitched cries, *zaṛârît,* [172]

[32] I have here omitted from this account of the *'oṭfe* this sentence, "Before the attack the tribal emblem Abu-d-Dhur is fastened to a camel which walks in the midst of the bravest youths on horseback." I cannot escape the impression that this sentence does not really belong here, and that it was interpolated by Musil unwittingly. For while it is clear that in his main account he described the general procedure with the *'oṭfe* of the Bedouin tribes, and not specifically that of the Ruwala, the reference to Abu-d-Dhur can contemplate only the Ruwala specifically. Moreover, were this sentence original, it would certainly imply that this tribal emblem, Abu-d-Dhur, which is fastened to a camel, is something quite apart and distinct from the *'Aṭfa,* the fancy litter, also borne by a camel, and that in these decisive battles there were therefore two parallel objects of the same kind and class serving precisely the same purpose. Such is certainly not the case. It must be therefore that the sentence which I have omitted was inserted by Musil inadvertently and confuses, and even misrepresents, the actual facts.

[33] The import of these words of the women in battle is obviously that the coward and fugitive shall never enjoy the privilege of marriage and sexual relations with them. Impliedly the thought or hope of such relations with these women, the most attractive within the camp, should serve as a stimulus to the warriors to fight intrepidly nor refrain from even the most extreme sacrifice of courage. This too is obviously the purpose of the baring of the breasts by the woman in the *'oṭfe,* when going into battle surrounded by the warriors of the clan or tribe. This is borne out by a number of battle songs which Musil recorded. The Tiyâha warriors, going into battle, call to their maidens:

> Loosen your braids, loosen them:
> Lay bare your breasts completely. (*Arabia Petraea,* III, 3)

A Ǧêheni woman, seeing her husband flee in battle, and unable to induce him to turn about, sang:

> Whoever desires my love
> Must press forward, when the coward fears.

[173] are heard for a great distance. In order to raise the courage and steadiness of his warriors the chief orders the 'Aṭfa', a fancy litter, to be placed on a she-camel and the handsomest of the girls to take her place in it. Throwing off her kerchief the maiden loosens her hair, unfastens the string holding together the dress under the throat, and seats herself in the litter. Her female companions, likewise, mount she-camels and shouting *zaṛârît* hasten to join the melée in order to encourage their relatives and friends. If it is impossible to withstand the superior strength of the enemy, they call out to the girl on the 'Aṭfa' to conceal herself, as the capture of the 'Aṭfa' by the enemy would mean the greatest disgrace for both the reigning kin and the whole tribe."

He recounts[34] the following incident which happened among the Beni Ḫâled, a tribe which camped by the Persian Gulf in the territory of al-Ḥasa, whose chief was Turki eben Ḥmejd eben 'Arej'er: "Turki's herds were suddenly attacked by the Fẓûl, a kin of the Ẓefîr tribe. Responding to the alarm cries, the riders hastened to defend the herds but encountered superior numbers and were slowly beaten back to the camp. In order to raise the courage and perseverance of his warriors Turki had a fancy litter fastened to a she-camel, in which his daughter had to seat herself.

He may sip my lips till they be dry
Without concern for my husband's nose. (*ibid.*, 390)

Elsewhere Musil records this battle-song:

Hellî-d̲-d̲wâjeb	Loosen the plaits of thy hair,
hellîhēn	Loosen them;
w-eṭla'i nhûdeč	And uncover thy breasts
kellîhen	Altogether.

Upon this he comments: "*D̲wâjeb* are a girl's hair plaits. She usually keeps them covered with her kerchief. *Hallat ad̲-d̲wâjeb* is said of a girl who has thrown the kerchief off her head and has unplaited and loosened her hair. This is done only by girls or young women accompanying the men into battle." (*Manners and Customs of the Rwala Bedouins*, 565).

Elsewhere (*ibid.*, 562) he says: "*T̲owb al-ṛawa'* is a woman's dress unbuttoned below the throat. It hangs loosely over the shoulders, disclosing both the throat and the breast. Thus the girl, who in a perilous fight encourages the men to persevere, arranges her dress."

[34] *Ibid.*, 214 f.

A virgin sitting in fancy litters and inciting warriors to fight is called 'Aṭfa', the same name being also applied to the litters. Throwing aside her kerchief, loosening her hair, and unfastening the clasp which held the shirt below her throat, she placed herself in the litter. Her girl friends, likewise, mounted she-camels and rendering at the top of their voices the sounds called onomatopoetically *zarârît*, mingled in the thickest of the fray. For a while they succeeded in bracing up the courage of both their kin and friends, but the superiority of numbers soon told. Fighter after fighter began to disappear, some being killed, many wounded; of others, again, the tired mares refused to obey any longer. [174]

"Finally the 'Aṭfa' and her female companions found themselves among the tents again. When it became certain that the enemy would capture the tents, the girls called to the 'Aṭfa' to hide, as it would be the greatest insult to the reigning family as well as to the whole tribe should the enemy capture the 'Aṭfa' too. Turki's daughter drove her animal in front of her father's tent, compelled it to kneel, jumped off and, unhooking the litter, tried to pull it inside; but the tent was already surrounded by the enemy, shouting: 'Seize the 'Aṭfa', seize the 'Aṭfa'.' Thoroughly frightened, the girl called on the 'Arej'er kin to help her, *tenḫa âl 'arej'er*, but their battle cry sounded only in a few places and at great distance.

"Seeing herself deserted by her own kin, the 'Aṭfa' caught sight of Fejṣal and his son sitting in the men's compartment of the tent with their servants, and appealed for help to them." Fejṣal and his men were strangers from a near-by village who chanced to be visiting the camp at the time of the attack. They responded immediately to the call of the 'Aṭfa' and drove off the enemy. The sequel of the incident, interesting though it be, has no import for our study and so need not be repeated here.

Elsewhere[35] Musil tells of a peculiar and seemingly portentous dream which the commander of a raiding troop of the Ka'âž'a had. He then continued: "Before long he attacked the Meṣâlîḫ, drove out their defenders, and, entering the camp by force, found himself before the chief's tent where the 'Aṭfa' litter was

[35] *Ibid.*, 396 f.

[175] standing, in which in times of danger the prettiest girl used to be seated in order to encourage the defenders to fight bravely and hold their ground. A cushion, *bedd*, such as is laid under the litter when fastened on the camel's back, was lying beside it, and also a long rope, *ğedi*, made of palm pith, hung down from it. Then at last did the commander understand the meaning of his dream. Laying the cushion, *bedd*, on the saddle of a strong she-camel, with the help of his comrades he placed the litter there, fastening it with some straps, making it tight with the *ğedi* rope, and rejoicing that he had taken from the Meṣâlîḫ clan their most precious possession, for once the 'Aṭfa' litter is lost it must not be used again."

Again[36]: "Râkân eben Meğlâd led out his Dahâmše to resist an attack of the 'Amârât. Recognizing, at last, their inability to oppose the superior strength of the enemy, Râkân's comrades chained themselves to the camel carrying the 'Aṭfa' litter. They fell to a man, the camel was also killed, and the 'Aṭfa' taken by Eben Haḏḏâl, the commander of the 'Amârât."

Later in his valuable book[37] Musil records the following poem or song:

Nešmijjeten tarčaḥ lena
w-ḥelw ṛazzat 'ûdaha
malbûsah rîš an-na'am
w-mdellelen ḳa'ûdaha
rašûšaha damm al-ḥamar
w-al-bizr ṭal' enhûdaha

A beauty is leaning towards us,
And how prettily she stands up in her litter
In ostrich feathers dressed;
She rides on a camel with gay trappings.
Stained by red blood is she,
And her breasts appear like lead bullets.

To this Musil appends the comment: "A young girl, with her breasts bared, sits in a fancy litter and during the fiercest fighting

[36] *Ibid.*, 546.
[37] *Ibid.*, 559 f.

encourages her countrymen to persevere."[38] The name, *'otfe*, is not used here, but that this litter was an *'otfe* is established with certainty by the picture of the beautiful maiden, standing erect, in the litter, borne by the gaily decorated camel, while she herself is adorned with ostrich feathers, in other words, is clothed as a bride,[39] and has her breasts bared; she is stained with blood, i. e., she has driven the camel into the midst of the battle. [176]

These various accounts make clear that, contrary to the opinion which we have encountered frequently, the institution of the *'otfe* has by no means practically disappeared from among the present-day Bedouin, so that only the Ruwala still preserve it, but that quite a good many clans and tribes still employ it.[40] Basically the *'otfe* seems to be a clan, rather than a tribal, emblem, and to be generally regarded as belonging to or at least in the immediate custody of the ruling chieftain or house of the the clan or tribe, since it is kept regularly either in or in immediate proximity to the tent of the prince or main chieftain. More-

[38] Cf. also Musil's account of Turkiyye, the daughter of the chief of the Fedan, when these were attacked by the Ruwala (*In the Arabian Desert*, 14 f.).

[39] So also Jaussen; above, p. 167.

[40] Thus Guarmani (*Northern Najd: A Journey from Jerusalem to Anaiza in Qasim*, 34 f.), writing in 1864, says, "I do not find *ootfe* any longer in use in the Neged. In Syria, only the Biscir of the Emir Heidal and the Ruola of Sceilan use it." To this Douglas Carruthers, editor of the 1938 edition of Guarmani's work, appends this note: "*Otfa*, like the *Markab*, a sort of battle-banner, consisting of a wooden cradle, ornamented with ostrich feathers, borne on camel-back. It leads the tribe in battle, and is then occupied by a Badawi maiden, "the living standard of her tribesmen in battle," who inspires the warriors to deeds of valour. According to Burckhardt this ancient custom was dying out, even in his day and is doubtless now extinct. The last one in use belonged to the Ruwalla." The evidence which we have gathered establishes firmly that, at least so far as the Ruwala are concerned, Carruthers was mistaken in his assumption that the use of the *'otfe* has completely died out; cf. especially Raswan's detailed account of the *'otfe* of the Ruwala, published in 1935, and therefore practically contemporaneous, given below. Probably more correctly Haefeli (*Die Beduinen von Beerseba*, 156 and note 229), whose account of the *'otfe* otherwise adds little to our knowledge, says: "This custom was practiced generally by the Bedouins in the days of marauding expeditions and enemy attacks. However, now with the gradual dying out of these practices it too is rapidly disappearing, and today in this section almost nothing is heard of it any more."

[177] over, we have found the opinion expressed more than once that in very remote times all Bedouin tribes or clans possessed each its own *'otfe*.

Likewise the following additional facts constantly present with the *'otfe* have come to light;

1. It is a kind of camel-saddle or *howdağ*, occasionally, if not usually, of tent-like shape, with a domed top, and is regularly adorned with ostrich feathers.

2. There are definite intimations that originally every clan or tribe had its own *'otfe*, and that in some way the clan or tribal deity was associated with it; something of this original divine nature and power seems still to linger in the *'otfe*.

3. The maiden within the *'otfe* is always one of the most beautiful of the tribe and of noble lineage, frequently, if not customarily, the sister or daughter of the chieftain himself.

4. She is usually, if not invariably, a virgin, and is arrayed as a bride, adorned in her best finery and especially decorated with ostrich feathers, and is attended, as a rule, by other maidens, mounted each upon her own camel.

5. She is looked upon, for the moment at least, as a person or being of superhuman nature and authority, equalling at least, if not actually surpassing, that of the chieftain himself and occasionally, so it seems, even exercising the right to choose the military leader in the impending battle. Her person is inviolable, either by her own people or by the enemy, if she be captured.

6. When first mounted in the *'otfe* she seats herself as if enthroned, as it were; but when actually going into the battle, she stands erect, with hair flying loose, straining to her full height, and bares her breasts[41] in the sight of all the warriors of her tribe,

[41] With this may be correlated the *ehda*-chant of the Tiyâha warriors when preparing for battle, cited above (note 33) (recorded by Musil also in *Arabia Petraea*, III, 375):

> Let down thy hair, let it down,
> And lay bare thy breasts completely.

Even though the Tiyâha today have neither *'otfe* nor *markab*, there seems to lurk in this chant a definite reminiscence of former days when they did possess, such an object.

and by her appearance, her gestures, and above all her cries, [178]
excites and stimulates them to superhuman efforts and sacrifices, even to the point of the death of the very last warrior.

7. The authority, honor and independence of the princely house and also of the clan or tribe are bound up with the possession and retention of the *'oṭfe*; these are forfeited if the *'oṭfe* is captured, and can be regained only with the recapture of the *'oṭfe.*

8. When captured the *'oṭfe* is deposited at the tent of the chief of the victorious tribe. Probably to forestall as completely as possible the potential regaining of a captured *'oṭfe* the victorious tribe usually destroys the *'oṭfe* of its enemy promptly. In this procedure it is encouraged by the seemingly well attested principle, that it itself can make no use of nor derive any advantage from the possession of its enemy's *'oṭfe.*

9. A new *'oṭfe* can be made to supplant an old one only by using as its nucleus a fragment of the old *'oṭfe*, in which, impliedly, as we have seen, something of the *mana* or supernatural or divine spirit of the old *'oṭfe* abides, and from which it may, of course, spread to the new structure.

10. The *'oṭfe* is employed only in major battles, where the very existence of the clan or tribe seems at stake, never in minor skirmishes nor on raids. It is also employed when the tribe is on the march from one camping-place to another or from one pasture-ground to another, and occasionally also in formal tribal processions and similar movements. It is always borne by a camel of fine appearance and great size and strength, usually white in color.[42]

11. Inasmuch as both litter itself and maiden within it bear

[42] Canaan, "Die 'Azazime-Beduinen und ihr Gebiet," *ZDPV*, 51(1928), 114. Among the Ruwala white camels, called *waẓḥa'*, are the most prized. (Musil, *Manners and Customs of the Rwala Bedouins*, 548). To meet white camels is a good augury (Guarmani, *op. cit.*, 110). We have seen (above, p. 6) that each year the Ruwala sacrifice a white camel to Abu-d-Dhûr. In a cuneiform text coming from the last quarter of the eighth century B.C. (published by Winckler in transcription and translation in *Altorientalische Forschungen*, I, 465) we read that Šamši, one of the conquered Arab queens, gave one hundred and sixty-four white camels as tribute to the Assyrian conqueror. It would seem that even in that relatively remote day white camels were thought by the Abar nomads to have an especial value or significance.

[179] the same name, *'oṭfe*, they seem in principle to be identified with each other and to partake of the same nature and powers.

12. Very clear intimations exist that the *'oṭfe* itself is regarded as possessing something of an innate, supernatural power to select the spot for the decisive battle or the road which the clan or tribe should take, and to drive the camel which bears it undeviatingly along this road, whether this lead into the heart of the battle or to the next nightly camping-place.[42a]

13. Closely related to these particular functions are certain powers of divination which the *'oṭfe* seems to possess, and also that, among some tribes at least, a sacrifice is offered annually to, or on behalf of, the *'oṭfe* to the clan or tribal deity, or his modern equivalent, thought to dwell in, or to be associated with, it.

That the sacred litter of the Ruwala is merely one, outstanding and particularly notable example of the *'oṭfe*, and not at all a peculiar object of altogether different character and category, despite its seemingly somewhat unusual shape and appearance, and its particular name, *Al-Markab*, is beyond all question. This conclusion is confirmed by Musil's most recent and fullest account thereof.[43] "The Rwala have no flag of their own. They go on raids without any special device; but when waging war, whether of aggression or defense, that endangers the whole tribe, they take with them a special kind of litter-called Abu-d-Dhûr or al-Markab. This is perhaps the old decorated litter, 'Aṭfa', destined originally for the prettiest girl, who used to lead the tribe to the decisive battle. But there is nobody now who can remember that a girl ever sat in it.[44] The Markab litter is constructed of stout poles, the frame being about 90 centimeters high, 270 centimeters long at the top, and 190 centimeters long and about 50 centimeters wide at the bottom. All the poles are wrapped round with ostrich feathers; to the upper poles are tied twelve short pegs, *zerânîž*, with plumes of bent ostrich feathers, *ṛalab*. To be loaded, the Markab is placed in the litter called *ḥaraǧ*, and this is tied to a camel with ropes, *mečârîb* . . . .

[42a] For this note see p. 113

[43] *Manners and Customs of the Rwala Bedouins*, 571–574.

[44] For a refutation of this statement see below, pp. 31–34.

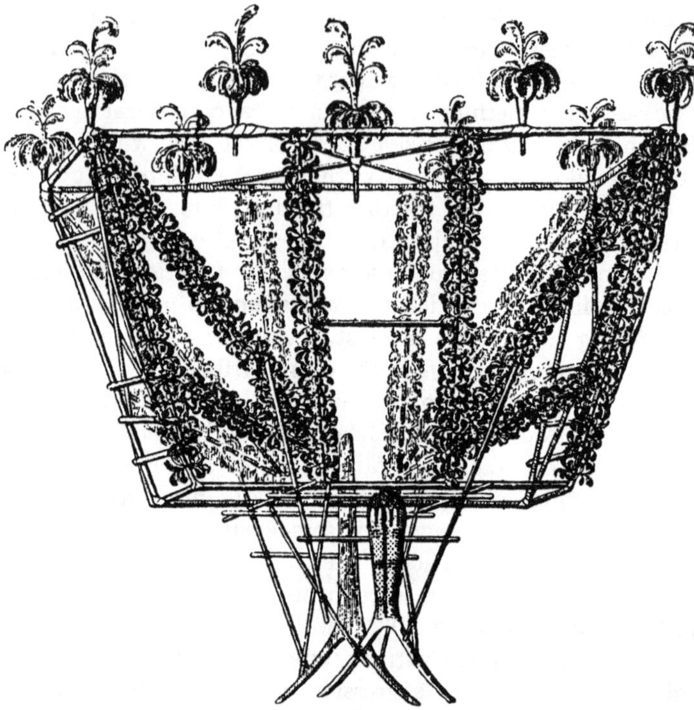

AL-MARKAB

Reproduced from Musil, *The Manners and Customs of the Rwala Bedouins*, with the ready and generous permission of the author and of the publisher, the American Geographical Society.

"The Rwala believe that the litter is called Abu-d-Dhûr, Father of Indefinite Periods of Time, because it is inherited from generation to generation, from age to age, *min ǧîlen ila ǧîl*, and that it will last forever. Al-Markab forms the visible token of princely power, and therefore this litter remains in the prince's tent all the time, in the part of the tent reserved for the women; bere it is guarded, day and night, both by the prince himself and hy his slaves, against everybody and especially against the prince's nearest kinsmen. For, if a revolt breaks out in the reigning kin against the prince, his opponents attempt first of all to snatch the Abu-d-Dhûr away from him, as he who has this emblem of the whole tribe in his possession must be recognized as

[181]

AL-MARKAB

Reproduced from Musil, *The Manners and Customs of the Rwala Bedouins*, with the ready and generous permission of the author and of the publisher, the American Geographical Society.

their prince. Should the enemy at war with the Rwala succeed in capturing the Abu-d-Dhûr, the respect for it would be entirely lost, and the Rwala would not use it again. To carry this litter, when the tribe migrates, an especially strong and docile camel, usually one of white color, is selected. The animal then, as a rule, walks between the laden camels and the herds, thus forming the center of all the migrating families.

"When attacked by an enemy in force on the march, the best fighters at once surround the Abu-d-Dhûr to protect it. If it seems that the enemy will push back the fighters resisting his attack and that he will break through to the pack camels, the commander of the chosen troop of fighters (called *ṣanam*) who defend the Markab will take the camel carrying this symbol by the rein [182] and lead her at the head of his troop against the enemy. The *ṣanam* are accompanied by girls seated on she-camels, who encourage the men to persevere, and behind them follow the women who threaten to beat to death any one who deserts the Abu-d-Dhûr and flees. So far no enemy has succeeded in defeating the Rwala sufficiently to take the Abu-d-Dhûr away from them. The prince, it must be said, is very prudent — the more dangerous the region through which the tribe has to pass when migrating, or where it encamps, the nearer together stand the tents of the various camps.

"When the Rwala engage in a war of *al-manâḫ*,[45] during which they move with all their herds and tents into an enemy's territory, the camel carrying the Abu-d-Dhûr walks at the head of the whole tribe, surrounded by warriors who follow every movement of the camel with closest attention. They belive that Allah gives signs by means of the Abu-d-Dhûr, from which the outcome of the fight can be foretold. Sometimes, in a dead calm, the ostrich feathers adorning the Abu-d-Dhûr begin to flutter. At other times the litter leans to the right or left, but suddenly straightens itself, remains quietly upright, and then rocks a few times from side to side. All this, the Rwala think, happens by the power of Allah, *ḳudrat min allâh*, who sends them help, *'enâje*, from al-Markab, where he is believed to seat himself for a while. The waving of the feathers and the straightening of the Abu-d-Dhûr are signs that Allah has touched it with his power.

"After each victory a camel is killed before the Abu-d-Dhûr in honor of Allah. This is also done every year, even if the Rwala have had no war to which the Abu-d-Dhûr had to be taken."

Later in his book[46] Musil gives an account of a bitter and critical war between the Ruwala and their arch enemies, the Beni Ṣaḫr, reenforced by the Ḥwêṭât and the Šarârât, in which the Ruwala with all their forces invaded the territory of their enemy. In this connection he speaks of the Abu-d-Dhûr "rocking on a camel ahead of their first column, the rest following in the

[45] I. e., a battle or war of major character, in which the very existence of the tribe is at stake; cf. *ibid.*, 540 f.

[46] *Ibid.*, 604–606.

183] customary order." Again[47] he quotes a long poem describing the reactions of the poet to a decisive battle fought between the Ruwala and the Muntifež, in which the following stanza occurs;

ǧawna ṣabâḥ wa-rčebow awlâd ṣa‘lân
ḥammâjet al-Merkab ‘an alli baṛâha

In the morning they came, and Ša‘lân's youths mounted their horses
To protect the Markab from all who might desire it.

To this he has appended the following note: "Al-Markab is sacred to all the Rwala. Should they lose it once only, should it be captured by the enemy, they would not be allowed to procure a new one, the emblem of their unity would be lost, and they would think that Allah had deserted them." Elsewhere[48] he cites a poem in which Al-Markab is used metonymically for Prince an-Nûri, the head of the Ruwala, and therefore the custodian of the sacred litter. He likewise cites a case where a member of another tribe "ran into the tent of Prince Saṭṭâm, grasped one of the poles of the *merkab* litter, and shouted: 'I stand under the protection of this pole, and nothing shall part me from it. By Allah's light and by Allah's right in this camp I put myself under thy protection, O Saṭṭâm.' "

The most recent account of the sacred litter of the Ruwala[49] records its existence in 1926, its nature, history and the manner of its use, by one who was privileged to observe it very closely and to acquaint himself with it authoritatively. Occasionally the author seems to distort matters slightly and even to draw somewhat upon his very fertile imagination in striving for romantic effect; but in the main his picture is unquestionably authentic. And inasmuch as in a number of details, and especially in two which are of extreme importance, he differs materially from data recorded by Musil, it is worth while to present his

[47] *Ibid.*, 623 ff.
[48] *Ibid.*, 631 f.
[49] Raswan, *Black Tents of Arabia*, 75–78.

account in full. He recounts the migration of the entire Ruwala tribe, consisting of some thirty thousand persons with approximately three hundred thousand camels, from their own grazing territory into that of the remotely kindred but bitterly hostile Aneze tribe, the Fid'an. Their own country had been devastated by an extreme drought; pasturage and water had disappeared almost completely; the camels were dying by the hundreds and the people themselves were thirsting; the very existence of the entire tribe was hanging in the balance. No recourse remained for them but to force their way boldly into the rich grasslands of their enemies, bordering upon the upper Euphrates. At this particular moment this procedure was doubly dangerous, since the Fid'an were merely awaiting the opportune moment to inaugurate war upon the Ruwala. After describing the slow migration from day to day, the difficulties in maintaining the camels, the chief wealth of the Ruwala, and other experiences, mostly bitter, incidental to this great migration, Raswan continues: [184]

"At the head of the advancing nation, in front of the center of the first line, strode one fawn-colored camel, bearing on its back a singular structure, adorned with hundreds of small tufts of black ostrich feathers and barbaric decorations. The large framework of acacia wood was balanced and secured on a saddle of special design. It was the *Markab*, the 'Ship', also called *Abu-Duhur*, 'Father of the Ages'— the Ark of Ishmael. It is the altar before which the Bedouins for centuries have made their votive and thank-offerings. There is only one such Ark in all Arabia. For ages past it has moved from tribe to tribe, as one conquered the other. The Ruala had held it now for nearly one hundred and fifty years, and to them it has become the symbol of their unity and their emblem of war,— the tribal Great Banner, as it were. This ancient and hallowed standard, the Ruala will tell you, has been moved by the spirit of Allah at critical periods in their history, especially in grave and decisive conflicts, to reveal to them when and where to face the enemy and join battle.

"This day, too, they expected to see God's presence and protection revealing themselves in mystic signs from the old frame on the camel's back.

[185] "Tra'd ibn Sattam[50] hurried with me to the sacred Standard, which rose high above the travelling-litters. We made our way through an agitated throng. The buzz of women's and children's voices intermingled with the grunting and complaining of laden camels. On nearer approach I noticed a group of women afoot, threading their way to the standard; they waved their head-cloths and kept up a high-pitched chant. They were escorting a young woman, walking sedately in their midst. It was Tuëma. Her beautiful, serene face was radiant and aglow with health. Her eyes under their long lashes were grave and devout, but she had a bright glance for Tra'd Ibn Sattam, who had chosen her out of all the Ruala maidens for the signal honour of riding in the *Markab*, and on recognizing me her cheeks dimpled with a smile.

"When Tuëma and her train of women had come up with the camel which bore the tribal symbol, a tall powerful animal led by a slave, she ran by its side for a space. The trilling and waving of the women rose to a joyous frenzy. Suddenly Tuëma broke away from her retinue, and with a running start grasped the camel's shoulder-girth and climbed nimbly on to its back and into the Palladium. In the left fore-corner of the sacred structure was a seat with a footrest, and on this she composed herself, enthroned on high like a desert queen above her people. Thereupon, she untied her head-cloth and her glorious tresses fell over her shoulders. At a sign from her, the escorting women, who had continued to walk beside the camels, climbed up again to their several litters.

"From the midst of the migrating multitude now came the sounds of shots fired in jubilation, and soon tribesmen were galloping forward from all directions. They assembled and in a body raced toward the *Markab*, Faris[51] at their head. Amidst the thunder of hoofs and the glint of carbines, there arose the wild chant of the young men as they pressed around their queen.

"Tuëma had risen and stood erect in the lofty frame. Her face became transfigured in an ecstasy of joy. Suddenly she put

[50] Acting as tribal chieftain in the temporary absence of the regular prince, Fuâz, the grandson of Prince An-Nûri ibn Ša'lân, of Musil's day.

[51] The destined husband of Tuëma.

both her hands to her throat and tore open her dress and broke [186] into jubilant song. With bared breast she rose, straining her supple body until she was poised high above the ark, holding aloft a bunch of snow-white ostrich plumes. She looked like a goddess — the bravest and most beautiful maiden of her great tribe. She cried to the youths words of passionate eloquence. She inflamed them with warlike ardour. She exhorted them to remember the heroes who once had chained themselves to this Standard by means of the iron shackles of their mares, so that they might not leave their queen, but defend her to the last breath . . . .

"Tra'd ibn Sattam took the leading rope of Tuëma's camel from the slave and led her past the marching tribe. For all the dire distress, a festive spirit animated the whole people. It was a festive day, for the Ruala had a queen again — a virgin in the sacred ark; and under her symbolic leadership they pressed forward to their destiny."

Elsewhere[52] Raswan gives the following history of the *Markab:* "To the Bedouins of Arabia, the *Markab* has a significance such as the Palladium had to the Trojans. They all hold the belief that the possession of this symbol, much like the Israelitish 'Ark of the Covenant,' means safety and power to the tribe holding it, while its loss spells disaster to the tribe and its subsequent dispersion. The Ruala have held it uninterruptedly for nearly a century and a half, but even today the sight of 'Ishmael's camel-throne,' with the chosen maiden sitting on it in times of war, will inspire them to greater heroism. The warriors composing its guard of honour are the picked troops of the tribe. They vouch for its safety with life and limb; they are, above all others, the heroes of Arabia.

"Before coming into the keeping of the Ruala, the *Markab* was held by the Amarat. More precisely, it was in the possession of the Ibn Hadhdhal family of that tribe until 1793. In that year the Wuld 'Ali, a tribe in alliance with the Ruala, made war on the Amarat. Jidua ibn Mubadir, a Rueyli then visiting the Wuld 'Ali, took part in the campaign. At the height of the decisive

[52] *Op. cit.*, 110.

[187] battle, so the tale is told, this Rueyli, with permission from the Wuld 'Ali chieftain, flung himself on the horsemen guarding the *Markab* (with the Amarat maiden enthroned in it), cut his way through single-handed, and with one blow of the sword cut off one of the legs of the camel bearing the emblem of the tribe, and brought it to the ground. With the sudden overthrow of the Holy Standard, the resistance of the Amarat also broke down and, terror-stricken, they suffered a crushing defeat . . . .

"After the defeat of the Amarat, the *sheykh* of the Wuld 'Ali presented the *Markab*, and with it Jidua's sword, now famous,[53]

[53] Of this famous sword another legend, accounting for its origin and unique character, is recorded by Raswan (*op. cit.*, 111 f.). "Of Jidua's sword — Thu'l-Hayyatu — "the-one-endowed-with-life"— there is also an older legend . . . .

"In the fifth century of the Hegira . . . . when the 'Anaza Bedouins were still grazing their camels south of Teyma at the Jabal Bird, it happened on the sacred pilgrim's road to Mecca from Damascus. Janda ibn Mubadir, an ancestor of Jidua, was travelling with his clan toward Khaybar . . . . One still dark night . . . . the air was suddenly filled with a terrific roaring. A mighty thunder-clap rent the sky, the ground trembled and swayed, and the whole world seemed to be tumbling . . . . From the midst of the dark heavens above there broke forth a light that shone over the quaking earth with swiftly growing brilliance, until in a moment it had equalled the luminous power of the noonday sun and surpassed its heat. It blinded men and beasts. The earth split; a sound of hissing, tearing, and crashing beyond the power of description filled the air, and a sulphurous smoke hung over the scarred earth.

"When morning dawned it was found that many persons had been struck dead . . . . A crater-like scar marked the place where an unusually large meteorite had buried itself. In addition, a number of men and camels had disappeared without trace into the bowels of the earth . . . .

"Janda ibn Mubadir and his war-mare . . . . lay dead before the wreck of his torn and partly burned tent . . . .

"Some years afterwards some bolder spirits among the Bedouins nerved themselves to examine the hole torn in the earth. To their joy, these Bedouins discovered that the rift, widened and cleared by them, began to fill with water. Bir er-Ra'ad (the Thunder Fountain) they named the well. During the excavation, they found small fragments of the splintered 'messenger-from-the-sky.' A son of Ibn Mubadir took one such fragment from the meteor and fashioned from it a sword two and a half feet long. It gleams today as it did then, as if it were brand-new. It is of a bluish tint without one rust stain, and fine silvery wavy marks run down the precious blade, which is as light as a feather. A silver-

to the Ruala, since it was a Rueyli who had overthrown the [188]
Markab and thus brought about the victory of the Wuld 'Ali. Since then this sacred emblem has been in the hands of the Sha'lan family and has accompanied the Ruala in all their victorious wars, a symbol of their dominant position among all the Bedouin tribes of Arabia."

The language of this account seems somewhat figurative and extravagant, and due allowance must be made therefore. The designation of the *Markab* as an altar, as the "ark of Ishmael," likened to the ancient ark of Israel, and as "Ishmael's camel-throne," must, of course, not be taken too literally, although, as we shall see later, even these terms are by no means without import for our study. The same holds true of Raswan's designation of the maiden within the *Markab* as a goddess.

In two exceedingly important details Raswan's account of the *Markab* differs from those of Musil and of the other travellers presented earlier in this study. His statement that the *Markab* was held originally by the Amarat and was taken from them in battle in 1793, almost one hundred and fifty years ago, contradicts absolutely the testimony of all the other records that an *'oṭfe*, taken in battle, cannot be used in any way by its captors, but is regularly destroyed. It is difficult to believe that Raswan's statement can be entirely correct. He may have misunderstood his informant somewhat, or else he allowed his romantic urge to lead him a bit too far in spinning out his fascinating story of the capture of the *Markab*. Raswan gives not the slightest intimation that he knew aught of *'oṭfe*'s in general and of the seemingly invariable principles underlying their nature and use. The

smith of Damascus made a handsome hilt and an equally handsome scabbard for it, and another artist engraved the blade with Arabic runes in gold.

" 'The Sword-of-Janda-and-Jidua' is thus, in the truest sense, a gift of heaven, and that is why it is called also 'The Sword of God' and 'The Life-endowed One'."

Needless to say, this legend cannot possibly be historical. None the less it evidences the extreme reverence with which the Ruwala regarded this object. In the course of the ceremonies which celebrated the marriage of Faris and Tuëma this sword was held over the head of the bride during the wedding procession. We shall have occasion later (cf. below, p. 123 f.) to compare this legendary sword with the sword of Goliath.

189] *Markab* is the only object of its kind with which he manifests the slightest acquaintance. Therefore it need not be too surprising that he should record a tradition which contradicts one of the basic principles of the *'oṭfe*. Furthermore, it would be startling indeed if the occasion of the capture of the *Markab* by the Ruwala could be fixed at this comparatively remote date with such precision as Raswan offers.

Moreover, two bits of evidence, recorded by Musil and cited in the quotations already given from his writings, tend to refute Raswan's statement. Musil heard the tradition from his informants that the *Markab* had come to them from Ruweil, their traditional, eponymous ancestor. This implies, of course, that Musil's informants believed that the *Markab* had been in their possession from the very origin of their tribe, and that accordingly they knew naught of a tradition that it had once belonged to some other tribe and had only from that source passed into their possession. There is no reason whatever to question that Raswan records accurately enough all that which he actually saw with his own eyes. But in the recording of traditions and other information gathered by hearsay or by systematic investigation undoubtedly Musil, with his rich experience and thorough technique, is the more reliable and authoritative chronicler.

In addition, we have from Musil the account of the capture of the *'oṭfe* of the Daḥâmše, with the implication that it was immediately destroyed, by the Eben Haḏḏâl clan of the 'Amârât, the very tribe and clan which, according to Raswan, had been the original possessors of the *Markab* up to 1793. It is hardly likely that within a period of less than one hundred and fifty years the established procedure of this tribe and of its immediate neighbors with regard to *'oṭfe*'s in general and of the *Markab* in particular, would have undergone such a radical change, viz., that less than one hundred and fifty years ago the principle would have obtained among them that a captured *'oṭfe* or *Markab* could be retained by its captors and regarded as a divine force among them working in their behalf, while today they hold that such a captured shrine must be destroyed by its captors. For these reasons Raswan's account of the passing of the *Markab* from the Amarat to the Ruwala, particularly with the obvious retention of all its orignal powers and authority, seems exceedingly doubtful; and yet it may not be dismissed too completely, and that all the more so since we shall, in the course of this study, have a close, partial parallel to such a procedure with an *'otfe.* [190]

On the other hand, despite Musil's statement that no one can remember that a maiden had ever ridden in the *Markab*, there is not the slightest reason to doubt the accuracy of Raswan's thrilling account of the placing of Tuëma, his heroine, therein; for this was not something of which he had merely heard a rumor or a tradition, but something which he saw with his own eyes, in fact an episode in which he was a certain, even though a minor, actor. Even making due allowance for some slight exaggeration in the account in order to heighten the romantic interest of his narrative, there can be no question that on this most critical occasion, when the very existence of the entire Ruwala tribe was at stake, when it, in sheer desperation, was invading the grasslands of its arch-enemy, and the decisive battle seemed most imminent, recourse should be had to this tribal palladium. All the sources other than Raswan have agreed that the Ruwala actually took the *Markab* with them into battle only on the very rarest of occasions, although the evidence is likewise ample that this was done on one or two occasions of which record is preserved, when the situation was not altogether critical. Actually there is no positive evidence that it was not customary for a Ruwala maiden to occupy the *Markab* on these rare occasions. We have heard only from writers who preceded Raswan that no one seemed to remember any occasion when this had been done. But inasmuch as this was the regular practice when the *'otfe* went into battle; inasmuch too as, as has been said, Raswan had apparently no knowledge whatever of *'otfe*'s in general and of the regular procedure with them, he could hardly have imagined the incident of Tuëma riding in the *Markab*; and finally, inasmuch as he was actually present at and a participant in the episode, there seems not the slightest ground for rejecting the evidence which he records.

From all this it is apparent, what the various accounts have, without exception, intimated, that the *Markab* of the Ruwala was an *'otfe*, possessing all the qualities and attributes of an *'otfe.*

[191] In the most literal sense therefore the statement, so oft repeated, that no tribe other than the Ruwala possesses an *'oṭfe*, is altogether incorrect. We have had ample evidence that within comparatively recent times, and no doubt still today, quite a good many clans and tribes do possess *'oṭfe*'s of their own, all with practically the same nature, purpose and power. Actually, however, the statement seems perfectly true that no tribe other than the Ruwala possesses such an *'oṭfe*. So far as our evidence goes, although we must admit that this is after all none too extensive and decisive, this is the only *'oṭfe* which has its own proper name, *Al-Markab*, or even more fully, *Abu Ẓhûr al-Markab*. It is likewise, so far as we can see at present, the one *'oṭfe* with which a deity, or what seems to have been a deity originally, viz., Abu Ẓhûr, is definitely associated. It is regarded with reverence by all the *zana* Muslim, i. e., the two very large tribes of the Ruwala and the Wuld 'Ali, one of the two main divisions of the great tribal group, the 'Aneze;[54] in other words it enjoys respect from, and authority among, a far larger group than any other *'oṭfe* of which we have record today. Moreover, it seems to be of utmost antiquity, a consideration which naturally enhances its reputation not a little. And the record of decisive victories in battle and attendant triumphs gained by the Ruwala is likewise a mighty factor in justifying the statement that none of the other present-day Bedouin tribes of Arabia Petraea possess such an object.

Moreover, there seems good reason to believe that the *Markab* differs in form and appearance quite decidedly from the ordinary *'oṭfe*. Burckhardt has recorded the fact that there are two related objects, one called *merkab* and the other *'oṭfe*. However, he seems to have confused the two, for his description of the *'oṭfe* applies rather to the *merkab*, and, on the other hand, his description of the *merkab* applies rather to the *'oṭfe*. Actually we have heard the name, *merkab*, applied only to the *'oṭfe* of the Ruwala, and that always with the article, quite as if this were really, not a common, but a proper noun, *Al-Markab*, the name or specific designation of this one particular *'oṭfe*. But if then this one particular *'oṭfe* of the Ruwala be the only one which deviates from

[54] *The Manners and Customs of the Rwala Bedouins*, 46.

the customary tent-like form of the *‘oṭfe*, with the domed top, of which Canaan speaks, then in another, very decided and significant respect, viz., that of form and appearance, this *‘oṭfe* of the Ruwala is unique; and this too justifies the statement that no other tribe possesses anything quite like it. And yet it is an *‘oṭfe* none the less. [192

Moreover, in connection with this unique *‘oṭfe* of the Ruwala we note again, in summary, that it is associated with Abu Ẓhûr, either a deity himself, or else a traditional name which developed, either by direct transmission or perhaps by corruption of the original name, from some old, almost entirely forgotten tribal deity, that at times Allah himself is supposed to take his place within the *Markab*, that regularly every year and likewise after each victorious battle in which it participates, a white camel is sacrificed to the *Markab*, or better to Abu Ẓhûr, associated with it, and the blood of the sacrifice is smeared upon the framework of the *Markab*. We note too the various, supernatural, semi-divine, or even completely divine powers, which the *Markab* possesses; it gives the signal for starting upon a migration and likewise the signal, and indicates the spot, for camping; it also frequently selects the site for the impending battle; it imparts oracles; it gives victory in battle; oaths may be sworn by it; the possession of it by a family establishes their title to princely authority within the tribe. It participates in formal tribal processions, and, occasionally at least, a virgin, the most beautiful and high-born maiden of the tribe, arrayed as a bride, the *‘Oṭfe*, as she too is called, occupies it, and for that moment sits enthroned in it, upon a seat on its left side, as if she were a queen or a goddess, leading her people either on the march or into battle or in formal, tribal processions. The capture of this *‘oṭfe* in particular would constitute an irreparable loss. It could never be replaced; and with it the honor and authority of the Ruwala, and within the tribe itself of the ruling family of Ibn Ša‘alân, jealously preserved through many generations, would be gone forever. We might almost say that the very existence of the entire tribe, at least upon the plane of dignity, self-respect and authority so highly esteemed by them, is inseparably bound up with the possession and retention of this peculiar object. It is

[193] indeed the palladium of the tribe. Finally we note the tradition, however none too well attested, that the maiden within the *'oṭfe* or *Markab* selects the warrior who is to lead in battle against the enemy from among the defenders of the sacred shrine.

So much then for the *'oṭfe*.[54a] We may now proceed to a brief consideration of the *maḥmal*.

iii. The *Maḥmal*

That the *maḥmal* too was a kind of *'oṭfe* playing a particular role, is beyond all question. This is apparent from every description of it. Maundrel[55] pictures the *maḥmal*, as he beheld it in 1699 at Damascus, about to set out for Mecca in the annual pilgrimage caravan, thus; "This is a large pavillion of black silk, borne by a huge camel; and on every side reaching to the ground it is adorned with gold fringes, and the camel ornamented with large ropes of beads, fish shells, fox tails, etc. Under this pavilion the Alcoran is placed with great solemnity, together with a new rich carpet, which the grand signior sends every year to Mecca, for the cover-

[54a] The name, عُطْفَة or عَطَفَة seems to defy etymological explanation. The basic meaning of the stem, عطف, is "to bend," then "to incline; to fold." (Lane, *op. cit.*, 2079–2082). May ("Ephod and Ariel," *AJSL*, LVI [1939], 49), quoting a personal communication from Sprengling, calls attention to the fact that "a derivative of the root from which *'utfa* comes is used for one of the divining or gambling arrows (of the pre-islamic Arabs), said by authors to be that one of the three (in the ancient Arab game of Meisir) which neither wins nor loses"; cf. also Lane, *op. cit.*, 2081b to عطوف. The connection of this idea with the *'oṭfe* is anything but clear. Perhaps in this connection, however, attention may be called to Musil's statement (above, pp. 6, 30), that at times *Abu Ẓhûr* is believed to bow itself unceasingly to the right, and that this procedure is portentous. Actually عطفة (Lane, *op. cit.*, 2081a) has the meaning, "an inclining," or even apparently, "that which inclines." But at the best this would be but a precarious etymological explanation of the term; yet none better suggests itself.

[55] *A Journey from Aleppo to Jerusalem*, in *A Compendium of the Most Approved Modern Travels* (1757), I, 104.

ing of Mahomet's tomb; and the old one is brought back in return, which is esteemed of inestimable value. The beast which carries this sacred treasure, is exempted from bearing burdens for ever after." [194]

Doughty writes as follows:[56] "I might sometimes see heaving and rolling above all heads of men and cattle in the midst of the journeying caravan, the naked frame and posts of the sacred *Mahmal* camel which resembles a bedstead, and is after the fashion of the Beduish woman's camel-litter.[57] It is clothed on high days with a glorious pall of green velvet, the prophet's colour, and the four posts are crowned with glancing knops of silver. I understand from grave elders of the religion, that this litter is the standard of the Haj, in the antique guise of Arabia, and yet remaining among the Beduw; wherein, at any general battle of tribes, there is mounted some beautiful damsel of the sheykhs' daughters, whose generous loud *Alleluias* for her people, in presence of their enemies, inflame her young kinsmen's hearts to leap in that martial dance to a multitude of deaths." Upon this I have remarked in my earlier work that the comparison which Doughty makes here between the *maḥmal* of the pilgrim-caravan to Mecca and the ancient Bedouin *'oṭfe* is suggestive indeed and leads to significant conclusions. It should be borne in mind that the *maḥmal* of both these passages is that of Syria.

The Egyptian *maḥmal* is described by Rutter[58] thus: "A mahmal (more correctly, mihmal) is literally a 'carrier'— a contrivance in which things are carried. The mahmal which is sent annually to Mekka from Cairo is a cubic box-like contrivance, measuring five feet in all three dimensions, constructed of a wooden framework covered with richly embroidered red brocade. This is surmounted by a conical tent-like top, of the same materials, which is some five feet high. At the apex of the conical top, and at each upper corner of the box, is a large gilded silver ornament, surmounted by a crescent. The bottom of the mahmal is so constructed as to allow of the contrivance being easily mounted on the saddle of the camel which bears it.

[56] *Travels in Arabia Deserta*, I, 61.

[57] I. e., a *howdaǵ*.

[58] *The Holy Cities of Arabia*, I, 168 f.

[195] "Mahmals similar to the Egyptian, but less magnificent, were formerly sent annually to Mekka by the Sultân of Turkey, with the Damascus caravan; and earlier, by the Caliphs of Bagdad; by the Imâms of the Yemen; by Ibn Rashîd, Prince of Hâil; by the Sultân of Darfur; and, upon occasion, by the Maharajah of Hyderabad."

Lane's description[59] of this same *maḥmal* is more detailed and informing:

"It is a square skeleton-frame of wood, with a pyramidal top; and has a covering of black brocade, richly worked with inscriptions and ornamental embroidery in gold, in some parts upon a ground of green or red silk, and bordered with a fringe of silk, with tassels surmounted by silver balls. Its covering is not always made after the same pattern with regard to the decorations; but in every cover that I have seen, I have remarked, on the upper part of the front, a view of the Temple of Mekkeh, worked in gold; and, over it, the Sultán's cypher. It contains nothing; but has two mus-hafs (or copies of the Kur-án), one on a scroll and the other in the usual form of a little book, and each enclosed in a case of gilt silver, attached, externally, at the top .... The Mahmal is borne by a fine tall camel, which is generally indulged with exemption from every kind of labour during the remainder of its life.

"It is related that the Sultán Ez-Záhir Beybars, King of Egypt, was the first who sent a Mahmal with the caravan of pilgrims to Mekkeh, in the year of the flight 670 (A.D. 1272), or 675; but this custom, it is generally said, had its origin a few years before his accession to the throne. Sheger-ed-Durr (commonly called Shegeret-ed-Durr), a beautiful Turkish female slave, who became the favourite wife of the Sultán es-Sáleh Negm-ed-Deen, and on the death of his son (with whom terminated the dynasty of the house of Eiyoob) caused herself to be acknowledged as Queen of Egypt, performed the pilgrimage in a magnificent 'hódag' (or covered litter), borne by a camel; and for several successive years her empty hódag was sent with the caravan

[59] *An Account of the Manners and Customs of the Modern Egyptians* (3rd ed.), 404 f.

merely for the sake of state. Hence, succeeding princes of Egypt sent, with each year's caravan of pilgrims, a kind of hódag (which received the name of 'Mahmal' or 'Mahmil'), as an emblem of royalty; and the kings of other countries followed their example. The Wahhábees prohibited the Mahmal as an object of vain pomp; it afforded them one reason for intercepting the caravan." [196]

Upon this I commented: This is the description of the Egyptian *maḥmal*. It is clear that Lane has given here, and in authoritative manner, the traditional account of the origin of this peculiar institution current in Cairo in the 19th century. According to this tradition the institution of the *maḥmal* is only approximately six hundred and fifty years old. The authenticity of this tradition is strongly questioned by Snouck Hurgronje,[60] who points out that in addition to this *maḥmal* from Cairo, and likewise the one from Damascus, to which Maundrel and Doughty refer, there were in ancient times various other *maḥmals*, representing the various parts and lands of the Moslem world and the princes who ruled over them. The *maḥmal* from Irak played an important role in the history of Mecca in 1320, but forty-nine years after the traditional date of the origin of the Egyptian *maḥmal*, and the *maḥmal* from Yemen played a similar role in 1380; and, as Snouck Hurgronje remarks, this was certainly not the first *maḥmal* which had come to Mecca from Yemen. In the light of these facts he asks very pertinently how it is possible that all the rival princes of Moslem states should have hit upon exactly the same method of representing themselves in the pilgrimage to Mecca, so very soon after the custom had been instituted by the Egyptian princess. He is therefore inclined to believe that the institution of the *maḥmal* must have had some different and more ancient origin. He furthermore cites De Goeje,[61] who suggests the possibility of some relation between the *'oṭfe*, the *maḥmal* and the old Arabic custom of carrying portable shrines upon a journey or into battle . . . . Snouck Hurgronje likewise cites the custom still observed in Djiddah, the sea-port of Mecca, that in the celebration of their folk-festivals the people of the different

[60] *Mekka*, I, 83 f.

[61] *Mémoires d'histoire et de géographie orientales*², No. 1, 180.

[197] quarters of the city make *maḥmals*, each quarter having its own festival and each its own *maḥmal*, and each trying to outdo its rival quarters in the fabrication of its *maḥmal*. These facts are significant. They point to the conclusion that the folk-tradition of the origin of the *maḥmal*, cited by Lane, is altogether unauthentic, and evidences no more than that the institution is of such antiquity that its true origin is entirely unknown to the modern Muslim.[62] Note should be taken too of the fact, repeatedly stated, that the *maḥmal* is the symbol of royalty.

Moreover, the facts cited by Lane, that, no matter how the details of the external adornment of the Egyptian *maḥmal* may vary from year to year, two details are constant, viz., the representation of the Ka'aba, or the Temple at Mecca, and the suspension of the two copies of the Koran upon the front side of the *maḥmal*-cover, coupled with the additional fact that, despite the Egyptian tradition that Sheger-ed-Durr occupied the first *maḥmal*, none the less all *maḥmals* are entirely empty, points to one significant conclusion, viz., that originally the *maḥmal*, whatever its earliest name among the Arabs may have been, was the litter in which the deity of the tribe or tribes to which it belonged was thought to ride upon the many wanderings of the nomad tribe. Nay more, since the *maḥmal* in the present day appears only in the annual pilgrimage to Mecca, a difficult and dangerous journey indeed, particularly in ancient, and in fact until quite recent, times, the thought suggests itself, that originally the *maḥmal* was believed to be the actual guide of the pilgrim-caravan through the difficult and dangerous desert; it was thought to be the divine power which selected the road which the caravan must take, in order to arrive in safety at its destination. The peculiar, sacred character of the camel which bears the *maḥmal* tends to confirm this hypothesis. And perhaps some slight additional confirmation thereof may even be found in the tradition that it was a woman, and a princess at that, who was the first occupant of the Egyptian *maḥmal*; for, as we have seen,

[62] This too is the implication of the information gathered by Doughty from "grave elders of the religion," that the *maḥmal* is "in the antique guise of Arabia."

the regular occupant of the *'oṭfe* was a maiden, and always one of the noblest maidens of the tribe. Unquestionably there is much probability to De Goeje's correlation of *maḥmal* and *'oṭfe.* [198]

This conclusion is confirmed by certain additonal considerations, all pointing to the original conception of the *maḥmal* as being of divine character, or at least as possessing divine powers. This is evidenced by an interesting account by Lane of how upon the occasion of the return of the *maḥmal* to Cairo, after having performed the pilgrimage to Mecca, during the procession of the sacred object through the streets of Cairo he ventured to draw near and not only touch, but actually lay hold of, the fringe of the *maḥmal* and walk beside it in this position for some distance. He was eyed with suspicion by the guard but was not interfered with. Other pious Moslems were permitted only to touch it with their fingers, which they thereupon kissed. This privilege which Lane thus arrogated to himself was regarded by his Moslem friends, to whom he revealed the experience, as a manifestation of unusual divine favor to him. Just to touch the *maḥmal* imparts *baraka* or divine blessing. This is likewise the implication of Doughty's statement,[63] "To rub and kiss the black stone built in the Kaaba wall is even now Mohammedan religion; in like wise you may see poor devout men in the northern Arab countries throng to kiss the *maḥmal* camel, returned from Mecca; and how they fervently rub their clothing on him."

Burckhardt's account of the *maḥmal*,[64] not cited in my previous study, supplements Lane's account in some important respects and in others even contradicts it. "The Mahmal . . . . is a high, hollow, wooden frame, in the form of a cone, with a pyramidal top, covered with a fine silk brocade adorned with ostrich feathers, and having a small book of prayers and charms placed in the midst of it, wrapped up in a piece of silk. When on the road, it serves as a holy banner to the caravan; and on the return of the Egyptian caravan, the book of prayers is exposed in the mosque El Hassaneyn, at Cairo, where men and women of the lower classes go to kiss it, and obtain a blessing by rubbing

[63] *Travels in Arabia Deserta,* II, 511.
[64] *Travels in Arabia,* II, 49–51.

[199] their foreheads upon it. No copy of the Koran, nor anything but the book of prayers, is placed in the Cairo Mahmal. The Wahábys declare this ceremony of the Hadj to be a vain pomp, of idolatrous origin, and contrary to the spirit of true religion; and its use was one of the principal reasons which they assigned for interdicting the caravans from returning to Mekka. In the first centuries of Islam, neither the Omeyades nor the Abassides ever had a Mahmal . . . . I believe the custom to have arisen in the battle-banner of the Bedouins, called Merkeb and Otfe, which I have mentioned in my remarks on the Bedouins, and which resemble the Mahmal, inasmuch as they are high wooden frames placed upon camels."

The first matter of significance in this account is the insistence that the book in the *maḥmal* was not a copy of the Koran, but rather a book of prayers and charms. Inasmuch as the publication of Burckhardt's book preceded Lane's studies by a number of years, it is clear that Burckhardt is not seeking to refute Lane's statement that in the *maḥmal* there were two copies of the Koran, one in book and one in scroll form, but rather that he was endeavoring to correct a tradition which must have been current in his day, and to which manifestly, a few years later, Lane gave full credence. Without questioning in the least the general accuracy of Burckhardt in recording the facts and data which he saw or heard, in a matter as specific as this undoubtedly preference must be given to the account of Lane, whose opportunities for ascertaining the facts with regard thereto were so much larger than those of Burckhardt.[65]

Significant in Burckhardt's account of the *maḥmal* is the fact that he found it decorated with ostrich feathers, obviously in much the same manner as, as we have learned, the *Markab* is decorated. Likewise his statement that on the road, i. e., of course, the road to Mecca, it serves as a holy banner to the caravan, agrees with our inference that we have here a reminiscence of the *maḥmal* acting as the divine guide of the *ḥaǧ* through the desert and selecting the road which the caravan was to travel

[65] Maundrell too has attested that a copy of the Koran was placed in the *maḥmal*. We will have another striking parallel to this procedure later (below, note 99).

until in safety it would reach its appointed goal. Even more significant is the explicit statement that the Wahhabys suppressed the *maḥmal* just because they regarded it as of idolatrous origin, i. e., undoubtedly as having its origin in the pre-islamic religious practice of the "Days of Ignorance"; this confirms our previously expressed inference. [200]

Likewise of importance is Burckhardt's statement that neither the Omeyades nor the Abbasides had a *maḥmal*, and that it was introduced only by Beybars, Sultan of Egypt about A.H. 670. This last is, as we have seen, the popular tradition, likewise recorded by Lane, the historic authenticity of which we have seriously questioned. Furthermore, as we shall see, Burckhardt's statement that the Omeyades did not employ a *maḥmal* must be qualified to a slight degree. But if his general statement be correct, then we would be compelled to infer that in all likelihood the Wahhaby contention that the *maḥmal* had its origin in the idolatrous practices of the pre-islamic Arabs is correct, that with the rise of Islam the use of the *maḥmal* or its pre-islamic antecedent was quickly suppressed by the Omeyade chalifs, in much the same manner and for precisely the same reasons as the Wahhabys suppressed it for a brief period near the beginning of the nineteenth century, and have suppressed it again in quite recent years,[66] but that the memory of it, and even its use in folk-custom also, persisted steadily, with the result that eventually its sanctioned and official use in approved Islamic rites was revived about 670 A. H. However, it is apparent that in so doing the *maḥmal*, or its antecedent, whatever it may have been, was thoroughly Islamized, so far as this was possible, by the substitution of the copy or, more precisely, the two copies, of the Koran for the object or objects which may have occupied the pre-islamic antecedent of the *maḥmal*, and by imposing a representation of the Ka'aba upon the outside, front portion of the covering. Otherwise, as we shall see, the institution has survived and persists in a form and manner of use which approximates very closely what must have been the form and manner of use of its pre-islamic antecedent in the "Days of Ignorance."

[66] Cf. Buhl, article *Maḥmal*, in *Encyclopedia of Islam*.

[201] Finally, of significance in Burckhardt's account is his direct and unqualified identification of the *maḥmal* with the *'oṭfe* and *Markab* of the present-day Bedouin.

Rogers' description of the *maḥmal*,[67] quoted in full in my previous study, may be repeated here in part, for illuminating corroborative evidence. "It is a large frame of wood, capable of being carried by a strong camel. When in the procession it is covered with a green veil, richly embroidered with ornaments and inscriptions in gold thread, and with heavy fringes and tassels. It is surmounted by silver-gilt knobs at the top and four corners, and a copy of the Kurân in a silver-gilt case is suspended from the top. Lane states that in his time the covering was black; but certainly for many years past it has been green . . . . The mahmil contains nothing."

This account confirms Lane's statement that the book suspended in the *maḥmal* is a copy of the Koran, although it seems to know of only one copy thereof suspended in the *maḥmal* instead of the two, of which Lane speaks. Its statement that the veil or covering of the *maḥmal* was green, instead of black, as Lane beheld it, corroborates the account of Doughty, cited above.[68] As Doughty remarks, green is the prophet's color; its use is still the peculiar prerogative of the traditional descendants of the prophet. Manifestly a certain implication of sanctity attaches to the use of this color for the covering of the *maḥmal* today. But this in turn raises the question, what may have been the color of the pre-islamic antecedent of the *maḥmal*.

Finally, Rogers says that "when in the procession it is covered with a green veil." Doughty too says, "it is clothed on high days with a glorious pall of green velvet." These two statements imply clearly that only on important, sacred occasions is the *maḥmal* covered with this green veil, that ordinarily it proceeds without this covering. This is corroborated fully by a statement of Burton,[69] "On the line of march the Mahmil, stripped of its

[67] In *The Academy* of March 31, 1883, 221 f.

[68] This veil or covering of the *maḥmal* is not at all the same as the covering for the *Kaaba*, likewise carried in the Egyptian *ḥaġ* caravan, with which it is frequently confused; cf. Buhl, *op. cit.*

[69] *Pilgrimage to Al-Madinah and Meccah* (Memorial ed., 1893), II, 65, note 3.

embroidered cover, is carried on camel-back, a mere framework." [202]
This framework, as the accompaning illustration shows clearly, is somewhat box-like in appearance, with the four sides and the bottom necessarily present constantly, but with the top open. In fact elsewhere[70] Burton says, "The often described 'Mahmil' is nothing but a Syrian Shugduf, royally ornamented." In its bare form, without the veil covering, the *maḥmal* seems to be box-like in the shape of its lower structure and also to have in general something of the form and appearance of the Ruwala *Markab*. This in turn suggests that the *Markab* may be naught but a form of the *maḥmal*, or rather of its pre-islamic antecedent, with the upper portion, the covering veil, permanently omitted. And inasmuch as it is immediately apparent that the suspension of the veil over the frame or substructure of the *maḥmal* is what gives to it a tent-like appearance, it is clear that, could we picture the *Markab* with a similar veil-covering, it too would have a tent-like shape and thus would approximate very closely the customary form of the ordinary *'oṭfe*, as Burckhardt has described this to us.[71]

THE *MAḤMAL* EN DÉSHABILLE
Reproduced from Burton, *A Personal Narrative of a Pilgrimage to Al-Madinah and Mecca*, London, 1893.

In his valuable work, *Le pèlerinage à la Mekke*,[72] Gaudefroy-Demombynes discusses the *maḥmal*, its origin, history and import in considerable detail. He relies in the main upon Lane's account and also upon that of a modern Moslem writer, Batanouni. His description is primarily of the Egyptian *maḥmal*. He records the

[70] *Ibid.*, I, 233 f., note 4.
[71] Above, pp. 46 f.
[72] Pp. 157–166.

[203] fact that the *maḥmal* is absolutely empty except for two little copies of the Koran, which may be in either book-form or else in the more archaic scroll-form. After discussing the authentic as well as the traditional history of the *maḥmal* and of the various *maḥmals* from different provinces of the Moslem world, of which the Meccan traditions make record, he concludes that the *maḥmal* seems to have enjoyed more of a political than a religious significance, in that it was always the symbol of authority, even of the supreme authority of the king or sultan. He remarks that the *maḥmal* has a marked resemblance to a richly equipped tent, and especially the tent of a tribal chieftain, and he follows Burckhardt in correlating it with the *'oṭfe* and the *Markab* and also with the litter of Aisha at the Battle of the Camel, in 656 A.D. He notes too that the ceremonies attendant upon the return of the *maḥmal* to Cairo at the end of the *ḥağ* are of quite as much importance as those incidental to its setting out. He likewise describes the manner in which the *maḥmal* formerly played an important role in the celebration of the local Egyptian festival of the Nile in Ragab of each year, and likewise the role played by "the mother of the cats," *umm el-quṭâṭ*, in the returning pilgrimage caravan. This was an old woman, clad only in a single garment, in other words nominally naked, who carried with her upon her camel five or six cats. Later the Egyptian government compelled the substitution of an old man for the old woman. This suggests inevitably the cult of the ancient Egyptian goddess, Bast, and indicates that into the traditional ceremonial of the Egyptian *maḥmal*, local rites, growing out of the practices of ancient Egyptian religion, have forced their way. The fact that certain of these rites were apparently associated with the cult of an Egyptian goddess rather than of a male deity, may not be without significance for this study, and so also the fact that "the mother of the cats" in the *maḥmal* procession was practically naked.

The latest description of the *maḥmal*, by Arthur E. Robinson,[73] adds but little to our present knowledge of this object. He records that the Wahhabys forbade the *maḥmal* entrance to the

[73] "The Mahmal of the Moslem Pilgrimage," *JRAS*, 1931, 117–127.

Hijaz in 1798–1814 and again from 1924 to the present day, and from this infers that the *maḥmal* must soon be completely discontinued and forgotten. He too holds that it as well as the *'oṭfe* are survivals of the precedent set by Aisha at the Battle of the Camel, but along with this he argues that it may have been originally a catafalque for the tomb of either Mohammed or Fāṭima at Medina, more probably of the latter. Perhaps the most valuable portion of his entire discussion is his quotation from a writer who, in his account of the *ḥaǧ* caravan, with the *maḥmal*, during the reign of Murad III (1574–1595), "described the Quran as carried from Cairo (and returned there) 'in a little chest made of pure legmane wood in likenesse of the ark of the old testament.' " This is a marked deviation from the later practice, as recorded by Lane, of suspending the Koran, in either one or two copies, from the apex of the *maḥmal*, either within or without. Not improbably this may have been the older practice. At any rate it suggests that the presence of the Koran within the *maḥmal* was from of old of primary, rather than of merely incidental, significance, that it was rather the purposed occupant of the *maḥmal*, and not merely a pious ornament thereof, and that it may well be the substitute which official Islam devised in the course of time to replace the woman, maiden, queen, goddess, sacred object or whatever else may have been the original occupant of the *maḥmal*, or, better, of its pre-islamic antecedent. [204]

The following seem to be the essential facts which characterize the *maḥmal*:

1. It is a tent-like structure, with a rounded or dome-like top, erected over a box- or basket-shaped base. As we have seen, Gaudefroy-Demombynes has remarked that in appearance it resembles the tent of a Bedouin tribal chieftain. Not infrequently upon the march the covering of the tent-like upper structure is removed. At such times the *maḥmal*, with only its basket- or box-like base and its framework visible, resembles not a little the *Markab* of the Ruwala Bedouin. We have seen that the *Markab* is actually only a particularly distinguished specimen of the *'oṭfe*, which lacks the otherwise customary tent-like superstructure of the *'oṭfe*.

2. The *maḥmal* is regularly mounted upon a *howdaǧ*, or

[205] woman's camel saddle, and seems actually to have some primary connection with this.

3. The *maḥmal* seems regularly to be without any human occupant, although the tradition of Sheger-ed-Durr does record the presence of a woman in it, at least upon one occasion.

4. However, regularly either one or two copies of the Koran are deposited, in one way or another, in the *maḥmal*, either in scroll or printed form, while tradition records the presence in the *maḥmal* of a manuscript copy of the Koran, deposited in a box of precious wood, and also, instead of the Koran, a book of charms or prayers.

5. The camel upon which the *maḥmal* is carried is of outstanding appearance and size, and, after the completion of his arduous task, enjoys certain privileges and is definitely regarded as possessing a measure of sanctity or holiness, which, of course, derives from its connection with the *maḥmal*.

6. Upon the pilgrimage procession to Mecca the *maḥmal* marches at or very near the head, and serves as a banner, as it were, and seems to manifest indications that at one time it was thought to select the road through the desert which the cortege should take.

7. A *baraḳa*, or condition of holiness and blessing, is acquired from touching the *maḥmal*, identical in every way with that acquired from touching the sacred black stone in the Kaaba at Mecca.

All these characteristics the *maḥmal* has in some degree in common with the *'oṭfe*. This establishes conclusively the hypothesis of De Goeje, that both *'oṭfe* and *maḥmal* are but variant forms of one and the same object, an object of manifestly sacred character.

Still other significant characteristics of the *maḥmal* must be recorded:

8. Tradition makes the *maḥmal* an institution approximately six hundred and fifty years old; but Snouck Hurgronje has questioned this and has established with reasonable certainty that the origin of the *maḥmal* must be sought in a much earlier time. In this connection Burckhardt's observation that during the period of the Omeyade and Abbaside caliphs the *maḥmal* was

unknown, or at least unutilized, and so seemingly forbidden, [206]
and also Gaudefroy-Demombynes' correlation of the *maḥmal* with the litter of Aisha at the Battle of the Camel acquire particular significance.

9. The Wahhabys have forcibly terminated the use of the *maḥmal* because of a supposedly idolatrous, i. e., pre-islamic, origin or connection. De Goeje has suggested that there must be some basic relationship between the *maḥmal* and the *'oṭfe*, on the one hand, and the old, pre-islamic, Arab custom of carrying portable shrines upon a journey or into battle. Burckhardt, Gaudefroy-Demombynes and Lammens[74] agree with this.

10. The *maḥmal* appears constantly as the symbol of royalty.

Accordingly but little doubt can remain that *'oṭfe*, *Markab* and *maḥmal* are all merely variant, surviving forms of some pre-islamic object of sacred character, which manifestly, in its original form and as employed in religious exercises, possessed a tent-like shape, was transported usually, if not invariably, upon a camel of outstanding size and appearance, was carried into battle or upon pilgrimages or in religious processions, and was thought able to give victory in important, critical battles and to select the site of battle or the road which the clan or tribe must take and the places where it must encamp upon its wanderings through the desert. The possession of this object established the authority of the clan or tribe, and within the tribe itself the authority of the clan or family which had the right of custody of this object. Within this tent-like structure, whatever it may actually have been originally, there must have been something of deep religious import, for which the copy of the Koran, or the two copies, within the *maḥmal* are, as has just been suggested, the Islamic substitute. Presumably too, as the Bedouin procedures with the *'oṭfe* and the *Markab*, and likewise as the vague tradition of the connection of the sultaness, Sheger-ed-Durr, with the *maḥmal* suggest, women were in some way associated with the original, ritual use of this pre-islamic, sacred object. This last inference is strengthened by the fact, recorded by Lammens,[75] that in the

[74] *Op. cit.*, 116 (cf. above, note 7).
[75] *Ibid.*, 119, note 1.

[207] cortege of the *maḥmal* at Mecca, two flute-players, *ṭabbāloūn*, play a role. This is all the more surprising and significant since, as Lammens likewise notes,[76] official Islam has rejected completely flute-playing as a religious rite. The presence of these flute-players may well have been one of the considerations which suggested to the Wahhabys that the entire ceremony of the *maḥmal* is of idolatrous origin and character and so prompted their abolition of it. Moreover, as Lammens has likewise pointed out, the playing of the flute as a religious rite among the Semites was usually performed by women. Manifestly we are herewith carried back to the period and practices of pre-islamic, ancient Semitic religion.

Here then is the place to ask what this early, pre-islamic antecedent of the *'oṭfe*, the *Markab* and the *maḥmal* may have been.

iv. The *Ḳubbe*

At the time of the preparation and publication of my initial study of this interesting subject I was not acquainted with the monograph of Lammens,[77] and not until some years after the appearance of my study did this work come into my hands. Its importance, particularly as a supplement to, or even as, in many very important details, a correction of, Wellhausen's *Reste arabischen Heidentums*, cannot be exaggerated. In this work the learned author discusses, in great detail and with wide and penetrating erudition, the cult of betyls or sacred stones among the pre-islamic Arabs, and with this the role of the *ḳubbe*, the small, sacred tent of red leather, in which these betyls were regularly housed, and in which they were transported upon camel-back in religious processions, the pre-islamic antecedents of the *ḥaǵ*, or rather of the *'umra*, or when the clan or tribe participated in a battle of extraordinary character. In more than one place

[76] *Ibid.*, 123.
[77] Cf. above, note 7.

Lammens, manifestly agreeing with Burckhardt and De Goeje, identifies the *maḥmal* and also the *'oṭfe* with the *ḳubbe*. He calls attention likewise to the significant fact that *ḥamala*, the verb used to describe the action of Abu Sufyan, the leader of the Koraish at Mecca, in carrying the images of the two goddesses, Al-Lat and Al-Uzza, in their sacred tent or *ḳubbe*, into the critical Battle of Ohod, is the same word from which *maḥmal* is derived. Here we may see definite indication of the close relationship of the *ḳubbe* with the *maḥmal*, and, in consequence, also with the *'oṭfe* and the *Markab*. [208]

The *ḳubbe* was regularly a tent, made of leather, red in color, with a domed top, terminating in a point. It was, as a rule, somewhat smaller than the ordinary tent for dwelling, of a size suitable for mounting upon the back of a camel, either for carrying in a sacred procession or for being brought into a battle of critical character, decisive for the fortunes of the clan or tribe. The betyls or sacred images of the clan or tribe were regularly housed in the *ḳubbe*, and in it they were carried into battle or in the sacred procession. In other words, the *ḳubbe* was the housing of the clan or tribal deities, as these were represented by, or embodied in, the sacred stones. Normally the *ḳubbe* stood in immediate contiguity to the tent of the clan or tribal chieftain; or, more precisely, at least for pre-islamic times, the tent of the clan or tribal chieftain was set up regularly next to the *ḳubbe*. Undoubtedly this contiguity symbolized primarily the favor and protection of the chieftain, and through him of the clan, of which he was the proper symbol and representative, by the clan or tribal deities embodied in the sacred stones. Conversely, too, this proximity of the *ḳubbe* to the tent of the clan or tribal chieftain was, viewed in a practical light, the sign of his authority over the clan or tribe.[78]

That the *ḳubbe* continued to be made of leather, and to be dyed red, even after the custom had become firmly established

[78] Cf. Robertson Smith, *Kinship and Marriage in Early Arabia*[1], 171. Accordingly the passing of the *ḳubbe* and of the betyl or betyls within it from one family or from one clan to another symbolized the passing of authority and of the privilege of leadership to the new possessors; cf. also Wellhausen, *Reste arabischen Heidentums*[2], 19, 21.

[209] among the nomadic population of Arabia of dwelling in black tents made of goats' hair, is convincing evidence of the antiquity of the institution; for, as Lammens has shown,[79] in the early days the Arabs employed leather for their tents and for all the utensils and contents thereof, while metal was used to only a very limited degree. Accordingly the tents in which their betyls were deposited were made of leather also. Eventually Yemenite fabrics supplanted leather for all profane uses, but, in conformity with the wide-spread principle of conservatism and opposition to change in religious matters, the use of leather persisted for sacred purposes; therefore the continued employment of leather, and also, no doubt, of the red color, in these ritual tents.

The *ḳubbe* was never carried upon a *ġazzu*, or marauding raid, nor into a battle of only minor significance. But into battles of major importance, especially when the fortunes, and even the destiny, of the clan or tribe were involved, the *ḳubbe* was brought and was carried into the thickest of the fighting. The purpose of this procedure was obvious. Thus the presence of the clan or tribal deities in the battle was assured, with a resultant promise of divine support and ultimate victory in battle.[80] The sight of the *ḳubbe* inspired the tribal warriors to superhuman deeds. Around it they would throng, especially when the tide of battle threatened to turn against them, and there put forth their most valiant efforts; for the *ḳubbe* must be safeguarded at all costs. Its capture by the enemy would constitute a major disaster.[81]

[79] Pp. 128–130.

[80] Wellhausen (*op. cit.*, 20 f.) gives an instance where the god, Jaghuth, went, i. e., was carried, into battle by his worshipers, the Madhig, but he makes no mention whatever of the *ḳubbe*, and seemingly, as Lammens claimed. failed altogether to appreciate the significance of this. Undoubtedly too, when Ġaḏîmah, the Laḫmite king at Ḥirah, would carry his two idols, aḍ-Ḍâribân (literally "the two smiters" or, perhaps more exactly and significantly, "the two givers of victory"), into battle, they were housed in a *ḳubbe*.

[81] A role quite comparable, and in fact practically identical, was played by the tribal banner or standard. At the battle of Ohod Abu Sufyân proclaimed, "The fate of the army depends upon the banner; if this sinks the army will be overcome. Therefore the bearer must be extraordinarily heroic" (Geyer, "Die arabische Frauen in der Schlacht," *Mitteilungen der anthropologischen Gesellschaft in Wien*, XXXIX [1909], 150; Geyer cites Ibn Hishâm for this). Cf. also

At the very least it would symbolize the impotence of the clan or tribal deities against the tribal deities of the enemy and their inability to protect their own tribe. The capture of the *ḳubbe* would mean also the capture of the tribal betyls and of the deities embodied in them by the enemy and their possible eventual use against their own original worshipers. [210]

The presence of the *ḳubbe* in battle, symbolizing the presence of the clan or tribal deities there, also permitted prognostication or divination during the course of the battle, undoubtedly not only to indicate in advance the probable outcome, but also to suggest, through divine revelation, procedures and maneuvers by which victory might be achieved. But for this service a properly qualified diviner or oracular priest, in constant attendance upon the *ḳubbe* and in close communion with the deities resident therein, was indispensable. Not uncommonly this oracular priest or *kahin*[82] was the tribal chieftain himself, who, as we have seen,

Tabari, *Chronicle*, III, 8 (translation from the Persian version by Zotenberg, III, 22): At the Battle of Bedr, a year earlier than the Battle of Ohod, the standard of the Koreish had been captured by the Muslims. In the interim between the two battles a new standard had been fashioned by the Koreish. This Abu Sufyân entrusted to the same warrior who had carried the standard at Bedr, with the injunction to guard this standard better than the last. That a new standard could be fashioned so readily, when the old one was lost, evidences that the standard possessed naught of the divine quality which characterized the *ḳubbe* and the *'oṭfe*, and that it was little, if anything, more than a profane symbol of tribal identity and a rallying-point for the tribe in battle. Note also the banners of the tribes of Israel referred to in Num. 2.1–17. This passage is from P, and is therefore quite late and has little real historic value. Yet it does indicate that even the P writers, about 400 B.C., preserved a distinct reminiscence of the desert, nomadic or semi-nomadic existence of the Israelite tribes and of their ancient customs and institutions. It is significant that in Num. 2.1–17 the tribal banners function as the rallying-points of the individual tribes, to indicate the precise order and place in the migratory caravan of Israel in which each would march and the precise place in the grand encampment where each would pitch its tents. For the tribal standard among present-day Bedouin tribes and its manifest relation to the *'oṭfe*, cf. Musil, *Arabia Petraea*, III, 376 f.; *The Manners and Customs of the Rwala Bedouins*, 571.

[82] Albright (*From the Stone Age to Christianity*, 18 f.), following Nöldeke and G. B. Gray, holds that Arabic *kāhin* is a term borrowed, just as is the Hebrew, *kohen*, from an original Canaanite *kâhin*. I dare not say that this is

[211] dwelt normally in immediate proximity to the sacred tent, and who might therefore function both as military leader and as oracular priest. But quite as frequently, so it would seem, in addition to the chieftain himself, the *ḳubbe* was ministered to by a special *kahin*, one who was presumably particularly expert in the techniques of divination, whatever these may have been.[82a]

not correct. But even if this be so, the fact remains, as we will see, that the Hebrew *kohen* was originally identical in character and function with the Arabic *kahin*, was primarily a soothsayer or diviner or consulter of the oracle rather than a priest, in the conventional sense of the latter term. This last he became only in course of a long cultural development. Therefore, as Gray suggests (*Sacrifice in the Old Testament*, 181 ff.), the term, *kahin* or *kohen*, must have had its origin in the early, desert, nomadic period of the cultural evolution of the Canaanite and Israelite peoples, or even in that remote, proto-Semitic period before the division of the Semitic stock into different peoples had begun, and must have designated just the type of functionary which the pre-islamic *kahin* and, as we will see, the primitive Israelite *kohen* also actually were. And if the term be primarily Canaanite, then it would seem to indicate that the Canaanites too had gone through precisely the same religious, cultural evolution as we will trace among the Israelites, but, of course, at a considerably earlier age, an evolution from a desert, nomadic stage of life and of religious belief and practice to that of settled existence in a rich, agricultural country.

[82a] And there seems to be no reason to believe that among the nomadic and semi-nomadic Arabs they were ever aught but relatively simple. Tabari (*Chronicle*, IV, 4; Zotenberg's translation from the Persian, III, 247–249) relates that during the Battle of Buzākha, fought in 11 A.H. (632 A.D.) Tolaiḥa, a *kahin*, sat at the door of his *ḳubbe* awaiting a revelation from Gabriel; but it did not come. Obviously the figure of Gabriel here represents an Islamization of the regular pre-islamic procedure of divination by means of the *ḳubbe* during a battle.

Musil (*Arabia Petraea*, III, 377) records the interesting and illuminating fact that still today when the people of Kerak go into battle they usually take with them a professional diviner. It is his task to pay expert attention to omens and portents, to ward off evil signs and effects, to give counsel to the military leader, and at times even to suggest the auspicious moment for attack. This he does not infrequently by an utterance couched in cryptic terms, quite after the manner of the ancient oracle. At times he will draw lines upon the ground with his staff, beyond which, presumably, the enemy will be unable to advance; in other words, in addition to his divinatory functions, he also practices magic on behalf of his people. That we have here a modern survival of the practice of the ancient *kahin*, persisting through the centuries despite the influence of Islam (cf. Lammens, *op. cit.*, 141), is self-evident. In this connection one cannot but be reminded of the role of Ahiyyah, the *kohen*, at the

Occasionally these functions were performed even by a *kahina*, a female oracular priest. [212]

As has been said, normally the clan or tribal chieftain's tent was set up in immediate proximity to the *ḳubbe*, and thus a relationship of utmost intimacy was established between him and the tribal deities. Because of this proximity of his tent to the *ḳubbe* and the implied closeness of relationship between himself and the divine occupants of the *ḳubbe*, the title *rabb ḳubbe* or *rabb bait*,[83] "master of the *ḳubbe*" or "master of the dwelling," was applied to him. Lammens has identified this title, and no doubt correctly, with the corresponding title, found frequently upon Nabataean inscriptions, *mara' baita'*, "lord of the dwelling." But this identification carries the institution of the *ḳubbe* and its divine contents backward in Arab life to the beginning of the present era and even, with reasonable certainty, to the earliest appearance of the Nabataeans upon the stage of history in the sixth, or, at the latest, in the fifth century B.C. In this connection it is not without importance that, in conformity with traditional Arab usage, not only the tent of the chieftain, the *rabb ḳubbe*, but also the *ḳubbe* itself, might serve as a place of asylum.[84] Impliedly the refugee thus placed himself under the protection of not only the chieftain and the tribe, but also of the tribal deities.[84a]

In addition to the *rabb ḳubbe* and the *kahin*,[85] the *ḳubbe* regularly had other attendants, particularly in times of action, i. e., in processions and in battles. These secondary ministrants were women. In processions the *ḳubbe* was usually attended by two women, likewise mounted upon camels and following the *ḳubbe* in the procession and playing the flute or tambourine.[86] And into battle the *ḳubbe* would be followed by women, again usually

battle with the Philistines (I Sam. 14.18–19), and that of Elisha in the war with Moab (I Ki. 3.10–20).

[83] Obviously *ḳubbe* and *bait* are synonyms here. The full title was *rabbu l-kubbati 'l-ḥamra'i*, "the master of the red *ḳubbe* (Lammens, *op. cit.*, 152).

[84] *Ibid.*, 158, note 3. [84a] Cf. above, p. 31.

[85] And, as has been said, the functions of these two personages were frequently combined in one individual.

[86] Cf. Lammens, *op. cit.*, 118 f. and above, p. 55.

[213] mounted upon camels, just as was the *ḳubbe* itself. They would function as the particular attendants and custodians of the *ḳubbe* during the battle and, when the struggle became hottest or the danger of defeat and capture of the *ḳubbe* greatest, these women would let their hair fly loose,[87] bare their bosoms, or even occasionally strip themselves stark naked, and, by their words and gestures and by the implied suggestion of the privilege of eventual marriage and sexual intercourse with them[88] would spur the warriors on to deeds of extreme heroism. These women were invariably of the noblest families within the tribe, usually the daughters of the chieftain himself. Marriage relations with them would therefore have been a privilege indeed, the mere prospect of which might well stimulate any warrior within the tribe to deeds of extraordinary daring. Usually too, though not invariably, so it would seem, these women were virgins. Their conduct during the course of the battle, and particularly at its height, when, as it were, the fortunes of their clan or tribe hung in the balance, bordered upon a state of frenzy. They must have seemed possessed, so we may say, by the spirit of the deity or deities of the *ḳubbe*, whose devotees, for the moment at least, they were completely. They were inspired battle-maidens in the most literal sense of the term.

Of unusual significance is the fact that customarily the deities of the *ḳubbe* were, not one, but two.[89] Usually two betyls or sacred

[87] For letting the hair fly loose as a symbol of actual nakedness on the part of women, cf. Lammens, *op. cit.*, 115 f.

[88] Cf. Geyer, *op. cit.*; also Lichtenstaedter, *Women in the Aiyâm al-'Arab*; also Musil, *Manners and Customs of the Rwala Bedouins*, 104, 147, 527, 557, 560, 565. In this connection the words of the beautiful girl of noble birth in the *'oṭfe*, with hair flying loose and naked breasts, addressed to the warriors in battle, "Whoever runs away today may nevermore receive aught from us" (above, p. 20 and Haefeli, *Die Beduinen von Beerseba*, 223, note 229), have more than passing significance. This was the practice within quite recent times; cf. above, note 33.

[89] Cf. Lammens, *op. cit.*, 103, 117–121, 143–147; Wellhausen, *Reste arabischen Heidentums*², 43, note 2; 68; 77, note 1; 244, note to page 43. It would seem that, from the quite incidental manner in which Wellhausen refers to the so oft recurring phenomenon of pairs of deities and betyls in the cults of the pre-islamic Arabs, he failed completely, just as Lammens contends, to appreciate the basic significance thereof. An interesting, and for this study illumi-

stones were deposited in the *ḳubbe*; and usually too they represented or embodied, not male, but female, deities, especially Al-Lat and Al-Uzza.[90] Just why there should have been this duality of deities and of sacred stones is still an unsolved problem; but the fact itself cannot be gainsaid. That female deities should have played a more significant role in connection with the *ḳubbe* than male deities was due in all likelihood to the preponderant role of female deities in the religious concepts and practice of the ancient Arabs. In other words this would seem to be an incident of the institution of the *ḳubbe*, rather than a basic principle. And it must be borne constantly in mind that the connection of male deities with the *ḳubbe* was by no means unknown. [214]

One other important function, significant for this study, was performed by or through the *ḳubbe*. In moments of crisis, when the existence of the clan or tribe seemed at stake, such as, for example, when an unduly severe drought made the pasturage inadequate for the subsistence of the camels, and it became necessary for the clan or tribe to seek new pasturing grounds, especially when such a migration was fraught with unusual danger or gave promise of becoming more or less permanent, then it was the *ḳubbe* which indicated that such procedure was expedient and even designated the auspicious moment for setting forth upon this migration. The *rabb ḳubbe* consulted the oracle of the *ḳubbe*, of which he was the custodian, and communicated

nating, instance of two deities or betyls constituting a single cult-unit or object of worship and religious functioning is recorded by Tabari (Chronicles, I, 752; in Zotenberg's translation of the Persian version, II, 11 f.) to this effect: Djadsîma had two idols of gold, which he called *Dhaizân*, and which he worshiped. When he undertook a war, he carried them with him, in the thought that they would bring him victory. With them he likewise practiced magic and divination. He once, with his large army, drew near to the Iyâdites and set up his camp. He had a tent of brocade pitched for his idols and had it guarded by ten men. When he marched he would have each idol mounted upon a camel and the ten men surrounded them . . . . During the night the Iyâdites sent ten men who made the guardians of the idols drunk and then carried the idols off and brought them to their tribe . . . . Djadsîma thereupon made peace with the Iyâdites and received his idols back.

[90] Cf. Winnett, "The Daughters of Allah," in *The Moslem World*, April, 1940, 1–18; also Wellhausen, *op. cit.*, 38, note 3.

215] to the clan or tribe the decision of the deity or deities housed therein. Thereupon the *ḳubbe* was loaded upon the back of the sacred camel. This act marked the precise moment when the tribal caravan would set itself in motion. Manifestly it was the clan or tribal deities, symbolized by the *ḳubbe* which housed them, which determined all this for the people. And, impliedly, it was these deities, lodged within the *ḳubbe*, mounted upon the sacred camel, which determined, not only the necessity of the migration and the moment of departure, but also the course which the journey should take, its duration and the precise place where the migration should end and the clan or tribe should take up its new settlement, whether temporary or permanent. Lammens even records one instance where, apparently, the sacred camel, bearing the *ḳubbe*, was allowed to wander freely, with the tribe following eagerly behind, to note where the camel would finally halt and where, accordingly, the new settlement would be located. The obvious implication here is that it was the deities within the *ḳubbe* which drove the camel irresistibly along the road which they selected and at the proper moment caused it to halt at the spot which they had chosen for the new abode of the tribe.[91] In

[91] *Op. cit.*, 117 f. The Banou Yād possessed a camel endowed with supernatural powers. In times of public calamity the entire tribe would abandon itself blindly to its guidance (*Kitab el-Aghâni*, XV, 97). With this may be compared the legend recorded by Tabari (Persian translation, Zotenberg, II, 464), that when, at the end of the Flight, Mohammed entered Medina, each of the inhabitants wanted the Prophet to lodge with him. But Mohammed bade them leave him alone, for his camel would know where it should halt. The camel marched to the spot where the mosque stands today. There it knelt down of its own accord, and the prophet dismounted. Jewish tradition has a similar legend with regard to the corpse of the prophet Hosea. Before his death, in Babylon, he expressed the wish to be buried in Palestine. His corpse was accordingly loaded upon a camel, which was left free to wander as it would, with the understanding that wherever the camel would halt, there the prophet was to be buried. The camel halted at Safed, in Galilee (Ginzberg, *Legends of the Jews*, IV, 261). Precisely the same legend is recorded of the corpse of Maimonides. Obviously the implication is that in every case here cited some higher, divine power drives the camel in the right direction and makes it halt at just the proper spot. For the Jewish tradition that the ark too had the power to carry or drive its bearers whithersoever it wished, cf. Ginzberg, *op. cit.*, IV, 6; VI, 172. note 15.

this connection the *rabb ḳubbe* functioned merely as the *kahin*, the oracular priest, of the deities within the *ḳubbe*, the proper intermediary between them and the tribe. But also, still in his role as intermediary, he could, on behalf of the tribe, address to the gods within the *ḳubbe* a plea or a summons, in the moment of the tribe's dire need, to function in its behalf, to bestir themselves, to consent to mount the sacred camel, of course, as always, within the housing of the *ḳubbe*, and lead the people on to safety and triumph, either in battle or upon a forced migration. Such a summons, as Lammens has remarked, must have paralleled closely the words regularly addressed to the ark by Moses, when setting out upon each successive stage of Israel's migration through the desert in search of its divinely promised new home, recorded in Num. 10.35–36. [216]

Manifestly the religious significance of the *ḳubbe* was not inherent in itself, but was derived entirely from the presence within it of the deities embodied in the betyls. It was they, and not the *ḳubbe* alone, which imparted oracles, led the tribe upon its migrations, determined the moment of setting out and the place of encampment, gave victory in battle and bestowed strength and blessing in general. The *ḳubbe* was but the housing or receptacle of these betyls and of the deities resident in them. But as such the *ḳubbe* became the natural symbol of these deities, and especially of their actual presence in moments of need, and thus, in its turn, acquired a large measure of sanctity, a sanctity which was secondary, it is true, but which was none the less real, absolute and effective. Thus the *ḳubbe* became itself an object of holiness and reverence but little less objective and compelling than the holiness and reverence of the betyls themselves.

Quite as significant for this study as the role which the *ḳubbe* played in the religion of the pre-islamic Arabs is the eventual procedure of Islam in dealing with it. In principle Islam sought, of course, to do away completely with the *ḳubbe* and everything connected with it, to obliterate it and its attendant rites and institutions from the practice of Islam and the memory of its adherents. But, as always, an institution as basic, as ancient and as deeply rooted as the *ḳubbe* was in the religious life of the early Arabs can never be eradicated completely. Some memories sur-

217] vive, and some details of ritual and tradition persist for ages. Usually these are reinterpreted in time in accordance with the new orthodoxy, and a new meaning and symbolism come to be attached to them. But the trained and discerning mind can easily detect what lies behind the new procedures and determine the real antecedents of the new institutions. Just so with the *ḳubbe.*

Mohammed himself continued to employ the *ḳubbe* of red leather,[92] as did likewise his adversary, Mosailima, both in battle and on the march, as a sign of supreme authority. The ancient betyls were, of course, expelled from the *ḳubbe* and, so far as possible, were done away with. The title, *rabb ḳubbe* or *rabb bait,* was abbreviated to *rabb* alone and applied only to the Deity. Similarly the term, *kahin,* fell into complete disuse, and the attendant practice of divination was terminated in all except a few isolated connections. But the *ḳubbe* itself survived, to indicate that all the former symbolisms, powers and prerogatives of the pre-islamic *ḳubbe* and of the deities housed therein were now summed up and embodied in the single person of the Prophet of Allah. Thus interpreted the *ḳubbe* even came to be designated as *ḳubbatu 'l-'islam,* "the *ḳubbe* of Islam," in order to distinguish it clearly from the former *ḳubbe* of the "Days of Ignorance." The *ḳubbe,* thus reinterpreted, continued for a brief period to be employed by the successors of Mohammed, the chalifs. Especially significant is the procedure of Moawiyya, the founder of the Omeyade dynasty, at the Battle of Siffin. In precisely the same manner as his father, Abu Sufyan, leader of the Koreish of Mecca against Mohammed at the Battle of Ohod, had set up the *ḳubbe* containing the betyls which symbolized Al-Lat and Al-Uzza, so once again Moawiyya set up a *ḳubbe* alongside of his tent. But whereas the *ḳubbe* of Abu Sufyan contained the betyls of the two goddesses and symbolized their presence in battle, the *ḳubbe* of Moawiyya was entirely empty and, so Lammens maintains, symbolized merely the supreme authority of the chalif.[93] This was a veritable "*ḳubbe* of Islam."

[92] Cf. May, "The Ark — A Miniature Temple," *AJSL,* LII (1936), 230.

[93] Still the consideration suggests itself, the validity of which, however, Lammens seems unwilling to admit, that the *ḳubbe* of Moawiyya at the Battle of Siffin may have symbolized the presence of Allah in the battle, in quite the

Equally significant was the procedure of Aisha at the Battle [218]
of the Camel. She took her place in a litter, a *howdağ*, mounted upon a sturdy camel. The litter was closed upon all sides and was protected with armor, as was the camel likewise. Within the litter Aisha had bared her breasts, and not impossibly had disrobed even further. With her in the litter she carried a copy of the Koran. In purposed and significant contrast to the procedure of pre-islamic days, she was attended by no maidens whatsoever. With the bridle of the camel held by one doughty warrior after another, as each was successively wounded or killed in the attempts of the enemy to capture the camel and its precious burden, Aisha was borne into the thickest of the melee. Particularly at the crisis of the battle, when it seemed as if her warriors were on the point of flight, Aisha bade the leader of the camel conduct it to where the danger was greatest. There her warriors rallied about the sacred litter; but all to no avail. Failing in repeated attempts to capture the camel and its burden, or at least to divert it from the field of battle, Ali finally commanded his warriors to hamstring the animal. This was done. As the animal sank to the ground, carrying the litter, with Aisha in it, with him, the battle was ended. Ali was the victor. Inasmuch as the person of Aisha was inviolable, Ali gave her, still in the closed litter, into the custody of her brother, Mohammed, son of Abu Bekr. As he inserted his arm between the curtains of the litter, his hand touched the naked breast of his sister, to her extreme consternation.[94]

same way as the *ḳubbe* of his father, Abu Sufyan, at Ohod symbolized the presence of Al-Lat and Al-Uzza in that battle. Naturally, however, in accordance with the basic principle of Islam with regard to the incorporeality of Allah, Moawiyya's *ḳubbe* would necessarily be empty. The very absence of a betyl or sacred stone of any kind and the consequent presence of an empty *ḳubbe* would be for Islam the most appropriate and effective symbolization of the presence of Allah in this critical battle.

94 This incident is not recorded in the Arabic text of Tabari, and has probably been suppressed there for obvious theological considerations. But the Persian version of Tabari (translation by Zotenberg, III, 661) does record it. The Arabic text does tell, however, that the *howdağ* of Aisha was kept fast closed and the covering drawn during the entire battle. In other words, though present in the *howdağ* and in the very midst of the battle in order to encourage

219] The procedure of Aisha in this battle is illuminating indeed. The litter was obviously the *ḳubbe* of the "Days of Ignorance."[95] It went into this critical battle in the same manner and for precisely the same purpose as did the ancient *ḳubbe*, to rally the hesitant forces at the moment of crisis and give assurance of victory. The significant difference was that now, under the influence of orthodox Islam, the betyls or images of the old gods were obviated completely, and Aisha took their place in the sacred litter. Moreover, the Arabic text of Tabari tells that the litter of Aisha was red in color, just as was the pre-islamic *ḳubbe*,[96] and this despite the fact that Mohammed himself had denounced red as the color of Satan.[97] Therefore that it was still the ancient *ḳubbe*, or rather an adaptation thereof to the principles of Islam, is beyond all question.

But it is equally apparent that Aisha not only substituted for the pre-islamic betyls in the *ḳubbe*, but also that, as the evidence of her bared breasts indicates, she combined with this in her single person the role of the ancient, pre-islamic battle-maiden. The role was now formal, rather than active; for, inasmuch as the litter of Aisha was kept closed and was even protected somewhat by armor during the entire course of the battle, it follows that she did not actually display her person to the gaze of her warriors. Therefore it must have been the consciousness of her presence rather than the manifestation of her physical charms, which was designed to spur her followers to

her warriors, contrary to established pre-islamic practice Aisha did not expose her person to their gaze. This was undoubtedly in conformity with the newly defined attitude of Islam with regard to women. But with the evidence of the Persian version of Tabari to support it, the presumption is reasonable that within the closed *howdaġ*, in conventional conformity with pre-islamic practice, Aisha had bared her breasts, and not impossibly had disrobed to an even greater extent; all the more reason therefore for keeping the covering of the *howdaġ* closely drawn.

95 Transformed, however, in reality, into a *howdaġ*, or woman's camel-saddle, with the litter mounted upon it. As Professor Torrey has kindly informed me, the Arabic text of Tabari actually calls it "the *howdaġ*."

96 My colleague, Dr. Franz Rosenthal, has very kindly checked the Arabic text of Tabari for me.

97 Lammens, *op. cit.*, 141.

acts of extreme heroism. All the more indicative then of the traditional role which she was playing is the fact that even within the privacy of the veiled litter she felt that it was still incumbent upon her to follow the old convention and bare her breasts. This is convincing evidence that, unable or unwilling as yet to dispense completely with the traditional *ḳubbe*, Islam had managed very early in its career to dispose of at least three of the to it most objectionable features of the cult of the *ḳubbe*, viz., the use of betyls, the presence of female attendants, and the practice of these women of exposing their bodies to the gaze of the warriors.[98] That by the time of the Battle of Siffin, but a few years [220

[98] Actually this is not the first instance where, under Islam, a woman took the place of the betyls in the *ḳubbe*. Tabari (Persian text, III, 6; translation of Zotenberg, III, 252–254) tells that Selma, the daughter of Malik, of the Banu Ghatafân, had been taken captive in a raid, which Mohammed had sent against her people, and had been brought to Medina. The Prophet gave her to Aisha, who, in turn, gave her her freedom and converted her to Islam. Finally she was permitted to return to her people, in order to convert her parents to Islam. After the death of the Prophet and during the caliphate of Abu Bekr, in order to exact blood-revenge for her brother, who had been killed some years previously in a marauding raid against the Prophet's camels at Medina, Selma and her Bedouins started an insurrection. Khalid ibn Walid marched against her. Selma, who obviously, despite her rebellion, adhered none the less to Islam and its tenets, took a leading part in the ensuing battle. She was seated in a litter, mounted upon a camel in the midst of her followers. Khalid, beholding this cried out, "Unless this camel is overthrown and the woman killed, we cannot conquer." Despite the offer of a reward of one hundred camels, no warrior dared undertake this task. Finally Khalid himself, supported by a few warriors, advanced towards Selma. After slaying one hundred of the warriors who guarded her, he hamstrung the camel. When it fell, Selma was thrown from her litter. Khalid slew her with his own hands.

It is clear that in this battle Selma played exactly the same role as did Aisha some years later at the Battle of the Camel, however, with this slight but significant difference, that apparently the curtains of her litter were open, so that she was visible to her warriors, and that the sight of her and the consciousness of her presence in the battle might spur them on to deeds of heroism. Whether or not her breasts were bared, is nowhere stated, but it is altogether probable. Obviously in this battle Selma in her litter played precisely the same role as did Tuëma, the Ruwala maiden in the *Markab*, or Turkiyye or the other Bedouin maidens, as recorded above. Equally obvious is the fact that already but a short time after the death of Mohammed the practice had become current in Islam of having a maiden of the highest birth and authority within

221] later, the *ḳubbe* was entirely empty, containing neither betyl nor woman, and that it was no longer actually carried into battle, but remained firmly planted beside the tent of the chalif, is manifestly but a further stage in the program of Islam of eradicating entirely the institution of the *ḳubbe*. That under the subsequent Omeyade and Abbaside chalifs it should have disappeared entirely and, officially at least, would seem to have been completely forgotten, is not at all surprising.

But institutions as basic and deeply rooted, as the *ḳubbe* certainly was in pre-islamic times, do not ever disappear readily or quite completely. Therefore we may well believe that the memory of the ancient *ḳubbe* persisted in certain circles, though what they may have been it is difficult to say. Accordingly it is not at all surprising that some six hundred or more years after the Battle of Siffin, when what would seem to be a, in some respects, rather heterodox dynasty occupied the throne of Egypt, the institution should have been revived, naturally in a somewhat modified form, in the *maḥmal* of Sheger-ed-Durr. Again we have the sacred tent, domed and with a pointed pinnacle, mounted upon a camel, participating, and perhaps, as has been suggested, even leading the way, in the sacred pilgrimage to Mecca. Here Sheger-ed-Durr manifestly plays much the same role as did Aisha at the Battle of the Camel, except for the fact that, naturally, during the entire course of the pilgrimage she remained presumably fully clad, and did not bare her breasts. Even more strikingly similar to the ancient *ḳubbe* is the traditional *maḥmal*; for, obviously, the two copies of the Koran, which

the tribe take the place in the *ḳubbe* or *howdaġ* when going into battle, which in pre-islamic times had been filled by the betyls.

It may be remarked in passing that the pre-islamic term, *ḳubbe*, seems to have speedily become distasteful to Islam, no doubt because of its intimate and inseparable association with the cult of the betyls, and to have been supplanted by the more general term, *howdaġ*. The practical identity of the *ḳubbe* and the *howdaġ* is apparent from Lane's definitions of both terms. *Howdaġ* he defines (*Arabic-English Lexicon*, I, 2885) as a kind of camel-vehicle for women, having a dome-like top (*muḳabbab*); or a camel-vehicle (*maḥmil*) having a dome-like top (*ḳubbe*), covered with pieces of cloth, in which women ride. *Ḳubbe*, in turn, he defines (*ibid.*, 2478) as a dome-like or tent-like covering of a woman's camel-vehicle of the kind called *howdaġ*.

are suspended in it, are the very natural and proper Islamic substitutes for the two betyls, which, as we have learned, were regularly present in the pre-islamic *ḳubbe.*[99] And, as we have just been told, already at the Battle of the Camel Aisha carried a copy of the Koran with her in her litter or *ḳubbe.* That the *maḥmal* is but a survival of the ancient *ḳubbe,* but superficially Islamized, is beyond question. [222

But that this same conclusion applies to the *'oṭfe* is equally certain. For, as we have seen, the normal form of the *'oṭfe* must have approximated closely that of the traditional *ḳubbe.* It too was shaped ordinarily very much like a small tent, mounted upon a woman's camel-saddle, or *howdaǧ,* and terminated in a point. Ordinarily, so it seems, there was nothing at all in the tent; but it too, like the ancient *ḳubbe,* was attended by maidens, the noblest born of the tribe, who went with it into battle, and by their presence there and their cries and gestures, incited the warriors to extreme efforts. The *Markab* of the Ruwala Bedouin, as we have seen, seems to be but a special type of *'oṭfe,* differing from the customary form of the latter only in the omission of the upper structure and the covering of the tent, but retaining the box-like lower structure, decorated with ostrich feathers. It was thus a kind of permanent combination of tent and woman's camel-saddle; in consequence as we have seen, it was not without the suggestion of a throne. And that the battle-maiden, with bared breasts, within the *'oṭfe* played precisely the same role as Aisha at the Battle of the Camel, with the two exceptions that, unlike Aisha, but quite like the pre-islamic battle-maidens, she was attended by other maidens of the tribe, each mounted upon a camel, and also that she exposed her breasts unhesitatingly and without embarrassment or shame to the gaze of the warriors

[99] Quite similar was the practice of the Sultan of Morocco who, we are told (cf. Goldziher, *Zahiriten,* cited from Lammens, *op. cit.,* 125), when he set out upon an important expedition at the head of his black troops, carried in solemn procession and amidst the most lively demonstrations of reverence, a copy of the *Ṣaḥīḥ* of Boḫārī. The volume, enclosed in a precious casket, had its own special tent, which was invariably set up beside the tent of the sultan. This is, of course, but another and a particularly illuminating instance of an Islamized *ḳubbe.*

[223] of her tribe, is self-evident. The role of the *'oṭfe* in battle or upon the migrations of the tribe in critical times is identical with that of the *ḳubbe* of the "Days of Ignorance." That therefore *'oṭfe* as well as *maḥmal* are naught but comparatively recent, semi-islamized forms of the ancient *ḳubbe*, can no longer be doubted.

v. Historical Forerunners of the *Ḳubbe*

In his treatment of the pre-islamic betyls and *ḳubbe* Lammens calls attention to two terracotta images, at present in the Louvre, described in detail by Cumont in his *Études syriennes.*[100] Both images come from Syria and, in all likelihood, date from near the beginning of the common era. The first image, in size 16 centimeters long and 12½ centimeters high, represents two female figures mounted upon a camel. The two figures are identical in every respect. They are elaborately gowned. Their hair falls in thick tresses over their shoulders and is surmounted by crowns. Their right hands are raised to the level of their shoulders with the palms outward, as if in blessing. Manifestly they represent two goddesses. They sit upon what is obviously a camel-saddle, a *howdaǧ*, which rests upon the back of the camel. The observer views the image as if from the camel's left side. But in order that both female figures may be completely visible, the artist has distorted his perspective and represented them as seated, so it seems, sideways along the ridge of the camel's back, so that both figures face towards the left side of the camel; in other words, he has conformed to the principle of frontality.[101] We must understand, however, that he certainly meant to represent the two goddesses as in reality facing forwards, seated one on each side of the camel, and so maintaining a proper balance

[100] In the article, "La double Fortune des Sémites et les processions á dos de chameau," pp. 273–276.

[101] Cf. also Ingholt, "Inscriptions and Sculptures from Palmyra, I" (*Berytus*, III [1936], 86, note 32).

in the camel's load, and with the *howdaǵ* extending across the camel's back, instead of along its length, as it seems at first glance.[102] Projecting above the right shoulder of the one figure and the left shoulder of the other figure a portion of what was unquestionably a tent or canopy may be discerned. The upper portion of the image is missing; but it is clear that this tent or canopy must originally have covered both figures. This tent rested, of course, upon the camel-saddle or *howdaǵ*. There is reason to believe that originally this tent or canopy was painted red.[103] [224

Cumont has assumed, though with a decided paucity of evidence, that these two female figures represent the Syrian Double-Fortune goddess, and that therefore we have two female figures exactly alike. Lammens, however, has questioned this conclusion and, with a far more convincing array of evidence, has identified these two divine figures with the Arab goddesses, Al-Lat and Al-Uzza. But, if this identification be correct, then it follows that the tent, which extends from the camel-saddle and covers them, is the pre-islamic *ḳubbe*. The two goddesses are then represented in a manner which conforms to practically all the details of the *ḳubbe*, as we, following Lammens, have formulated them. They are seated in a *ḳubbe*, which rests upon a camel-saddle or *howdaǵ*, mounted upon a camel, which, as the position of its legs indicates, is actually marching. It follows therefore that this image represents these two goddesses as either being carried into battle in the customary manner, or participating in a migration or, as Cumont maintains and Lammens endorses, in a sacred procession. In only one respect do they differ from the picture of the *ḳubbe* and its contents, which we have reconstructed, viz., in that instead of being betyls, or shapeless, unmodeled sacred stones, they are carefully carved and decorated figures. However, with their Syrian provenience this is precisely what we would

[102] For a more effective representation of the correct mounting of the *howdaǵ* upon the camel's back, cf. the relief depicting a sacred procession of a horse and a camel from the temple of Bêl at Palmyra, reproduced by Seyrig, "Antiquités syriennes," *Syria*, XV (1934), plate XIX, discussed in greater detail below (pp. 74 f.).

[103] Cf. Ingholt, *op. cit.*, 86.

[225] expect; for, as Wellhausen has observed,[104] all carved images of Arab deities in the "days of ignorance" were imported from Syria.

This identification of Lammens finds strong confirmation in the second terracotta image.[105] Here again we have two female figures mounted upon a camel-saddle, which rests upon the back of a marching camel. Again the two figures and the camel-saddle are represented in distorted frontal perspective, as if mounted on the ridge of the camel's back and facing his left side, when, again, we must understand that the artist meant to suggest that the saddle extended across the camel's back and that the two figures were seated one on each side of the camel. Again protruding from the two ends of the camel-saddle and rising above the heads of the two figures is a tent or canopy. The two figures are fully clothed, but the necks of the garments of both seem to be wide open, almost, or even quite, as if their breasts, or at least the upper portions of their bosoms, were bared. A part of their hair seems to be arranged in a heavy braid, coiled tightly about the top of the head, but the remainder, unbound, falls loosely upon their shoulders. The one figure is playing the double-flute; the other is tapping upon a square drum.[106] It is impossible not to identify these two figures, precisely as Lammens has done, with the *ṭabbaloun*, the two flute- and tambourine-playing women in

[104] *Op. cit.*, 72, 102. In this connection attention must be called to the golden bracelet worn by Nazih, in the *Sirat Antar* (translation of Terrick Hamilton, III, 279 f.), upon which were represented the two goddesses, Al-Lat and Al-Uzza, and upon which was inscribed likewise the name of the Lord of heaven and earth, i. e., undoubtedly Ba'alšamēm (cf. Eissfeldt, "Ba'alšamēm und Jahwe," *ZAW*, XVI [n. F.] [1939], 1–31). This inscription indicates unmistakably a Syrian origin for this golden bracelet. In just what form the two goddesses were represented upon it is not indicated in any way; but it would not be too far-fetched to assume that it was in much the same manner as in this terra-cotta image.

[105] Published also by Rostovtzeff, "Dura and the Problem of Parthian Art," *Yale Classical Studies*, V (1935), figure 16; cf. also p. 183.

[106] Ingholt (*op. cit.*, 86) tells of another terra-cotta in the Ny Carlsberg Glyptothek, Copenhagen, which likewise shows a camel bearing a palanquin, also with traces of red paint, in the tent of which two women may be seen beating the tambourine. This is obviously, as Ingholt maintains, a representation almost identical with that just described.

the train of the *ḳubbe*, and, still later, of the *maḥmal*, at Mecca. [226]
Certainly these two figures do not represent goddesses; for, unlike the two figures of the first image, they are uncrowned, and the acts, which they are represented as performing, are obviously of a ritual, worshiping character. If it be correct that they are depicted with bared, or half-bared, breasts, then, beyond all question, they represent the attendants upon the *ḳubbe* and the sacred images within it, as these went into battle or, as in this case, participated in a sacred procession.[107]

Still another representation of the *ḳubbe*, upon a bas-relief from the temple of Bêl at Palmyra,[108] is significant for this study. Here the *ḳubbe* is a low, tent-like structure, which rests upon what seems to be a decorated rug, laid crosswise upon the back of a camel. This *ḳubbe* still shows traces of having been painted a bright red. The camel is led in what is obviously a ritual procession. The camel's bridle is held by a man, with the hand which grasps the bridle raised above his head, who strides along in the procession in front of the camel. From the camel's neck is suspended a small, round ornament or ritual object, which De Vaux compares,[109] very properly, with the Midianite camel-ornaments of Jud. 8.26. Immediately behind the camel, and seemingly participating in the procession, quite as if they were the customary attendants of the *ḳubbe*, are three female figures, each

[107] In *op. cit.*, figure 17, Rostovtzeff has published another closely related terra-cotta image, which likewise comes from Syria and dates from the same period and has the same background, and which is likewise at present in the Louvre. It too represents two female figures, apparently kneeling, rather than seated, in exactly the same tent-like structure as in the other image. However, this tent-like structure, despite the fact that its base is identical with the tent-base of the first image, does not rest upon the back of a camel. Instead it has a perfectly flat bottom, intended obviously to permit the image to stand firmly upon a flat surface. This image might therefore very well represent a *ḳubbe* resting on the ground, as, as we have learned, was its normal state when not in action. These two female figures are clothed exactly like those in the first image, and again with necks and upper portions of their bosoms bared. Their hair too seems to be arranged in a manner closely similar to that of the two figures in the other image. Here both women are playing on tambourines.

[108] Published by Seyrig; cf. above, note 102.

[109] "Sur le voile des femmes dans l'orient ancien," in *RB*, 44 (1935), 405, note 2.

[227] heavily veiled.[110] Seyrig claims to see within the *ḳubbe* traces of a recumbent figure, presumably a sacred image. This is, however, by no means certain, although it is difficult to conceive of a *ḳubbe* being represented in pre-islamic times as empty. What seem to be spectators hail the procession, and especially the *ḳubbe* and whatever its contents may have been, certainly the chief cult-object in the procession, with arms upraised in somewhat the same gesture as is made by the man leading the camel. Obviously it is a gesture of homage to the *ḳubbe* and its contents.

As the invariable mounting upon camel-back indicates, these are all unquestionably representations of the *ḳubbe* of the pre-islamic Arabs. All come from the Roman period, and, in all likelihood, from the second or third centuries A.D. All come from Syria or the region of Palmyra, in which districts, because of extensive caravan traffic, Arab cultural influence was strong at this time.[111] This evidence establishes then that during this period, antedating the rise of Islam by three or four centuries at the very least, the cult of Al-Lat and Al-Uzza and of the *ḳubbe*, with all the customary attendant paraphernalia, rites and institutions, must have flourished in Syria, no doubt chiefly among the nomads of the northern desert and those peoples and communities which participated in the far-reaching caravan traffic of that day.[112]

This conclusion is corroborated by the term, *mara' baita'*, recurring oft in Nabataean inscriptions and designating the pos-

[110] Seyrig (*op. cit.*, 160) holds that these three women were only spectators, and not participants in the procession. De Vaux (*op. cit.*) supports the opposite hypothesis. He establishes that already in the pre-islamic period Arab women, especially of the upper class, were regularly veiled in public. He contends that, notwithstanding its provenience from the temple of Bêl at Palmyra, the scene here depicted is peculiarly Arabic, and that the three veiled female figures conform fully to contemporary Arabic custom. That these women participate in this procession heavily veiled, instead of with bared bosoms, is not surprising, since here they follow the *ḳubbe* on foot in the procession, i. e., they have only a semi-active part in the ritual, instead of riding in a *ḳubbe* itself in the role of active attendants upon the cult-object.

[111] Cf. Rostovtzeff, *Caravan Cities*, 91–119.

[112] Cf. Winnett, "The Daughters of Allah," *The Moslem World*, April, 1940; also Rostovtzeff, *op. cit.*, 209.

sessor or guardian of a sacred tabernacle.[113] This Nabataean *bait* [228]
must have been identical with the pre-islamic *bait* or *ḳubbe*, while the full title, *mara' baita'*, was, of course, the Nabataean equivalent of the Arabic *rabb ḳubbe* or *rabb bait.* But this title and the institution which it evidences must have been current among the Nabataeans already in their nomadic and semi-nomadic days, preceding their eventual settlement in Transjordan and the development by them of a sedentary life there.[114] This carries the *ḳubbe* and all its religious associations back to at least the fourth or fifth centuries B.C. and, quite probably even earlier.

From a statement of Diodorus[115] we may infer that the Carthaginians too employed the sacred tent, at least when they went into battle, no doubt battles of a critical nature. He records an instance of a fire breaking out in the sacred tent and from there spreading to and destroying the tent of the chief military commander, which must therefore have been pitched immediately adjacent to the sacred tent. This caused great consternation in the camp, quite as if it was an augury of evil. This institution the Carthaginians must, of course, have derived from their Phoenician ancestry.

What seems to be a still older instance of the *ḳubbe* and its sacred image is recorded by Sanchuniathon.[116] He tells that in the early period, following shortly upon creation and the birth of both gods and men, a certain Agroueros or Agrotes had a wooden statue, which was highly venerated, and a shrine or portable temple, drawn about in Phoenicia by yokes of oxen.

[113] Cf. Rostovtzeff, *op. cit.*, 52 f. Ingholt (*op. cit.*, 83–88) has published an inscription coming from Palmyra, and not improbably from the temple of Bêl there, which records the erection of a *ḳubbe* in honor of the deity, "Blessed is his name forever." This may well have stamped the person who erected the *ḳubbe* as a *mara' baita'* and as one of high rank and authority among his people. Ingholt makes no attempt to date the inscription, but unquestionably it may be assigned with reasonable certainty to the second or third centuries A.D. (cf. Rostovtzeff, *op. cit.*, 91–119).

[114] Dalman (*Petra*, I, 72; II, 53) records another significant detail of the *ḳubbe*-cult among the Nabataeans, viz., that they had a predilection for the worship of betyls in pairs.

[115] XX, 65, 1 (ed. Dindorf); quoted from Gressmann, *Mose und seine Zeit*, 242.

[116] Cf. Cory, *Ancient Fragments*, 9.

[229] This shrine or portable temple must have been, of course, the housing of this wooden statue or idol. When it travelled in this manner, it must have been placed upon a cart or wagon. Moreover, it is a reasonable inference from the specific wording of this narrative that the oxen were supposed to draw the portable shrine, with the idol in it, not upon a regular, pre-arranged itinerary, but rather that they went in whatever direction and halted at whatever place the deity within the shrine would compel them. In other words, the procedure with this portable shrine, mounted upon a wagon or cart and drawn by oxen, driven by the deity within the shrine, parallels exactly the procedure with the ark, after the discomfiture of the Philistines, recorded in I Sam. 6. But it also parallels sufficiently closely the procedure with the pre-islamic *ḳubbe* and the later *maḥmal* and *'oṭfe* to establish the identity of these various sacred objects.

But with these evidences of antiquity for the *ḳubbe* and all that was associated with it, it is but a relatively short step from the fifth century B.C., or even somewhat earlier, back to the twelfth or thirteenth century B.C. and to the consideration of the corresponding institution or institutions in ancient Israel. And first the ark.[117]

vi. The Ark

In the previously oft-cited article I endeavored to show that the history of the ark falls into three distinct periods. The first period was that of the pre-Palestinian desert life and migrations of the tribe or tribes, with which the ark was originally associated, and of the early settlement of these tribes in Palestine. This period extended through the reign of David and actually to the erection of the Temple at Jerusalem by Solomon.

The second period in the history of the ark was coincident with the existence of the first Temple, and ended with the destruc-

[117] Lammens (op. cit., 159) correlates the ark with the pre-islamic *ḳubbe* and suggests that it was in his role as *rabb el-bait* that Moses would recite the summons to the ark recorded in Num. 10.35 f.

tion of the Temple by the Babylonians in 586 B.C. and the [230]
resultant disappearance of the ark. It was during this period, and beginning quite early in the period, that the ark came to be transformed, in tradition at least, if not in actual fact, from what it had been originally, whatever that may have been, to the box-like container of the two tablets of the decalogue[118] and likewise, as the result of the religious reformation in 899 B.C., during the reign of Asa, took the place within the *d^ebir* of the Temple, and as the most sacred object of the cult thereof, of the golden image of Yahweh, seated upon a throne, which had stood there originally.[119]

The third period in the history of the ark was associated with the post-exilic Temple at Jerusalem, particularly from the period about 400 B.C., or perhaps a decade or so earlier, when the Priestly Code was formulated and made authoritative, and when, in connection with the official promulgation of this code for the Jewish community of Judaea, it seems that the Temple was rebuilt extensively, in conformity with the somewhat new pattern of the sanctuary which the Priestly Code set forth.[120] Once again the nature of the ark was reinterpreted, at least partially. It continued to be regarded as the box-like container of the two tablets of the decalogue, now called the "tablets of testimony"; but in addition thereto it recaptured something of the character of the sacred object which it had supplanted in the Temple of Solomon, and so was regarded likewise as the throne of the Deity. This was, in fact, its major role in the Temple scheme of the Priestly Code, while its role as container of the sacred stone tablets became secondary.

The Priestly Code represented the ark as standing in the holy of holies, beneath the overshadowing wings of the two cherubim. Upon the top of the ark was the golden cover, the *kapporet*, the so-called "mercy-seat." It was upon this that the Deity was con-

[118] So also, in part at least, Ed. Meyer, *Die Israeliten und ihre Nachbarstämme*, 214.

[119] For a detailed account of this reformation and of the role of the ark therein, cf. "Amos Studies, III," 100–134.

[120] Cf. "Supplementary Studies in the Calendars of Ancient Israel," 72–146.

[231] ceived as seated, enthroned in solitary majesty, invisible to human eye.[120a] Into the holy of holies and into the presence of the Deity, and therefore into close proximity to the ark, only one human being was permitted to enter, the high-priest, and that only once each year, upon the recurrent Day of Atonement;[121] and that too only enveloped in a cloud of incense, to the end that he might not behold too closely that which was assumed to be within the holy of holies, and as a result of such temerity perhaps lose his life.[122]

Actually therefore, despite the provisions of the Priestly Code, whether there was really an ark within the holy of holies of the post-exilic Temple is none too well attested. And if there was an ark there, we have only the vaguest idea of what it was like. But of this we may be sure, that in any case it was not the ark of the pre-exilic period, of the sanctuary of David and of the Temple of Solomon. That original ark had certainly disappeared, if not sooner, then, at the very latest and beyond all doubt, in the destruction of the first Temple in 586 B.C. A full century and three quarters had elapsed between the disappearance of the true ark and the formulation of the Priestly Code's half-imaginary reconstruction thereof. Not improbably the authors of the Priestly Code had only a vague tradition of what the ark had really been. Not improbably also even this vague and unreliable tradition they did not hesitate to modify more or less to meet their own peculiar purposes. Too much importance may therefore not be attached to the account of the ark in the Priestly Code in the endeavor to determine what the original ark really was. This last is our present task. Our primary concern in this study

[120a] Not at all improbably a like concept obtained with the empty *ḳubbe* which Moawiyya set up in immediate proximity to his own tent at the Battle of Siffin. While physically empty, Allah may well have been thought to be present invisibly in the *ḳubbe* in order to give victory to the cause of his worshipers (cf. above, note 93).

[121] Originally the New Year's Day; cf. "The Three Calendars of Ancient Israel," 22–58.

[122] Cf. Lauterbach, "A Significant Controversy between the Saducees and the Pharisees," *HUCA*, IV (1927), 173–205, and my "A Chapter in the History of the High-Priesthood," 13–24.

is with the nature and role of the ark during the first period of its history. [232

During the early period of the sojourn of the tribes of Israel in Palestine the ark stood at Shiloh, in the territory of the tribe of Ephraim. It was obviously the principal cult-object of the important sanctuary there and was ministered to by a levitical priestly family,[123] the names of three members of which are preserved in the biblical records, Eli and his two sons, Hofni and Phineas. It is reasonable to infer, from the fact of its location at Shiloh, that the ark had been originally the cult-object of Ephraim alone, or, in the pre-Palestinian, desert period, of the antecedents of this tribe, whatever they may have been. However, it seems that during the period of Ephraimite hegemony over the tribes of Israel, or at least over the tribes of Central Palestine, during the decades immediately preceding the Philistine conquest, the ark acquired somewhat more than merely local or tribal significance. It came apparently to be regarded as the major cult-object, and its sanctuary at Shiloh as the central sanctuary and source of oracular revelation, of all the tribes which constituted the then federation of the tribes of Israel.[124]

[123] Descended from Moses, as at least early post-exilic tradition had it, presumably through the young Levite whose story is recorded in Jud. 19. The evidence for this positive statement I hope to present upon some other occasion; meanwhile cf. below, note 228, pp. 128 f.

[124] At the time of the Philistine wars this federation consisted of at least Ephraim and Manasseh. Benjamin had certainly been a member of this federation earlier, but had completely severed its connections therewith, at the most but a few decades previously, as the result of the intertribal war recorded in the earliest literary stratum of Jud. 19–21. Therefore in the early Philistine wars Benjamin did not participate at all. It held severely aloof; and this, together with its topographical situation, caused the Philistines to pass it by when they conquered the territory of Ephraim and Manasseh and subjected it to their rule. This enabled Benjamin to maintain its tribal strength unimpaired and so to carry on its own war with the Philistines under Saul some fifty years later. (cf. below, note 137. This chronology is based upon considerations of Samuel's apparent age at the time of each of these two wars. During the former he was still a mere lad, while during the latter he was well advanced in years and even approaching his death. There is a rabbinic tradition that at the time of his death Samuel was fifty-two years old [Num. Rab. (ed. Wilna), III, 7]. Albright [*Archaeology and the Religion of Israel*, 103 f., 210 f.] would date the Battles of Ebenezer and the resultant destruction of Shiloh at *circ.*

[233] 1050 B.C., or a little earlier. I would date them some fifteen years earlier than this [cf. below, notes 143 and 174]. Albright likewise regards Shiloh as the central sanctuary of all Israel. I regard it as the central sanctuary of only the tribes of Central Palestine, i. e., of Israel proper, or, at the very most, of Central and Northern Palestine. This would also account adequately for the manifest reluctance and eventual failure of the northern tribes to rally strongly to Saul's standard after his initial victory over the Philistines, as, quite obviously, both he and Samuel had confidently expected [despite the statement of I Sam. 14.21–22]).

Whether the tribes north of the Valley of Jezreel were actually linked in any degree with this federation at the time of the Philistine wars cannot be determined with certainty. That at the time of the Battle of Ta'anach Issachar, Zebulon and Naphtali, north of the Valley, had joined with Machir, Ephraim and Benjamin, south of the Valley, in united resistance to the common Canaanite enemy, is convincingly evidenced by Jud. 5. But how long this early and quite extensive coalition of Israelite tribes persisted after the battle, is not certain. It endured probably long enough to ensure the breakdown of the power of the Canaanite city-states in the Valley and the immediately adjacent sections of Palestine and the termination of all danger from that direction. Apparently by the time of Gideon and the Midianite inroads it had dissolved completely, or at least almost so.

Seemingly too after the dissolution of the premature and short-lived political organization which, following upon Gideon, Abimelech effected, the leadership in the affairs of the tribes of Central Palestine passed to Ephraim. In fact Jud. 8.1–3 evidences that even before Gideon the Ephraimites had exercised a definite intertribal hegemony, of which they were intensely jealous, and that the Gideon regime represented merely a brief interlude therein. Jud. 12.1–7 illustrates clearly the arrogant manner in which the Ephraimites exercised this hegemony, at least in Central Palestine, west of the Jordan, and even to an extent to the east of the Jordan. This Ephraimite intertribal hegemony, which had begun even before Gideon, continued until the Philistine triumph.

All the evidence indicates that it was primarily this federation of tribes of Central Palestine which was subsumed under the name, Israel, and that too as far back as the time of Mernephtah. The name itself seems to have been somewhat elastic in application, to have designated primarily the federation as such, and to have had a broader or narrower connotation with the expansion or contraction of tribal membership therein and resultant cooperative action.

At the time of the Battle of Ta'anach, as Jud. 5 indicates, the term, Israel, embraced not only Ephraim, Machir and Benjamin, but also Issachar, Zebulon and Naphtali. As we have seen, the common Canaanite danger drew these six tribes into the federation. But at the time of the later, intertribal war, of which we read in Jud. 19–21, the connotation of the term, Israel, seems to have narrowed again and to have covered little more than Ephraim and Manasseh and to have definitely excluded Benjamin. So it was still at the time of the Philistine wars.

This sanctuary, so it would seem, was not at all a *ḳubbe*, a tent,[125] but a much more pretentious structure, a *bait* or a *hekal*.[126] It had its doors and doorposts.[127] The doors were closed regularly at night and opened again in the morning. The ark stood apparently in the sanctuary proper, which was illumined during the night by a lamp of sacred character.[128] Within this sanctuary and seemingly in immediate proximity to the ark, in order that he might be in constant attendance upon it, should a revelation from the Deity come at some unforeseen moment, when Eli, the chief priest, was not present, slept the young Samuel, in discharge of his duties of priestly apprenticeship.[129] The abode of Eli, house or tent, whichever it may have been, was immediately adjacent.[130] In other words, Eli dwelt in the same close proximity to the ark as did the pre-islamic Arab tribal head to the *ḳubbe* or as the Ruwala tribal chieftain to the *Markab*. This proximity must have [234]

[125] Despite the application to it in I Sam. 2.22b, unquestionably by editorial hands, of the term, *'ohel mo'ed*.

[126] I Sam. 1.7, 9, 24; 3.3; cf. Jud. 18.31; so also Luther, in Ed. Meyer, *Die Israeliten und ihre Nachbarstämme*, 135; Sellin, "Das Zelt Jahwes," in *Kittel Festschrift*, *BWAT*, 13 (1913), 174; Gressmann, *Mose und seine Zeit*, 88 f.

[127] I Sam. 1.9; 3.15.

[128] I Sam. 3.3.

[129] For the same practice, of the priest sleeping in the sanctuary of Al-Galsad in Hadramaut, in close proximity to the idol, in order to be prepared to receive an oracle at any moment, day or night, whenever the deity would choose to speak, cf. Wellhausen, *Reste arabischen Heidentums*², 55. Actually the role of Samuel as the youthful priest and apprentice to Eli is altogether secondary and probably in some measure unhistorical. Unquestionably it is patterned after the role of Moses as the oracular priest of the "tent of meeting" (cf. below, pp. 131–161, with his apprentice too never departing from the sanctuary (Ex. 33.11). So here Samuel plays the role of priestly apprentice to Eli, while the sanctuary, in turn, is represented as, and is even called specifically, *'ohel mo'ed* (cf. also Josh. 18.1, 8-10; Ps. 78.60, and above, note 125). Actually in relation to the ark Samuel played no priestly role whatsoever. Its priests were Eli and his two sons, Hofni and Phineas (cf. I Sam. 1.3b). Within the original ark-pericope of I Sam. (for the analysis cf. the commentaries, and also Press, "Der Prophet Samuel," *ZAW*, XV[n. F.] [1938], 177–225) Samuel does not appear at all. None the less even in the secondary sections of I Sam. 1–6, in which the youthful Samuel functions as priestly apprentice, there are here and there some reminiscences of the ark and of the ancient sanctuary at Shiloh which seem to have positive historic value, although they must be used with discrimination.

[130] I Sam. 3.2–5.

[235] been due primarily, of course, to Eli's role as the oracular priest of the ark. But when we remember that as a rule the pre-islamic Arab tribal chieftain was also the *kahin* or oracular priest of the deity or deities of the *ḳubbe*, we may see some indication of close relationship between the role of Eli as the priest of the ark and that of the pre-islamic *kahin* as the oracular priest of the *ḳubbe*, and see likewise in the proximity of Eli's abode to the ark a token of the very high authority which he exercised within his community and tribe, and even, no doubt, within the federation of Israelite tribes of Central Palestine. But this suggests, in turn, that, not the actual sanctuary at Shiloh, but only the ark within it, played for the tribe of Ephraim, and perhaps even for the tribal federation likewise, somewhat of the role of the *ḳubbe* for the pre-islamic Arab tribes.

This suggestion is confirmed by abundant evidence. From its normal place in the sanctuary at Shiloh the ark was carried into battle in order to give the hosts of Israel victory over their enemies. But it was not carried into ordinary battles.[131] In the first

[131] In this connection it may be asked very properly, why there is no record of the presence of the ark at the Battle of Ta'anach in either Jud. 4 or 5. The answer to this question is suggested by Täubler, "Die Spruch-Verse über Sebulon," *MGWJ*, 1940–41, 1–37. Täubler establishes that in this battle it was the tribes of Zebulon, Issachar and Naphtali which were most immediately threatened by Sisera, ruler of Haroshet Haggoim, and were therefore the leading participants in the battle (cf. above, note 124). Ephraim, Machir and Benjamin played only a secondary role therein, that of sympathetic allies. They themselves were in no immediate danger, since their territory lay to the south of the Valley of Jezreel, at some distance from the center of the coalition of Canaanite city-states which Sisera had effected, and so for them this was not, strictly speaking, a decisive battle. Therefore there was no reason for the presence of the ark there. Despite the gloss, Jud. 4.4b–5a, Deborah was probably from Issachar (cf. 5.15aα) and not from Ephraim, while Barak was certainly from Naphtali (cf. 4.6, and for ויששכר in 5.15aβ read וכנפתלי). Barak, who probably cherished ancient, nomadic custom, made his acceptance of leadership, to which he was summoned by Deborah, conditional upon Deborah's accompanying him and his men into battle (4.8). This she did, and, in the role of battle-maiden and at the critical moment in the battle, she chanted a song in order to stimulate the Israelite warriors to deeds of extraordinary heroism (5.12). That even previous to this battle Deborah was recognized as a *n^ebi'ah*, i. e., a female diviner, undoubtedly equivalent to the pre-islamic *kahina*, is attested by Jud. 4.4–5.

Battle of Eben Haezer, when manifestly the Israelites confidently anticipated a complete and easy victory over the Philistine enemy, the ark remained in Shiloh. Only after this initial defeat and after they had thus been made to realize the power of the Philistines and the magnitude of the danger which now confronted them, did the federated tribes have recourse to the ark, and bring it from the sanctuary at Shiloh to the field of battle, in the custody of its two regularly attendant priests, Hofni and Phineas, the sons of Eli.[132] But it is plain that with the advent of the ark on the field of battle the Israelites were still fully confident of victory,[133] while, on the other hand, the Philistines are represented as being dismayed and losing confidence, for, as they exclaim, "Their god[134] has come unto them to the camp."[135] Obviously the Philistines are here represented as seeing in the ark either the deity of Israel or else, what seems far more likely, and, as we will see, is the correct explanation, the container of the god or gods of Israel. [236]

None the less the Philistines persist, and in the second Battle of Eben Haezer they gain a complete and decisive victory over Israel. The ark is captured and its two attendant priests are killed. The capture of the ark marks the end of the struggle and the complete conquest of the Israelite tribes of Central Palestine[136] and the subjection of their entire territory, at least as far as the northern border of the Valley of Jezreel on the north and Beth Shean to the northeast, to Philistine domination, a domination so thorough and rigid that it endured for almost three quarters of a century, until finally the tables were turned upon the Philistines by David. It must have seemed to the Israelites of Central Palestine that in the two battles their god had proved no match for the gods of the Philistines, and that also, with the capture of the ark and its removal to Philistine territory, their god had been forcibly carried away from their land and from their midst, so that they were now left a people without any god to protect and

[132] I Sam. 4.1 ff.

[133] V. 5.

[134] Or perhaps "their gods," with G^B.

[135] Vv. 6–9.

[136] Of course not including Benjamin; cf. above, note 124.

237] prosper them, weak, helpless, impotent. How completely their spirits were crushed and their faith shattered is proved conclusively by their failure to rally to Saul's banner, as unquestionably he had anticipated they would do, after his initial victory over the Philistines.[137] The ark was the visible symbol of the presence

[137] Despite the statement of I Sam. 14.21–22. If these two vv. have any historical value at all, they indicate only that the exhilaration of these northern tribesmen, resulting from Saul's victory over the Philistines, which impelled them to flock to Saul's standard, was but momentary and subsided almost instantaneously, so that they deserted him quite as quickly as they had joined him. It must have been this fact more than aught else, which, almost from the start, spelled the doom of Saul's warfare against the Philistines. He must have realized from the outset that his own little tribe of Benjamin, which could as yet hardly have regained its normal strength after the disastrous intertribal war of a few generations earlier (cf. above, note 124), was too weak alone and unaided to cope successfully with the Philistines. He must have counted from the very beginning upon a significant initial victory over the Philistines to revive the spirit of the conquered Ephraimites and Manassites and draw them to his standard. Only in this way could he hope to gather a force strong enough to wage an aggressive offensive war against the Philistines. The defection of these northern tribesmen and the hopelessly low state of their spirit and courage disappointed all his expectations and upset his plans completely. With only his own tribe of Benjamin to support him, he was compelled to wage a defensive war, one largely of guerrilla character, against the Philistines. Not once did he dare invade the Philistine lowlands and engage there in pitched and decisive battle with them.

Only at the very end of his life, realizing no doubt how rapidly his malady was growing upon him, and appreciating apparently that not one of his sons was worthy to succeed him and carry on the war with any promise of eventual success, he resolved, in sheer desperation, to stake everything upon one pitched battle in the enemy's own territory, which it had conquered, in the Valley of Jezreel, near Mt. Gilboa. Victory in this battle would have given him control of the Philistine avenue of communication with their great fortress at Beth Shean, from which largely, so it seems, the Philistines maintained dominion over the tribes of Central Palestine. Had he succeeded in this battle, and in the ultimate capture of Beth Shean, these tribes might have been sufficiently enheartened to rally once again, and this time permanently, to his banner. But the odds against him were far too great and the battle went against him. He lost his life, and the army was decimated by the Philistines. But a remnant thereof escaped into Trans-Jordan. The territory of Benjamin too, for the most part, now came under Philistine control.

But had at the very outset the spirit of the Northern tribesmen been different, Saul's campaign, certainly not unreasonably conceived, might well have succeeded. It was the dispiritedness and lack of faith of these Northerners,

of their god in their midst and the guarantee of their continued [238]
political independence and power under his protection. Its capture meant not only the conquest and departure of their god from among them, but also their loss of independence and subjection to a foreign people. Obviously the ark played in this respect too precisely the same role for Israel as did the *ḳubbe* for the pre-islamic Arab tribes.[138]

But what must have been contary to all normal procedure on the part of both Israelites and Philistines, the capture of the ark and its carrying off as a trophy of victory to the Philistine cities did not by any means terminate its divine power and functioning. Even in the midst of a foreign land the deity or deities of the ark were able to affirm their potency and authority, and that too over the very people which had captured their cult-object and likewise over their gods. No doubt the tradition of the events

convinced no doubt by the loss of the ark that Yahweh had forsaken them, which doomed in advance Saul's war for freedom.

Still further evidence of the completely crushed spirits of these Northern tribesmen may be seen in their total failure to respond to the appeal for help of the people of Jabesh Gilead (I Sam. 12.3). It is apparent that the messengers of Jabesh Gilead came to Saul's town only towards the end of the seven days respite granted them by the Ammonite king, and only after they had vainly appealed for support among the communities of Ephraim and Manasseh, the true Israel at this moment (cf. v. 3 and above, note 124), and also in the procedure imposed upon these Northern tribes by their Philistine masters recorded in I Sam. 13.19–21.

[138] This is unquestionably also the implication of the statement in II Sam. 5.21, that after the Battle of Baal Perazim the Philistines left their idols upon the battlefield, so that they were captured and carried away by David and his men. This indicates that this battle must have been regarded, by the Philistines at least, as decisive. The capture of the Philistine idols by David was the complement of the previous capture of the ark by the Philistines, and evidenced to Israel how completely David had turned the tables upon the Philistines. Quite properly therefore the narrative of the bringing up of the ark to Jerusalem follows, in II Sam. 6, almost immediately upon the record of David's capture of the Philistine idols. The capture of these idols and the presence of the ark in the new national sanctuary at Jerusalem must have symbolized concretely to Israel, and especially to the tribal federation of Central Palestine, whose allegiance was a matter of constant concern to David throughout his entire reign, how absolute was David's triumph over the Philistines, what a mighty warrior and able king he was, and the magnitude of their debt to him for his deliverance of them from Philistine dominion.

[239] attendant upon the sojourn of the ark in the various Philistine cities, recorded in I Sam. 6, is the result of certain expansion and embellishment; but beyond all question basic to it is the broad outline of fact formulated above. The actual events, whatever their specific nature may have been, served to establish indubitably for both Philistines and Israelites, and perhaps even more for the former than the latter, that the deity or deities of the ark were indeed potent at all times and places, and this too with a power which transcended that of the Philistine deities.[139]

[139] Not at all improbably, this was one of the most cogent considerations in David's bringing the ark from Kiryat Yearim to Jerusalem. For he recognized fully that his first major task as king of united Israel was the conquest of the Philistines and the reversal of the relations which had obtained between them and Northern Israel for approximately a half-century. And what could he do better to reassure his own people of ultimate victory, and likewise to dismay and dishearten the Philistines, than to bring up to Jerusalem, into the national sanctuary which he had just established there, the very palladium of those same Northern tribes, which fifty years or so earlier had so completely discomfited the Philistines, and this too within their own territory, and thus to identify the original Yahweh of the ark with the national Yahweh of the new sanctuary at Jerusalem? Mindful of their inability a half-century earlier to withstand the power of the deity of the ark, the confidence of the Philistines in their ability to successfully resist David, particularly if the present consecution of narratives in II Sam. 5–8 is significant and David had already gained several important victories over them (II Sam. 5.16–25), must have been greatly diminished, if not broken completely. Just this is the implication of II Sam. 8.1, "And after these things David smote the Philistines and conquered them." Recognizing that II Sam. 7 is a post-exilic interpolation (I hope to establish this thesis conclusively in a different connection), and that accordingly 8.1 was originally the immediate continuation of 6.23, and that therefore "after these things" refers to the various incidents attendant upon the bringing of the ark up to Jerusalem, recorded in II Sam. 6, the full import of II Sam. 8.1 becomes clear. Undoubtedly in thus bringing the ark up to Jerusalem and depositing it in the new national sanctuary there David was influenced by various considerations. But among them this of the effect of this procedure upon both the Northern Israelites and the Philistines, must have been of major importance. It was a master-stroke of military strategy and political statesmanship. Also in no small degree the possession of their ancient cult-object and its constant presence in the national sanctuary, in immediate proximity to his own palace, must have strengthened immeasurably David's claim to sovereignty over the none too submissive and loyal Northern tribes; for in such proximity to the residence of the chief or ruler the ark was still the symbol of supreme authority and leadership within the tribe and the nation.

And within the Philistine country one other function, which, [240] we have inferred, was characteristic of the pre-islamic *ḳubbe*, the ark continued to perform, viz., that of selection of the road which it wished to take. That this important power was inherent in the ark, and already in the pre-Canaanite, desert period was thought to be a regular function of the deity resident in or associated with it, is convincingly attested by the little fragment of an independent narrative of the journey through the desert, preserved in Num. 10.33.[140] Now, once again, and under quite comparable circumstances, the ark discharged the same function. For, fulfilling the test which the Philistines proposed, in order to determine to their complete satisfaction whether it was really the Israelite deity resident in the ark, who had brought the various misfortunes upon them, as they half suspected, or whether instead it might have been only a series of fortuitous circumstances with which the ark had no connection whatever, the ark chose the road which led away from the territory of the Philistines and back into Israelite country, and this too despite the fact that, had purely natural and normal forces prevailed, the ark would have remained within the bounds of Philistine territory and dominion.[141] Not only did this outcome of the test demonstrate conclusively to the Philistines that it was the ark, or rather the Israelite deity within the ark, who had thus discomfited them so disastrously, and that too even within their own land and after they had mistakenly believed, as they now recognized, that they had gained a great victory over him and his people, but also it reveals in no uncertain manner what the real, original nature of the ark was, and how close its affinity to the pre-islamic *ḳubbe*.

When the ark came to Beth Shemesh after its departure from the Philistine country, the cows which were drawing the cart stopped of their own accord, quite as if they knew that this was the appointed end of their journey.[141a] There the ark was set upon a great stone in the open field, and there the men of Beth Shemesh sacrificed to it the two cows which had drawn the cart, and which

[140] Cf. "The Oldest Document of the Hexateuch," 39–51.

[141] For the implication of all the details of this narrative recorded in I Sam. 6 cf. "The Book of the Covenant, I," 18–20.

[141a] Cf. above, note 91.

241] had, so it seemed, offered themselves for this sacrifice.[141b] Obviously they recognized it, as it approached their town, and felt themselves greatly blessed by its presence among them. Manifestly its divine character was known to them even before its advent. And this divine character and its quality of inviolable taboo were impressed upon them all the more when they ventured upon an unhallowed act, viz., to look within, of course in order to ascertain what the ark really contained or perhaps, even more probably, whether its original contents, whatever they may have been, were still there and had not been removed by the Philistines.[142] By their very words they affirmed that the deity of the ark was Yahweh, and that He was thought to dwell in it. To them His presence among them seemed to promise as much of danger as it did to the Philistines; and so they sent the ark on to Kiryat Yearim.

There the ark was deposited in the home of Abinadab, impliedly one of the most substantial citizens of the town, whose house was situated upon the hill. This was a fitting place for the repository of the cult-object, and therefore the sanctuary, of an important and powerful deity, such as, it was now recognized, the god of the ark was in truth; for this hill constituted a high place, as it were. There one of the sons of Abinadab was consecrated as the priest of the ark; and there the ark remained for many years,[143] and the priesthood thereof descended to at least

[141b] With this sacrifice of these cows to the ark cf. the annual sacrifice of a camel to the *Markab* by the Ruwala (above, pp. 6, 15, 30).

[142] Cf. "The Book of the Covenant, I," 283.

[143] I Sam. 7.2 says explicitly that the ark remained in the custody of Abinadab and his family for twenty years. However, this passage is recognized by most scholars as a gloss, and its historic authenticity is open to serious question. Actually the residence of the ark in Kiryat Yearim must have endured for approximately a half-century; for it is clearly implied that it could have been in the Philistine country for only a brief period. Its captivity by the Philistines and the attendant destruction of Shiloh must have taken place when Samuel was still a lad. Samuel must have been well advanced in years when he anointed Saul as king. The entire reign of Saul ensued, near the end of which Samuel died. David was established upon the throne when the ark was finally brought up to Jerusalem. Certainly a period of approximately fifty years is not too much to assume for these successive events (cf. above, note 124). This assumption would account for the fact that when the ark was

the grandsons, and perhaps to members of the family later even [242]
than the third generation after Abinadab.[144] Undoubtedly the presence of the ark brought blessing to at least the household of Abinadab, if not to the entire community of Kiryat Yearim. At any rate during its three months sojourn in the home of Obed Edom, the Gittite, in the course of its journey from Kiryat Yearim to Jerusalem, the ark wrought good fortune for Obed Edom and his entire household. Manifestly when treated with proper ritual consideration, the presence of the ark was an unfailing source of blessing to those in whose custody it stood.[145]

It is self-evident that, in bringing the ark up to Jerusalem and depositing it in the national shrine which he had erected there, in immediate proximity to his own palace, David had more

brought up to Jerusalem, Elazar, the son of Abinadab was apparently no longer its ministering priest, but in his place functioned two obviously still young men, Uzza and his brother (reading for אַחָיו, אָחִיו with Budde and following Budde in his identification of this brother with Zadok; *ZAW*, XI [n.F.] [1934], 42–50), both descendants of Abinadab (II Sam. 6.3–7) and therefore no doubt sons, or even grandsons, of that Elazar who had been the first priest of the ark at Kiryat Yearim. Just as the ark was carried into the Battle of Eben Haezer by its two priests, Hofni and Phineas, brothers and sons of Eli, so now the ark was escorted from Kiryat Yearim to Jerusalem by its two priests, likewise brothers (cf. "A Chapter in the History of the High-Priesthood," 14).

[144] Cf. II Sam. 6.3, where בְּנֵי is to be interpreted as "male descendants" rather than in the literal meaning, "sons."

[145] Similarly among the Yezidis, when the peacock-image is sent around the country in the custody of a Qauwâl, in order to collect money for the maintenance of the shrine of Sheich 'Adî, it is carried in a saddle-bag upon the back of the horse upon which the Qauwâl rides. It is usually protected by a red coverlet. When the Qauwâl arrives at a village, a kind of auction is held, and to the highest bidder is awarded the privilege of having the sacred image pass the night in his house (Empson, *The Cult of the Peacock Angel*, 138–140). While not explicitly stated, the obvious implication is that the presence of this image in a house confers blessing (*baraka*) upon it and its inmates. Various details of this procedure suggest that this sacred peacock-image of the Yezidis may have developed out of an original betyl of the pre-islamic Arab type or some cult-object of quite similar character, in particular the manner of transportation of the image, its being covered by a red cloth, and its power to work blessing upon those in close proximity to it. It reminds us too, and quite strikingly, of Sanchuniathon's account of the wooden image of Agroueros (cf. above, pp. 76 f.).

[243] than one purpose in mind. On the one hand, the now constant presence of the ark in direct contiguity to his palace, would presumably bring blessing upon him and his household, even as it had upon the household of Obed Edom and impliedly upon that of Abinadab. Not improbably it would even bring abundant blessing upon the royal city, Jerusalem, "the City of David," as it was now popularly known.[146] But even more, in accordance with the long established implication of the presence of a cult-object such as, as is becoming more and more patent, the ark actually was, and conforming to the old, desert tradition, for which David had such profound reverence,[147] the presence of the ark immediately adjacent to David's own abode stamped him as the supreme personality, the highest authority, within the city and the nation; in other words, the custody of the ark by David and his family was a visible and potent title to his position as king. In precisely the same manner as, as we have seen, the *ḳubbe* was regarded in no small measure as the immediate possession of the tribal leader and his family, rather than of the tribe itself, so now the ark must have been regarded as very largely the possession of David and his family, rather than of the nation at large, and as the proof and guarantee of his royal authority over the nation, assured to him by Yahweh, the deity of the ark. Undoubtedly it was for this reason that, in David's initial flight before Absalom, Zadok brought out the ark, impliedly to accompany David upon his flight and thus to give assurance, first of Yahweh's constant presence with him and His protection of the king from all danger, then of ultimate victory over Absalom in the decisive battle soon to be fought, and finally of David's persistent and unyielding title to the throne.[148] Obviously the ark

[146] II Sam. 5.7–9; cf. also Alt, "Jerusalems Aufstieg," *ZDMG*, 4 (1925), 15.

[147] Cf. Lammens, "La vendetta chez les Arabes," in *L'Arabie occidentale avant l'Hégire*, 202.

[148] Cf. the statement above (p. 28) of the procedure among the Ruwala, "For if a revolt breaks out in the reigning kin against the prince, his opponents attempt first of all to snatch the Abu-d-Dhûr away from him, as he who has the emblem of the whole tribe in his possession must be recognized as their prince." The fact that David sent the ark back to Jerusalem almost immediately after its arrival may well attest that with advancing years this great and progressive king gradually outgrew many of the pastoral, nomadic or semi-

had the same close, personal relation to David that the pre-islamic *ḳubbe* had to the tribal chieftain. [244

But at the same time the ark, deposited in the new national sanctuary at Jerusalem, had a national significance. It was the cult-object, the palladium, of the entire nation.[149] This is evidenced conclusively by the presence of the ark in the decisive battle between the Israelites and the federated Ammonites and Aramaeans, when, to no small degree, the very existence of the still quite young Israelite nation hung in the balance.[150] Manifestly the ark was there to guarantee victory to the Israelite army. It was the very same role which the ark was wont to play of old, not only at the Battle of Eben Haezer, though there with unexpected results, as we have seen, but likewise in the still earlier period of Israelite history, and even out in the desert in the pre-Canaan days of nomadic or semi-nomadic existence.[151]

But still more, the presence in the new national sanctuary at Jerusalem of the ark, the ancient cult-object and palladium, as we have seen, first of Ephraim and then of the federated tribes of at least Central Palestine, possession of which implied supreme authority and sovereignty over these tribes, must have symbolized and given concrete effect to David's kingship over these tribes. The biblical evidence establishes clearly that these northern tribes were always impatient of the dominion of David and his dynasty. True, under the stress of Philistine rule, they

nomadic institutions of his boyhood and early manhood and the principles which underlay them.

[149] I have suggested elsewhere ("The Oldest Document of the Hexateuch," 125, note 119; "The Book of the Covenant, I," 65, note 78; 122, note 154) that in David's national tent-sanctuary in Jerusalem not only the ark of Ephraim but also the ephod of Benjamin, the brazen serpent and the cult-objects of various other tribes were deposited, in order to give concrete and visible demonstration to the principle that the national Yahweh of Israel, from the time of David on, was the sum total and somewhat of a composite representation of all the older tribal Yahwes. In this respect this tent-sanctuary was a kind of Israelite pantheon in precisely the same manner as was the Kaaba at Mecca just before the rise of Islam (Cf. Wellhausen, *Reste arabischen Heidentums*[2], 77 f.; Lammens, "Le Culte des bétyles," etc., 146 f.).

[150] II Sam. 11.11; cf. also 10.12, where, following the generally accepted emendation of Klostermann, we should read עיר for ערי.

[151] Num. 10.35–36.

[245] had turned to David after the death of Saul and invited him to become their king and deliverer.[152] But it seems that barely had the Philistine danger passed, when they began to rue their agreement with David and to seek an opportunity to repudiate his authority over them and to regain their political independence. The struggle between David and Absalom eventuated, so it seems, in an earnest attempt on the part of the Northern tribes to sever their political relations with the South.[153] Despite the crushing of their successive rebellions by David, these Northern tribes never gave up hope of ultimately achieving the desired political independence. And eventually, immediately after the death of Solomon, they attained their goal. It is apparent therefore that especially to David the appeasement of the Northern tribesmen and their adherence to the kingdom was an ever-present, serious problem. He may well have conceived, therefore, particularly in the early days of the United Kingdom, that his possession of the ark, the ancient symbol of supreme authority over these Northern tribes, would strengthen not a little his claim to kingship over them. Therefore we can well understand the pains he took to bring the ark from Kiryat Yearim to Jerusalem with fitting ceremonial and to there deposit it in the new national sanctuary, the shrine of the national Yahweh, whom he had actually called into being. Its presence there symbolized more concretely than aught else that the Yahweh of the ark, the Yahweh of the Northern tribes, was completely one with the national Yahweh, the Yahweh of the new Israelite nation, and that these Northern tribes were now an integral part of this new nation, which David had created, and that David was their king, chosen by them and approved by, and enjoying the favor and support of, Yahweh, their God.

Thus up to and through the reign of David the ark retained practically all of its original, pristine character, rooted in the desert, nomadic or semi-nomadic life of the Israelite tribes.[154] It

[152] II Sam. 5.1–3.

[153] II Sam. 15.1–6; 16.3; 18.6 f.; 19.9–13, 42–44; 20.1.

[154] The affinity of the ark to the *ḳubbe* is so close and unmistakable that it is impossible to accept the hypothesis of Dibelius, that the ark cannot have

was not until the reign of Solomon, the erection of the Temple and the removal of the ark thither from the national tent-sanctuary of David that it began to be regarded as a cult-object of altogether different character from what it had been originally.[155] Into the record of this, the second period of the history of the ark, we need not enter here. [246]

It suffices for our purpose to have established firmly that during this entire first period of its history, in the pre-Canaan, desert days as well as in the period of evolving settled existence in Palestine and adjustment to the agricultural civilization of the Palestinian environment, the ark retained all the characteristics and discharged all the functions of the pre-islamic *ḳubbe*. It imparted oracles. It participated in decisive battles and gave assurance of victory to its people. It could select the way it wished to go and could drive its carriers, whether human or animal, irresistibly along this road. It could designate the successive camping-places for its people on their journeying through the desert.[156] Normally it abode in a sanctuary, either a tent or a house, in immediate proximity to the dwelling-place of the chief priest, a town grandee, or the national ruler, and this very proximity of the ark was an important and undeniable title to the very highest authority. Moreover, like the *ḳubbe* the ark too had its female attendants who performed some kind of ritual ministration to it.[157] Above all else, precisely like the *ḳubbe* and the still earlier palanquins, mounted upon camel-back, reproduced in Syrian art, the ark was thought to symbolize the actual presence of Yahweh, and undoubtedly even to contain a sacred

been of desert origin, but must rather have been of either Canaanite or Egyptian ancestry or perhaps even of Babylonian provenience (*Die Lade Jahwes*, 115 ff.). Westphal (*Jahwes Wohnstätten*, *BZAW*, XV [1908], 55–59) likewise holds that the ark cannot have had a desert origin. This is also the conclusion reached by Gressmann, though in a manner most surprising, particularly after acknowledging his acquaintance with Lammens' illuminating study of the *ḳubbe* (Hoffmann-Gressmann, "Teraphim," *ZAW*, 40 [1922], 86–94).

[155] For this transition cf. "The Book of the Covenant, I," 37–72 and "Amos Studies, III," 118–122.

[156] Cf. Num. 10.33 and "The Book of the Covenant, I," 14–21.

[157] I Sam. 2.22; cf. Ex. 38.8.

[247] stone,[158] or, still more probably, even two sacred stones, even as we see a pair of deities depicted in the Syrian palanquins, and also, as we are told, the deities within the *ḳubbe* were usually represented, and as the Nabataeans too usually worshiped their sacred stones or betyls, in pairs.[159]

As was to be expected, the settled, agricultural environment of the ark in Palestine, so completely different from the desert, nomadic culture in which the ark had its origin, could not but affect the character of the ark, after its entrance into Palestine, to no small degree. In place of the relatively simple tent-housing of the desert period,[160] the ark came now to dwell in a much more pretentious, permanent sanctuary, whether the *bait* or *hekal* at Shiloh, the house of Abinadab upon the hill at Kiryat Yearim, the house of Obed Edom the Gittite on the way to Jerusalem, the tent-sanctuary of David at Jerusalem or the magnificent Temple of Solomon. It was no longer borne in solemn ritual procession or upon its journeyings through the desert upon camel-back, as, as we will soon see, must have been the original practice with it. Instead it seems to have been carried normally by its functioning priests, regularly two in number,[161] or else, particularly during the process of ordinary transporation and when not in the discharge of a specific ritual function, upon a cart drawn by oxen.[162] The women who had in the desert period ministered to the ark and the sacred images which it contained, now became,

[158] So also Luther, in Ed. Meyer, *Die Israeliten und ihre Nachbarstämme*, 214, note 2.

[159] Cf. above, note 114. Perhaps in the figures of the two cherubim, so intimately and seemingly indispensably associated with the ark (In I Ki. 6.23–28; 8.6–7 the two cherubim were integral parts of the *d*^{e}*bir* of the Temple, and beneath their outspread wings the ark was deposited. In the P code [Ex. 25.18–22; 37.6–9] the two cherubim were permanently attached to the *kapporet*, the golden cover or lid of the ark, and so were integral parts of the ark itself.) we may see a reminiscence of the two sacred stones or betyls or divine images originally associated with the ark. In some, and on the whole rather striking, respects, they do remind us not a little of the two goddesses in the Syrian palanquins.

[160] Cf. II Sam. 7.6.

[161] Obviously the minimum number needed to carry a ritual object such as the ark was; cf. I Sam. 4.4; II Sam. 15.24, 29.

[162] I Sam. 6.7–12; II Sam. 6.3–6.

at least according to the tradition which has survived, partici- [248]
pants in rites of sacred prostitution.[163] And ultimately the two sacred stone images within the ark became transformed, under the force of evolving theology and tradition, into the two, still sacred, tablets of the decalogue. That this transformation of the ark in its new and somewhat unnatural, Palestinian, agricultural environment should have taken place in this manner is not at all surprising. More surprising perhaps is that this transformation should have evolved so slowly, and that still in the comparatively late post-exilic period so many of the original desert, nomadic characteristics of the ark should have been persistently discernible.

However, despite all these seeming points of contact, and even of identicity, of the ark with the *ḳubbe* and its closely related cult-objects, the *maḥmal*, the *'oṭfe* and the *Markab*, one consideration seems to defeat all attempts at such identification. We have seen that the *ḳubbe* and these various related objects were all tents or tent-like structures, while seemingly all biblical evidence suggests unmistakably that the ark was a box, or at least a box-like structure, in which the two sacred stones were deposited. In fact the description of the ark in Ex. 25.10–22 and 37.1–9 is precisely that of a box, two and one half cubits long, one and one half cubits wide and one and one half cubits deep, lined both inside and out with gold and covered by a lid of just the proper size, two and one half by one and one half cubits, made of gold, called the *kapporet*. Immediately after its fabrication the two tablets of testimony were deposited within the ark, and after this the golden *kapporet* or lid was set firmly in place. Above the *kapporet* and at its two ends were attached the two golden cherubim. All this is the plan of the ark set forth in the Priestly Code, a product of the period about 400 B.C. It is self-apparent that to these Priestly writers the ark was a box primarily; but at the same time a box which, once the two tablets of testimony were deposited in it, was never to be opened again; the sacred character of this box and the two heavy golden cherubim above the lid would have effectively guarded against that.

[163] I Sam. 2.22.

[249] But this very consideration suggests that the ark of the pre-exilic period, and particularly the ark which had stood at Shiloh and had had such remarkable experiences in the Philistine country and in Israelite territory, until it was eventually deposited in the Temple of Solomon, could hardly have been precisely identical with the ark of the Priestly Code; for had it been, then certainly the people of Beth Shemesh would not have found it such a simple, easy and natural thing to raise the heavy lid and open the ark in order to see what it might contain. In certain, very significant respects the ark which came from Shiloh into the Philistine country and thence to Beth Shemesh must have been quite different from the box-like structure of the Priestly Code.

Actually outside the name, *'aron*, and this picture of the ark in the Priestly Code there is little in the entire biblical record which suggests that the ark must have been basically a box-like structure. True in II Ki. 12.10, 11 and II Chron. 24.8, 11 *'aron* seems to designate a box with a door or lid, through an aperture of which money could be dropped, while in Gen. 50.26 the word designates a coffin. Etymologically the word, ארון, seems to yield no satisfactory and convincing interpretation, and therefore likewise no indication of what it might have connoted originally.[164] However, there is good, and even convincing, evidence that originally the *'aron* was basically not a box-like, but rather a tent-like, structure, precisely as we would expect after having noted the unmistakable relationship of the ark to the pre-islamic *ḳubbe*.

In the first place it is of some significance to note that in the now well known representation of the departure of the ark from the Temple of Dagon at Ekron, upon the wall of the synagogue

[164] Meissner ("Babylonische Leichenfeierlichkeiten," *WZKM*, XII [1898], 61 f.) correlates ארון with Akkad. *(aban)a-ra-nu*, which he translates "grave"; but this is very doubtful, especially since the word is cited neither in Delitzsch, *HWB* nor in Meissner's own *Supplement*. Many years ago Redslob suggested, though purely hypothetically, that Aaron (אהרון) was but a personification of the ark (ארון), and this suggestion was repeated half-heartedly by Winckler, (*Geschichte Israels*, I, 72, note 2). Later in the same work (II, 95) Winckler identified the ark with the coffin of Tammuz, and held that, just as the dead and about to be reborn Tammuz rested in the coffin, so the newly-born Yahweh rested in the ark.

at Dura, the ark is mounted upon a small cart, drawn by two [250]
cows, precisely as in the biblical narrative. But instead of in any way suggesting the appearance of a box, the ark is plainly a small tent, facing forwards on the cart, and with the front curtains or face of the tent closed, thus concealing whatever may have been inside. It can hardly have been accidental that the artist of this painting disregarded completely what in his day must have been the established and conventional conception of the ark, viz., as a box-like structure, the ark of the Priestly Code, and instead represented it as a small tent. He must have had some cogent reason, based upon ancient, unorthodox tradition current among Jews who dwelt away from Jerusalem and the centers of life and tradition of normative Judaism,[165] which, despite the authority of the Priestly Code, told persistently that the ark had actually been a tent-like structure. Otherwise he could never have ventured upon this unorthodox and daring representation of the ark.

Equally interesting, and perhaps equally significant, is the term which regularly designates the manner in which the ark was transported, viz., נשא,[166] for this verb is the precise Hebrew equivalent of the Arabic حمل, which, as we have seen, is the term which regularly designates the manner in which the preislamic *ḳubbe* was transported upon camel-back, and from which the name, محمَل or محمِل, for the closely related tent-like cult-object of the mediaeval and modern pilgrimage to Mecca, is derived.[167]

[165] That there were such unorthodox traditions and practices current in Jewish communities away from Jerusalem and the center of normative Judaism, in Galilee for example, traditions and ritual practices which preserved ancient, pre-Priestly custom and ceremonial, I hope to demonstrate upon some other occasion.

[166] *Passim*; even in Num. 10.35 for בנסע is it well to read, with *G*, *V*, *S* and all three Targums, בנשא or even בהנשא, "when the ark would raise itself."

[167] Still another verb, used seemingly in a somewhat technical sense in connection with the ark, נוח, is of significance in this connection. For נוח seems to have regularly designated the act of returning the ark to its normal and proper place, after it had been taken therefrom (נשא) in order to function as palladium in battle, as guide upon a migration, or in some other like capacity; cf. Num. 10.36. The corresponding Arabic verb, نوخ , in IV and X (cf. Lane, *op. cit.*, 2865) has the meaning, "to cause a camel to kneel (so that those riding

[251] Perhaps the most convincing evidence of the original tent-like character of the ark may be found in the interpretation of the term ארגז. The word occurs only three times in the entire Bible, in I Sam. 6.8, 11, 15, and in all three cases in precisely the same connection and meaning. These passages tell that when the Philistines returned the ark to the Israelites, or rather put it to the test, the outcome of which was that it did return to the Israelites, they placed the golden images of mice and hemorrhoids, which they had made, in the ארגז at its side. Two questions are implicit here, just what was the ארגז, and also just what is the meaning of מצדו, "at its side."

In an interesting and stimulating article[168] the late Professor Sapir endeavored to prove that ארגז is a Philistine rather than a Semitic word, and that it designated the box-like upper structure of the Philistine ox-cart, as we see it depicted upon Egyptian monuments. In truth the fact that the word is used in the Bible only in this one passage and only in connection with the transportation of the ark and its accompanying objects upon this Philistine ox-cart lends not a little initial reasonableness to this hypothesis. Moreover, as Sapir contended, the Hebrew word, has no semantic relationship with the Semitic root, רגז, at least none immediately apparent, and might therefore be a loan-word; and if so, then in all likelihood from the Philistine.

But this assumption that ארגז designated the box-like superstructure of the cart is altogether inferential, and the etymological interpretation of the term, which he proposes, is forced and artificial, largely evolved, so it seems, in order to support a preconceived and quite ingenious hypothesis. Moreover, to establish his hypothesis Sapir must resort to three rather violent proced-

upon it may dismount or its burden be removed)" (cf. also Doughty, *Arabia Deserta,* II, 63), and the derived noun, مناخ, means accordingly "a place where camels kneel for unloading," therefore "a resting-place for camels, particularly for the night," and secondarily "a resting-place for men"; cf. Num. 10.33. A still further, and apparently modern, semantic development of the Arabic مناخ is "a decisive battle" (literally "battle-field"), in which the *'otfe* is normally present; cf. Musil, *The Manners and Customs of the Rwala Bedouins*, 54, 534, and especially 540 f.

[168] "Hebrew *'ărgaz* a Philistine Word," *JAOS*, 56 (1936), 272–281.

ures. He contends, in the first place, that בארגז מצדו in v. 8 means [252]
"in the box [and] at its (the ark's) side," and not, as it is usually interpreted, "in the box at its (the ark's) side." This latter thought, he claims, could be expressed only by בארגז אשר מצדו But in this he is certainly not correct. Quite frequently in Hebrew prose, and very frequently in Hebrew poetry, אשר is omitted and is implied in the pronominal form and in the context. Sapir is constrained to this forced interpretation by the exigencies of his hypothesis, which maintains that the ארגז, being the superstructure of the ox-cart, had no immediate connection with the ark itself.

In the second place, he seeks to establish that both vv. 11 and 15 are interpolations, in whole or in part, for, as he admits, they imply a meaning for ארגז which is hardly compatible with that of a part of the cart itself. Actually they do much more than this. V. 11 implies clearly that the ארגז was placed in the cart along with the ark, therefore that not only was it in no way identical with the cart or a part of it, but actually it must have been something similar or related to the ark, and even connected with or attached to it, which was placed in the cart along with it. This is likewise the implication of v. 15, which states, after v. 14 has already told that the cart was chopped up in order to provide the fuel for the sacrifice of the cows which had drawn it, that the ark and the ארגז "which was with it" were set upon a great stone in the field, and there, i. e., before the ark, the men of Beth Shemesh offered a sacrifice to Yahweh, i. e., of course, to Yahweh of the ark. The fact that the ארגז was not destroyed with the cart proves that, contrary to Sapir's hypothesis, it was in no wise a part of the cart. It is not at all improbable that v. 15 is an interpolation; and in fact it is generally so regarded by scholars. But while it does seem that v. 11b is somewhat corrupt, there is no good reason for regarding the v., in what may have been its original form, as an interpolation. In fact, were it an interpolation, it would be necessarily a substitute for something else which stood in the same place originally and expressed practically the same thought; for the thought is absolutely indispensable to the narrative. Moreover, even were both vv., 11 and 15, interpolations, none the less they would still evidence that the inter-

[253] polators plainly regarded the ארגז as having some immediate connection with the ark, and not at all as the designation of the superstructure of the cart, as Sapir contends. The vv. and their unmistakable implication cannot be disposed of so cavalierly as Sapir would do.

And finally, to establish his thesis Sapir must explain away the article which is used with ארגז in its very first occurrence, in v. 8; and this he fails to do in convincing manner. The immediate and most probable implication of the article, with which the word, הארגז, is used in all three passages, is that the ארגז was something well-known, so well known in fact that it needed no further definition or identification; and it could have been well known in this manner only if it had been some regular and indispensable part or accessory of the ark. What could it have been? The one thing which is certain from the context is that it was a receptacle of some kind, in which such objects as the golden images of mice and hemorrhoids, given to the deity of the ark, could be deposited. More than this I Sam. 6 does not tell us.

However, in Arabic a word, رجازة, occurs, apparently a quite uncommon word, and yet adequately confirmed. Lane[169] defines the word thus: *A certain vehicle for women, a thing smaller than the* هودج: or *a* [*garment of the kind called*] كساء, *in which is a stone* ([in the CḲ *a white stone*,]) or *in which are put stones, and which is suspended to one of the two sides of the* هودج *to balance it when it inclines*: so called because of its commotion: or *a thing consisting of a pillow and skins*, or *hides*, *put in one of its two sides for that purpose* . . . . : or *hair*, or *red hair* or *wool*, *suspended to the* هودج *for ornament*. Obviously the word, رجازة has a twofold connotation. On the one hand, it designates a certain vehicle for women, similar to but smaller than a *howdaǧ*, in other words, a kind of small tent, which was carried upon camelback. But this is precisely what the *ḳubbe* was. On the other hand,

[169] *Op. cit.*, 1036. In a Ras Shamra epic poem, (cf. Gordon, "A Marriage of the Gods in Canaanite Mythology," *BASOR*, 65, Feb., 1937, 29–33, l. 43), בערגזים occurs. Gordon suggests a possible connection with ארגז only, however, to immediately reject it. Nor would the word in its context there fit in any way the meaning which we have established for ארגז.

it designates a kind of pouch or receptacle, in which stones, and [254]
especially, so it seems, white stones, or other heavy objects, were deposited, and which was attached to one of the two sides of the *howdağ* in order to balance it when it inclined and threatened to topple over, and which served likewise as a decoration for the *howdağ*. In other words, رجازة. could designate both a kind of *howdağ*, of small size, however, or the pouch appended to it, in which stones or presumably other similar objects, particularly if their weight was comparable to that of stones, and so suitable for balancing the *howdağ*, were deposited. Etymologically رجازة is related to رجز,[170] "commotion, agitation, consecutiveness of motions," in other words, "swaying, rhythmic swinging," and so connotes that which hangs down from the *howdağ* and swings back and forth with the stride of the camel. Obviously the word is of pure Semitic origin and not borrowed.

It is impossible not to coordinate, or even to identify, the ארגז of I Sam. 6.8, 11, 15 with this رجازة. Despite Sapir's unconvincing argument, the fact remains that v. 8 says unmistakably that the ארגז was "at the side," or even "from the side," of the ark, while both vv. 11 and 15 establish that the ארגז was connected with the ark in such inseparable manner that wherever the ark was set, whether in the ox-cart or on the rock at Beth Shemesh, the ארגז, with the golden images in it, accompanied it.

But if we must identify the ארגז with the Arabic رجازة, then it follows necessarily that the ark was conceived of in I Sam. 6, not as a box or a box-like structure, but somewhat as a *howdağ*, a female camel-saddle, with, of course, something mounted upon it in precisely the same manner as the *ḳubbe* of the pre-islamic Arabs was regularly mounted upon a *howdağ*, and in such way as to be practically inseparable from it, so much so in fact that, as we have seen, whenever the *ḳubbe* or the *maḥmal* or the *'oṭfe* was removed from the back of the camel which was carrying it, the *howdağ* was removed with it and the two together were deposited in, or beside, the tent of the tribal chieftain. So close was the connection in fact, as we have seen, that the term, *ḳubbe*,

170 Lane, *op. cit.*, 1036b.

[255] as commonly employed, included both sacred tent and camel-saddle as one single, unified cult-object.[171] In precisely the same way the Hebrew term, ארון, must have designated both the camel-saddle, to which the ארנו was attached, and the sacred object mounted upon it; and this sacred object must have been, basically at least, not a box-like structure at all, but a small sacred tent, in other words a *ḳubbe*.[171a]

But if this identification of ארנו and رجازة be admitted, then no other conclusion is possible; the tent-like form and character of the original ארון, are established beyond all question,[172] and the full implication of the terms, נשא and נוח[173] to describe the mounting of the ארון upon its bearer, obviously originally a camel,[174] when it went into battle, and its removal from

[171] So also in Syriac; cf. Payne-Smith, *Thesaurus*, under ܡܣܒܠܬܐ.

[171a] For this note see p. 114.

[172] In one other detail of the equipment of the ark a relationship to the Semitic camel-saddle may be noted. The ark was provided with two staves or long poles, one on each side, and extending beyond its two ends. By means of these staves the ark was carried by human carriers. These staves were called בדים. But the Arabic camel-saddle also had its بد (plu. بدود) (cf. Euting, "Der Kamels-Sattel bei den Beduinen," *Nöldeke Festschrift*, 395; Musil, *Manners and Customs of the Rwala Bedouins*, 396; Boucheman, *Materiel de la vie bedouine*, 38) or بداد, two long leather strips or pads set upon the camel's back, one on each side of the hump, upon which the saddle rests, and which protect the camel's back from being galled. Etymologically בדים seems to be derived from بدّ, "to be far apart; to be widely separated," i. e., then "to be on opposite sides."

[173] Cf. Num. 10.35–36, reading for ובנוחו with *G* and *Sam.* ובמנוחו; cf. also above, note 167.

[174] This assertion implies, of course, that camels were known to and used by the Israelite tribes of Central Palestine or their forebears out in the desert previous to their entrance into Palestine. This runs completely counter to Albright's recently proposed hypothesis, that the culture and use of the camel by Semitic nomad tribes in the Arabian desert began at some time towards the end of the thirteenth century B.C. or even somewhat later (*From the Stone Age to Christianity*, 120 f.; *Archaeology and the Religion of Israel*, 96–102, 206, note 58). Were this hypothesis correct, it would follow necessarily, just as Albright contends, that, even granting an actual desert origin and pre-Canaanite, desert, nomadic culture for the Israelite tribes of Central Palestine, previous to their entrance into Palestine, these tribes could not have known the camel, and that therefore the ark could not have been a small, tent-like object

camel-back and its being deposited in the customary place of [256]
safe-keeping, after the battle was completed and won, is now self-evident. Equally firmly established is the unmistakable

mounted upon a woman's camel-saddle, a *howdaġ* (Was this the כר הגמל upon which Rachel sat [Gen. 31.33], or was that object, in which Laban's teraphim were deposited, identical rather with the ארון? Or did כר הגמל, like the Arabic رجازة, designate both the woman's camel-saddle and the small tent upon it, in other words the palanquin or *maḥmal* plus the pouch suspended from it, in which heavy objects, such as stones, golden images and even teraphim could be carried? In Arabic كر designates the leather piece, either in front or in back, which connects the two wooden side-pieces of the kind of camel-saddle called رحل, which is used regularly by women [Lane, *op. cit.*, 2601]. If this was the כר הגמל of the biblical narrative, then we may perhaps infer that the teraphim which Rachel stole were two in number, that they were of no great size, and that perhaps she concealed them, one in the front כר and the other in the rear כר; this is, however, a remote conjecture), and that in consequence our entire hypothesis of the origin and primary character of the ark would be shattered at one stroke.

However, Albright's hypothesis rests upon dubious and unconvincing grounds. Despite his oft-manifested inclination to regard the patriarchal narratives as basically historical, he ignores completely the afore-mentioned narrative of Rachel and her father's teraphim, in which the woman's camel-saddle plays an integral and indispensable role. (Note also that in this narrative the כר הגמל, precisely like the *'otfe* and the *Markab*, was kept regularly in the woman's tent, and also that for Rachel to remain seated in or upon the כר הגמל, even within the privacy of her own tent, seemed a perfectly natural and normal procedure. The כר הגמל must then have been a suitable and convenient resting-place for a woman in Rachel's condition, a palanquin or *howdaġ* in other words, of course with the small tent-like structure atop it.) Likewise in the narrative of Gen. 24 camels play an integral role. This establishes conclusively that the authors of the J code, which Albright would date unduly early, between 925 and 750 B.C. (*FSAC*, 190), believed firmly that camel-culture was an established institution in the period of the patriarchs (cf. also Gen. 30.43; 31.17; 32.8, 16; 37.25); and they were scarcely so far removed from the thirteenth century B.C. as to commit so gross an anachronism and speak of camels in the patriarchal age, if this culture had begun only in or after the thirteenth century B.C. and after the majority of the Israelite tribes were already settled in Palestine.

Actually the chief basis of Albright's hypothesis is his claim that the account of the Midianite raid or *ghazzu*, recorded in Jud. 6–8, is the very first record of the use of camels in all Semitic literature. This is probably correct, if we ignore, as Albright does, or else regard as purely legendary, the afore-

[257] desert, nomadic origin of the ארון. That the artist of the wall-painting of the Dura Synagogue had a reliable tradition behind him is now clear. Perhaps the intimate caravan connections,

cited references to camels in the patriarchal narratives of Genesis. Albright dates these Midianite raids and the victory of Gideon at about 1080–1060 B.C. In consequence he dates the short-lived reign of Abimelech at *circa* 1050 B.C., and shortly *after* the Battles of Eben Haezer and the fall of Shiloh at the hands of the Philistines. But, even despite the rather uncertain archaeological evidence which Albright adduces to support his argument, his dating is quite gratuitous and ignores well-documented historical considerations. It implies that the Philistine war, the Battles of Eben Haezer and the conquest of Shiloh took place either during or else immediately after the judgeship of Gideon; but this is inconceivable. It is impossible to assign the brief kingship of Abimelech over Shechem to the period when Philistine dominion was firmly established over all of Central Palestine north of the territory of Benjamin and as far as the Valley of Jezreel and Beth Shean. Albright's dating of the Philistine war at about 1050 B.C. and of Abimelech's reign as somewhat later, conforms to his seemingly constant inclination to reduce all early dates in Israelite history to the latest possible moment and to crowd historical events into the briefest space of time. As stated above (notes 124 and 143), I would date the Philistine war at about 1065 B.C., and upon practically the same evidence which Albright adduces, would fix Gideon's time and that of the Midianite raids at about 1120 B.C., approximately a century and a half after the Israelite tribes had established themselves in Central Palestine.

Albright further assumes tacitly, and this is the weakest point in his argument, that the culture of the camel by Semitic desert-folk could not have begun much earlier than what he claims to be the earliest Semitic literary record of camels, viz., not long before 1050 B.C. Through this tacit and gratuitous assumption he reaches his conclusion that Semitic camel-culture could not have begun before the end of the thirteenth century B.C., i. e., about 1200 B.C. But this is a gross *non sequitur*. The narrative in Jud. 6–8 implies clearly that the use of camels by these Semitic nomads was a well established and highly developed institution at the time of the Midianite raid. Knowing the slow tempo of normal cultural evolution in the desert, the natural inference is that camel-culture must have been practiced by Semitic nomads and have reached a fairly advanced stage of development at least several centuries before the Midianite raid, whatever the exact date thereof may have been. And if so, then there is no reason whatever to believe that the culture and use of camels was not well known to the Israelite tribes during the period of their desert sojourn before their immigration into Central Palestine near the beginning of the thirteenth century B.C. In fact there is no adequate reason to question the knowledge of the camel by Semitic nomads and semi-nomads, as the patriarchs are represented as being, already in the so-called patriarchal age. Correspondingly there is not the slightest ground for believing that already in their desert

through Palmyra, of Dura and its population with the desert [258]
and desert life and institutions[175] helped to keep this tradition alive among its probably none too orthodox Jewish citizenry, even despite the influence of the Priestly Code upon the transformation of the form and character of the ark in orthodox Jewish belief and practice. After all the institution of the *ḳubbe*, with the two sacred stone images in it, and mounted upon camel-back was, as we have seen, well-known and real in the caravan life of Palmyra. It need not be surprising therefore that the contemporary Dura artist should have comprehended clearly just what the ארון really was, and so should have represented it as a small tent mounted upon the Philistine ox-cart, only, however, unlike the Palmyrene representations of the *ḳubbe*, which we have noted, with the front curtains closed, since the episode in the narrative recorded in I Sam. 6.19 implies that the ארון was closed and therefore could not be readily looked into, without some deliberate act of opening the concealing curtain or tent-flap.[176]

One problem remains, and then our identification of the ארון with the *ḳubbe* may be regarded as decisive, viz., to account for the tradition which transformed the original tent-like ארון into a box-like structure, and this too to such a degree that all memories of the original, tent-like form were completely forgotten in orthodox Jewish circles, and the term, ארון, came in time to denote not merely the sacred object itself, but also the collection-box set up in the Temple by Josiah and also the coffin of Joseph.[177]

period these Israelite tribes, who eventually settled in Central Palestine, were not acquainted with the woman's camel-saddle, the forerunner of the later *howdaġ*, and the sacred tent, the forerunner of the later *ḳubbe*.

[175] Cf. Rostovtzeff, *Caravan Cities*.

[176] This curtain or tent-flap might well have been designated originally as כפרת (cf. Arab. كفر, "to cover, to conceal"), just as well as, at a much later time, the golden cover of the ark of the P code; cf. "The Book of the Covenant, I," 35, note 41. In other words, the P writers may well have cherished a tradition that, in addition to בדים (cf. above, note 172), the ארון had a כפרת or "cover"; but, of course, since they conceived of and represented the ארון as a box, naturally they could make of that כפרת only the lid of the box instead of the tent-flap, as it may well have been at first.

[177] As has been said, the etymology of ארון defies all assured explanation. Therefore it is impossible to determine with absolute certainty whether from

[259] But this is not a difficult task. For, as I have shown elsewhere,[178] the religious reformation in the Southern Kingdom in 899 B.C. was directed very largely against the still quite new and foreign-seeming Temple of Solomon in Jerusalem, against the golden image of the enthroned Yahweh standing in the *d^ebir* of the Temple, and against the solar cult of the Temple, largely Phoenician-Canaanite in character, and altogether different from the traditional, pastoral Yahweh-cult of the Southern herdsmen and small farmers. As one of the procedures of this reformation the golden image of Yahweh was removed from the Temple[179] and destroyed, and in its place the ארון was set up in the *d^ebir* of the sanctuary. The substitution of the ארון, of the desert origin of which the people must have still been fully aware, for the golden image of the enthroned Yahweh, the Phoenician origin and character of which were self-evident to everyone, must have symbolized popularly the triumph of the old, traditional, pastoral religion over the newly introduced and still largely foreign Phoenician-Canaanite agricultural religion.

In time the character of the ארון underwent an inevitable transformation. The tradition of the enthroned Yahweh in the *d^ebir* persisted somehow, despite the triumph of the prophetic, pastoral party and the destruction of the golden image. Inevitably therefore the ארון in the *d^ebir* came to be regarded as the throne of Yahweh, and, in turn, the two sacred stones, the ancient betyls, within the ארון were transformed, in tradition, into the two tablets of the decalogue.[180] With the completion of this twofold process the ancient ארון had now become the ark of the Priestly Code, and of even somewhat earlier, pre-exilic tradition.

the very first ארון had the meaning, "box; box-like structure"; but it does seem most probable.

[178] Cf. "The Oldest Document of the Hexateuch," 98–119; "Amos Studies, III," 100–134.

[179] I Ki. 15.12–13; II Chron. 15.16.

[180] With this far-reaching transformation of the two betyls, originally kept in the ארון יהוה, the box-like tent-shrine, into the two tablets of the decalogue, we may safely compare the transformation of the two betyls or images of the pre-islamic *ḳubbe* into the two copies of the Koran, regularly suspended in the *maḥmal*, or to the copy of the *Saḥīh* of Boḫārî suspended in the *ḳubbe* of the Sultan of Morocco (cf. above, note 99).

It was now both a divine throne and also a container; and in this double role what more natural, and this all the more so since, within the *d^e^bir*, it was no longer visible to the general public, than that, as a container, it should have come, and that too rather speedily, to be regarded as having box-like form, and that ultimately all memory of its original, tent-like form and character should have disappeared completely in orthodox or normative Jewish circles? That it should have survived, however, in Dura, on the periphery of Jewish religious and cultural life, and where direct contact with desert life and tradition was never interrupted, need not surprise us too greatly. [260]

That the biblical ארון, the cult-object of Ephraim, then of all the tribes of Central Palestine, and eventually of the entire Israelite nation, was of desert, nomadic origin, and that it was at first a tent-like structure, housing the two betyls or sacred stones, that, in other words, it was of precisely the same form and character and functioned in a ritual manner in precisely the same way as the pre-islamic *ḳubbe* and its more modern forms, the *maḥmal*, the *'oṭfe* and the *Markab*, and that it was, in fact, the historical forerunner of the *ḳubbe*, may now be regarded as firmly established.

The realization that הארון, or the ark, to employ once again the conventional translation of the term, was originally, basically not a box-like structure, but rather a small tent-shrine, regularly mounted upon a woman's camel-saddle, enables us to take one further step forward, to interpret in a somewhat new light a troublesome biblical passage, and in so doing to find additional and strong confirmation of the correctness of our major thesis. As we have seen, הארון was identical with, or at least was one particular object of that general class of sacred objects designated by the Arabic term, *ḳubbe*. Actually the term, קבה, occurs only once in the entire Bible, in Num. 25.8, where its primary implication seems to be "a marriage-tent," i. e., the special tent in which, according to Bedouin custom,[180a] marriage was con-

[180a] Burckhardt, *Notes on the Bedouins and Wahâbys*, 61; Stevens, *Folk-Tales of Iraq*, 234. It is noteworthy that the Bedouin marriage-tent is pitched at quite some distance from the camp, precisely as Ex. 33.7 records was Moses' practice with the "tent of meeting" (cf. below, p. 143).

[261] summated; in this particular instance the tent in which the sexual act, incidental to the celebration of the festival of Baal Peor, was performed.[181] A synonym of קבה is חפה, found, however, in the entire biblical literature only three times, twice with the explicit connotation of "marriage-tent,"[182] and once, in Isa. 4.5, as a synonym of סכה in the following v. It is this last word which claims our attention here.

Sellin has directed attention[183] to Amos 5.26, although he has missed almost completely the real import of the v. Actually this v. must be interpreted in conjunction with v. 27a for its full meaning to be appreciated. The general context is perfectly clear. The prophet, speaking in the name of Yahweh, has denounced Israel, the Northern Kingdom, scathingly for its manifold sins and repeated faithlessness towards its god, and proclaimed the doom which Yahweh will bring upon His rebellious people. They must leave their present home, Palestine, Yahweh's land, and go into exile, far away into a strange and, to them, completely unknown country, far beyond Damascus, and there they must wander about in search of a new place of settlement. But how can an entire people wander about in a strange and unknown country with reasonable assurance, and how will it at last find its proper place for resettlement? V. 26 gives the definitive answer to this question. There is no need to repeat here the numerous interpretations of this seemingly difficult v. given by various scholars. The ready possibility of, by a slight change of the vocalization of the two words, seeing in סכות and כיון the gods, Sakkuth and Kaiwan, has led scholars far astray from the real, and now almost self-evident, meaning of the v. In fact, recognizing that v. 26b must be a gloss,[184] we see that this glossator himself, whatever his date may have been,[185] misinterpreted these words as

[181] Notice the force of the article, הקבה, i. e., the well-known tent of a certain kind, regularly associated with the peculiar sexual rites of this festival; cf. also Ingholt, "Inscriptions and Sculptures from Palmyra, I," *Berytus*, III (1936), 85–88).

[182] Joel 2.16; Ps. 19.6.

[183] "Das Zelt Jahwes," *Kittel Festschrift*, *BWAT*, 13 (1913).

[184] So Wellhausen, G. F. Moore, Guthe, Schmidt, Zeydner and Nowack (to a certain extent); cf. Harper, 130.

[185] Certainly not later than the third century B.C., since in this in-

the names of deities, and so not only misrepresented the meaning of this v., but likewise led practically all subsequent biblical scholarship more or less completely astray. [262]

Actually the interpretation of the v. is perfectly simple. In addition to recognizing v. 26b as a gloss the only textual emendation necessary is to read for סִכּוּת, with *G*, *Σ*, *V*, *S* and *Syr. Hex.*, and to a certain degree *A* also, סֻכַּת.[185a] Furthermore, we must recognize that it is quite possible to interpret צלמיכם as a dual. The vv. then say, "And you will take up the tent of your king and the base of your two images — and I will drive you into exile beyond Damascus." The "tent of your king" is obviously the sacred tent which served as the symbol of royalty, and which, for precisely one of the reasons because of which, as we have learned, David was so concerned to bring the ark, the sacred tent, up to Jerusalem, was kept constantly in close proximity to the royal residence. Whether Jerobeam II actually possessed such a royal symbol, corresponding to the *ḳubbe* of the pre-islamic Arab tribal chieftain, or whether the language here be merely figurative, it is, of course, impossible to determine.[186] But even if the language be only figurative, none the less it evidences conclusively the existence in ancient Israel of the sacred tent-shrine, the סכה, the precise counterpart of the old Arabic *ḳubbe*, employed as the regular and proper symbol of supreme authority.[187]

terpretation he is followed more or less completely by *G*, *A*, *Σ*, *Θ*, *V*, *S* and *T*.

[185a] Also *The Fragments of a Zadokite Work*, 9.6–7 (cf. Charles, *Apocrypha and Pseudepigrapha of the O.T.*, II, 816) must have read סֻכַּת, since it speaks of "the tabernacle of the King." It likewise interpreted כיון as in the construct state with צלמיכם, since it speaks of "the כיון of the images"; to its author כיון must accordingly have had some such meaning as "base," just as we propose. In his translation of this passage Charles failed completely to appreciate these readings. This evidence, and especially the reading סֻכַּת, coming from near the end of the first century B.C., is of more than passing significance for this study.

[186] In the same way the symbolic figure of the sacred tent as the mark of the authority of the king and his dynasty is basic to the utterance ascribed to Amos (9.11), but dating certainly from the early post-exilic period, "I will set up the tent of David, which is fallen," i. e., "I will restore the Davidic dynasty."

[187] It is readily comprehensible why in Ps. 27.5; 76.3; Lam. 2.6 the Temple at Jerusalem is likened to a סכה.

263] Moreover, within this tent were two sacred images, symbolic of the deity, or even of two deities, precisely as in the ancient Arabic *ḳubbe*, as we have seen, and, as now seems practically certain, likewise in the ancient ark. These two images rested upon a כיון,[187a] a base, which, whatever it may actually have been, corresponded closely to the *howdağ*, the woman's camel-saddle, upon which, as we have seen, the ark, and also the Arab *ḳubbe*, was regularly set. Moreover, the verb here used to express the idea of taking up the sacred tent and starting upon the journey is נשא; and, as we have seen, this verb, precisely like the Arabic حمل, was the technical term regularly employed to describe the placing or loading of the ark or the *ḳubbe* upon the back of a camel and setting forth upon a journey or pilgrimage. In other words, vv. 26–27 give us an exact description of the ancient tent, its equipment and the regular procedure therewith, and likewise suggest one of the major functions which both ark and *ḳubbe* normally performed, viz., to lead the people upon a migration through a totally unknown country, to select for them the road which they must travel, and to indicate for them the place of their ultimate settlement. The meaning of this passage is now perfectly clear. And in a way these two vv., thus interpreted, provide the final link in our chain of evidence of the original nature and function of the ark.

But one question concerning the ark remains to be answered, viz., why, if it now be granted that the ancient ark was a tent-like, rather than a box-like, structure, should it have been designated by the express name or title, הארון, "the box"; for it may now be conceded that the primary meaning of ארון is "box" or "ark." That the ארון contained originally two sacred stones, betyls in all probability, is no adequate answer to this question; for, as we have seen, among the early Semites the customary container or housing of these betyls was a small tent and seldom, if ever, a box. There is no direct evidence whatever bearing upon this question, and so it can be answered only by conjecture.

[187a] Inasmuch as כיון here is a hapaxlegomenon, and so not altogether above suspicion, it may not be amiss to emend it to the closely related and much more common word, מכון, "base, fundament."

Our conjecture is that הארון was a proper name, the specific designation of one particular object of outstanding significance among a large number or class of similar objects, viz., clan or tribal tent-sanctuaries. We have seen that the *'oṭfe* of the Ruwala Bedouin bears such a specific title or name, *Al-Markab*, literally "the riding-vehicle" *par excellence.*[188] That the ark, as we have seen, originally the cult-object, or the container of the cult-object or objects, of the tribe of Ephraim, and later the palladium of the federated tribes of Central Palestine, was in its day quite similarly a tent-shrine of inter-tribal character, and therefore of supreme significance, is now firmly established. What more probable therefore than that it should have come to be designated, and that too at a relatively early moment in its history, by a specific title, its own proper name, which distinguished it immediately from all other similar clan or tribal tent-shrines and accorded to it the recognition of supremacy, which its outstanding role justified? [264

Just why, however, it should have come to be designated as הארון, "the box," is not absolutely certain. Quite probably, how-

THE *MAḤMAL* IN GALA ATTIRE
Reproduced from Lane, *The Manners and Customs of the Modern Egyptians*, London, 1842.

[188] According to Lane (*op. cit.*, 1145) مركب connotes any kind of vehicle borne by a camel or other beast."

[165] ever, there was something distinctive in its peculiar shape or appearance which suggested this name, and thus distinguished it fittingly from other tent-shrines of a somewhat different shape or appearance, yet of the same general class of clan or tribal cult-objects. We have seen that the *maḥmal, en déshabille,* as Burton puts it,[189] i. e., stripped of all its appurtenances and therefore reduced to its mere framework, or sub-structure, resembles a box much more than a tent. This box-like form of its lower section is even more apparent in the photograph of the *maḥmal* in normal dress here reproduced. We have noted likewise that the Ruwala *'oṭfe, Al-Markab,* which Raswan intuitively correlated with the ancient ark of Israel, has much more the appearance of a box or basket than of a tent. It seems therefore very probable that something peculiar about the shape or appearance of the ancient ark may have suggested its proper and distinctive name, הארון "the box," or ארון יהוה, "the box of Yahweh."

We have just suggested that the name, הארון, may have been the special designation or title of a particular clan or tribal tent-shrine, of which, by implication, there must have been others in ancient Israel. We must now determine whether this hypothesis is valid, and if so, just what the generic name for this class of cult-objects may have been.

[189] *Pilgrimage to Al-Madinah and Mecca,* I, 233; cf. above, p. 202, and also the accompanying photograph of the *maḥmal* in full dress.

[42a] An illuminating instance of the supernatural, divinatory power thought to reside in a camel, believed to be mounted and driven by some divine agency is recorded by Wellhausen, *Muhammed in Medina, das ist Vakidi's Kitab al-Maghazi,* 267, viz. that Mohammed once encamped where his camel lay down, and there built the mosque (at Khaibar). For other significant instances of this same principle see *ibid.* pp. 125, 147. The classical, and at the same time the most extreme and illuminating, example of such divinatory precedure is recorded by Lucian (*De Dea Syria,* 36; Tooke's translation, pp. 456 f.): "But all these oracles are delivered only through the mouths of priests or prophets: none except the Apollo at Hierapolis moves itself, and performs the whole operation of the diviner from beginning to end without extraneous aid. The method of it is this. When he intends to deliver an oracle, he begins to stir upon his seat; and the priests immediately lift him up. If they fail to do so, he begins to sweat, and moves himself into the middle of the Temple, down among the congregation. But when they have hoisted him upon their shoulders, he drives them all round in a circle, leaping upon one after the other.

vii. The Ephod [26

We suggest tentatively that the generic name for the ancient Israelite tent-sanctuary, with its betyls or divine images, was אפוד. We must now test this hypothesis.

At last he places himself facing the high priest, and asks him after the interrogatories to which the answer of the god is required. Would he say, No; he goes back. But if his response is to be, Yes, he drives his bearers forwards, with the motion of a coachman guiding his horses."

Perhaps this narrative in all its details should not be taken too seriously. It is difficult to refrain from inferring that Lucian has here given his mischievous fancy somewhat loose rein. But be that as it may, this much is clear, that basic to the entire narrative is the principle, obviously current in certain more or less primitive forms of Semitic religion, that the deity may impart an oracle by driving his bearers, i. e., the bearers of his image or representation, whether idol or *'oṭfe*, in this or that direction and making them halt where and as he chooses.

[171a] A distinct reminiscence of the ארנו may lurk perhaps in Deut. 31.24–26. The passage is from RP. It records Moses' command to the Levites, the bearers of the "Ark of the Covenant of Yahweh," to deposit "this book of the law," i. e., impliedly Deuteronomy, at the side of the ark, that it might be there as a witness. The implication seems to be that "this book of the law" is to be deposited beside the ark in its place in the Temple at Jerusalem. I Ki. 8.4–11 and its parallel passage, II Chron. 5.4–10, record that the ark was deposited in the Temple by the priests. However, II Chron. 5.4–5, especially when compared with I Ki. 8.3–4, establishes fairly conclusively that in its original form this passage told that it was the Levites rather than the priests who bore the ark, and who therefore deposited it in the Temple. In this respect this narrative in its original form was in agreement with Deut. 31.24–26 as to who bore the ark and presumably who deposited it in the Temple. It is apparent that in their present form both I Ki. 8.4–11 and II Chron. 5.4–10 have undergone drastic textual revision in the interest of the priests over against the Levites. Furthermore, the insistence of I Ki. 8.9 and II Chron. 5.10 that in the ark there was naught but the two tablets which Moses had placed there at Horeb is of more than passing significance. In the first place, the use of the name, Horeb, rather than Sinai, suggests that there is an old, pre-Priestly tradition basic to this narrative. In the second place, the later strata of P represent the two tablets within the ark as the testimony; therefore the name, "the two tablets of testimony." But this contradicts the statement of the obviously older P narrative of Deut. 31.26, that "this book of the law," placed

[1] Basing himself upon the fact that for ארון האלהים in I Sam. 14.18 *G* read האפוד, Arnold,[190] contending that the reading of *MT* was correct, sought to prove that in every case throughout the entire Bible where *MT* reads אפוד or האפוד it should be emended to ארון or הארון or some corresponding construct connection of אָרון, and that ארון was the generic term for the specific class of cult-objects in question.[191] Arnold's hypothesis has not found general acceptance; and indeed it could not have been accepted, for the weight of evidence is overwhelmingly against it. But undoubtedly Arnold was on the right track in contending that there must have been some generic name for this class of objects; and if he had reversed his argument and reached the conclusion

at the side of the ark, was to serve as the testimony. The very insistence of the statement in I Ki. 8.9 and II Chron. 5.10, that in the ark was naught but the two tablets seems almost a purposed refutation of the statement of Deut. 31.26 about the presence of "this book of the law" there and of its function as witness.

But this older P narrative would hardly have told that "this book of the law" was merely deposited at the side of the ark, without covering or protection. The natural implication is that it was deposited in some suitable receptacle at the side of the ark. Indeed this seems implicit in the word, מצד; for normally "at the side of the ark" would have been expressed by לצד הארון. I suspect therefore that in its original form the narrative in Deut. 31.24–26 told that "this book of the law" was deposited בארגז מצד ארון ברית יהוה, precisely the same expression as in I Sam 6.8, and that perhaps this was even the actual original reading, and that בארגז was omitted purposely by late P editors for obviously theological reasons.

But if this hypothesis be correct, then, unquestionably, the tradition of the ארגז, and with this the concept of the ark as a tent-like structure, must have persisted in Palestinian Jewish circles until well into the post-exilic period. Therefore it could have been only Pg writers who, about 400 B. C., coined the fiction that the ark was a box rather than a tent. Realizing this, it is easy to comprehend how the tradition of the tent-like form of the ark could have persisted in such peripheral circles of the Jewish people as the Jewish community of Dura as late as the third century A. D.

[190] *Ephod aud Ark*: *Harvard Theological Studies*, III (1917).

[191] Actually ארון in the sing. absolute state occurs only twice in the entire Bible, II Ki. 10.12; II Chron. 24.8, and in both passages designates the box or chest which Joash set up in the Temple to receive contributions for rebuilding the Temple. Actually therefore, contrary to Arnold's conjecture, ארון is used nowhere in the Bible to designate a class of cult-objects, of which the ark at Shiloh was merely one example. On the other hand, אפוד is used in Jud. 8.27; 17.5; 18.14; I Sam. 2.28; 14.3 (?); 23.6 (?); Hos. 3.4 in just this generic sense.

that אפוד was this generic name, and הארון was really the proper [2]
name of one specific and outstanding object of this class, he would undoubtedly have been happier in his conclusion.

As is well-known, in the biblical writings אפוד designates three different objects.[192] In the Priestly Code it is an outer garment of peculiar character, worn by the high-priest, to which the breastplate, in which were the *'urim* and *tummim*, was attached. In four passages, I Sam. 2.18; 22.18;[193] II Sam. 6.14; I Chron. 18.27, it is used in connection with בד to designate a garment of the simplest and most primitive type, a small piece of cloth apparently, girded about the waist, serving as a kind of apron, and really leaving the wearer practically naked, worn by priests or persons functioning as priests.[194]

[192] Cf. Sellin, "Das israelitische Ephod," *Nöldeke Festschrift* (1906), 699 ff.; Arnold, *op. cit.*, 7–9.

[193] Although the term, אפוד בד, in I Sam. 22.18 is supported by all the versions except G^B, which omits בד, I believe that the original read merely אפוד, and that בד is here a gloss. Note that in I Sam. 2.18; II Sam. 6.14 the verb used with אפוד בד is חגר, "gird," which is precisely what we would expect. On the other hand, the term, נשא אפוד (without the article) is used in I Sam. 14.3 in the connotation, "a priest," more specifically "a priest" of the sanctuary at Nob. Just this is the meaning required in I Sam. 22.18. But if then בד be a gloss here (so also Arnold, *op. cit.*, 125, note 1), and since, moreover, I Chron. 18.27 is based directly upon II Sam. 6.14, it follows that actually in the entire Bible we have only two authenticated instances of the אפוד בד; but they are so well authenticated that there is no reason whatever to question the existence and use of such a cult-garment in ancient Israel. It is significant that the last mention of the אפוד בד is in connection with David. None the less Ex. 20.26 evidences that until at least the middle of the ninth century B. C., i. e. until 841 B. C., the time of the composition of the *d*^{e}*barim*-section of the Book of the Covenant (cf. "The Oldest Document of the Hexateuch," 115–119; "Amos Studies, III," 225–240) the priest of Yahweh functioned regularly at the altar in some kind of a simple cult-garment similar to the אפוד בד, which left his private parts exposed, at least from below. Ultimately, as Ezek. 44.18 and Ex. 28.42; Lev. 6.3 (P) evidence, advancing culture provided for the wearing of a trouser-shaped under-garment by the priest who functioned at the altar.

[194] No doubt closely related to the Old Assyrian *epâdâtum*, a simple garment worn by both men and women (cf. Albright, in *BASOR*, 83 [Oct. 1941], 39 f. and note 10 on p. 40), and practically identical with the Arabic *izār*, the garment of primitive simplicity donned by the pilgrim to Mekka, the moment he enters the sacred territory (cf. Wensinck, *Some Semitic Rites of*

[3] Elsewhere אפוד seems at first glance to designate something made out of metal, usually precious metal, and which was an object of worship by the people. Accordingly the majority of scholars have assumed, though somewhat gratuitously it will appear, that the ephod was an idol. However, Sellin has demonstrated quite convincingly that the ephod cannot possibly have been an idol.[195] What then might it have been?

The ephod plays a significant role in three important episodes in biblical history, all of them belonging to the period antedating the establishment of the kingdom by David. This suggests quite naturally that the ephod was an object of primitive cultic significance in Israel, and that, after the establishment of the kingdom, its role steadily declined and eventually died out completely.

The first, and perhaps the most illuminating, instance of the ephod is in the well-known story of Micah, the Ephraimite, and the migration of the Danites, in Jud. 17–18. As is now generally recognized, these chapters contain two main strata, the major and older of which designates the cult-object of Micah as אפוד ותרפים, while the secondary source designates it as פסל or פסל ומסכה.[196] Despite this duplication of terms in both strata the narrative tells clearly that only one, single cult-object is involved. The repeated designation of this cult-object in the secondary stratum as פסל, establishes with certainty that this cult-object was an image or idol; and correspondingly תרפים, of the primary stratum, always designates an idol or idols. It is true that מסכה, the second term, linked with פסל in the secondary stratum, also designates an idol, a molten image, made usually of gold or silver. But this does not justify the inference that correspondingly אפוד must likewise designate an idol. The constant association of אפוד with תרפים may well indicate that, since the תרפים were certainly idols,[197] the אפוד was some other object regularly associated with

Mourning and Religion, 65 f.). It was actually not much more than a girdle, so that the person wearing it was practically naked (II Sam. 6.23).

[195] *Op. cit.*, 706–711.

[196] In *MT* of 18.20, 30, 31 only הפסל; in 17.4; 18.14, 17, 18 פסל ומסכה, though in 18.17, 18 the two words are separated by intervening words.

[197] Whereas *G* usually renders תרפים as *τὸ θεραφειν*, in Gen. 31.19, 34, 35 its rendering is *τὰ εἴδωλα*. *V* renders תרפים throughout Jud. 17–18 and also in Hos. 3.4 *teraphim*, but elsewhere regularly *idola*.

them; and if so, then what could it be more probably than the housing of these idols, the tent-shrine in which they regularly reposed? [4]

Jud. 18.14, 22 indicate that Micah was no ordinary person, but was rather the head of a settlement, probably composed of his own clan, which consisted of a number of houses. Among these was one particular structure, called a בית אלהים, i. e., a sanctuary, in which the אפוד ותרפים were deposited by Micah.[198] This seems to have been also the house in which the young Levite, Micah's priest, resided.[199] Obviously the relationship of this priest to the אפוד ותרפים is precisely the same as that of Samuel to the ark in the sanctuary at Shiloh.[200] He is the interpreter of the oracle of the אפוד ותרפים[201] and so must remain constantly in proximity to the cult-object, so that he might always be ready to receive the oracle, whenever the deity would choose to speak.

The possession of this particular cult-object is manifestly the source of Micah's power and authority within his clan, as well as the source of the power and dignity of the clan itself; for when it is stolen by the migrating Danites, Micah gathers his clansmen in an earnest resolve to recapture his idol; and when challenged by the Danites, Micah accuses them of having stolen his gods, and then he adds, very significantly, with them gone "what have I left?"[202] Obviously the אפוד ותרפים played for Micah and his clan precisely the same role which the pre-islamic *ḳubbe* played for the Arab chieftain and his clan or tribe.

Moreover, the eagerness of the Danites to acquire possession of this cult-object is of more than passing significance. They were in process of migration from their original home to the southwest of Ephraim, and were seeking a new home in the far north of Palestine. The implied historic background of this incident is clear. The Danites were the first Israelite tribe to come into actual conflict with the Philistines. They had not participated in the

[198] Jud. 17.5. On the other hand, 17.4, from the secondary stratum, states that the פסל ומסכה was deposited in the house of Micah himself.

[199] Jud. 18.14–15.

[200] I Sam. 3.3 ff.; cf. above, p. 82.

[201] Jud. 17.10.

[202] Jud. 18.24.

[5] Battle of Taanach[203] and apparently had had little or no part in the federation of the tribes of Central Palestine and had as yet developed little sense of kinship with them. Accordingly they seem to have had to cope with the Philistines entirely alone, unaided by the other tribes of Israel. This struggle between Dan and the Philistines provides the historical setting of the Samson-myth.[204] But despite the statement of Jud. 16.30, it is patent that in this struggle, probably protracted over quite a number of years, the Danites were eventually worsted[205] and, finding themselves unable to maintain a dignified and independent existence in their original place of settlement in southwestern Palestine, they resolved upon the quite desperate procedure of migration in search of a new home. A further implication is that, in their unsuccessful and even catastrophic struggle with the Philistines, they had even lost their tribal god or gods, however these may have been represented. The Philistines had probably captured these, just as a generation or so later, as they pushed northwards and northeastwards through Palestine, they captured the ark of Ephraim, and as, in turn, their own gods were eventually captured by David.[206] The Danites were left therefore in forlorn plight. Without either tribal gods or tribal home they were indeed desperate. Hence their migration in search of a new place of settlement; and hence likewise the eagerness and lack of scruple with which they stole the idol of Micah and thus acquired for themselves a new tribal deity and also, in the person of the young Levite, a new tribal oracular priest. The further implication of the narrative seems to be that it was the אפוד ותרפים which guided these Danites upon their migration onwards and ultimately gave them victory over the original inhabitants of Laish. In other words, it would seem that for these migrating Danites the אפוד ותרפים played precisely the

[203] Jud. 5.17.

[204] Note that, according to Jud. 16.31, the grave of Samson was located in that very district from which, according to Jud. 18.2, 11, these six hundred Danites migrated.

[205] And perhaps even almost decimated; for the implication of the narrative of Jud. 18 seems to be that these six hundred men were all that were left of this once powerful tribe after its struggle with the Philistines.

[206] II Sam. 5.21; cf. above, note 138.

same role which the ark did for Ephraim originally and ultimately for the federated tribes of Central Palestine, which the *ḳubbe* did for pre-islamic Arab clans and tribes, and which the *'oṭfe* does for present-day Bedouin tribes. [6]

In Jud. 8.27 the ephod which Gideon made and set up in Ophra, his home city, functioned in quite similar manner. The reference to the ephod here is brief. Gideon made the ephod out of the gold which had been taken by him and his followers as booty from the conquered Midianites. It became an object of worship, so the text says, by all Israel. No more than this; and yet the narrative says very much.

Merely the ephod is mentioned here as having been made by Gideon, and there is no record whatever of teraphim. Yet almost invariably teraphim are associated with the ephod; and there is no good reason to doubt that this ephod too had its teraphim. The occasion of the making and setting up of this ephod was of deep significance. The conquest and annihilation of the Midianites had terminated a great tribal danger, which had obviously for many years affected all the clans of Manasseh, and not improbably had threatened more or less directly other neighboring clans and tribes. It is quite comprehensible therefore that, as Jud. 9.22 f. states, these various clans should have gathered at Ophra and invited Gideon to become their king. According to the narrative Gideon declined their invitation. In all likelihood the influence of the nomadic or semi-nomadic way of life, none too far removed in point of time, was still too strong upon Gideon to permit him to regard the institution of kingship, with its absolute power and authority, with sympathy. None the less it is clear that thereafter Gideon continued to exercise until the day of his death a certain, large authority over his own tribe and at least over the immediately adjacent clans in addition, an authority which represented that of the tribal chieftain *par excellence*, and in some respects no doubt, as the attempt of his son, Abimelech, to make himself king in Shechem would seem to suggest, approximated that of a king of a little Palestinian city-state or tribal group. In fact, as Jud. 6.35; 7.23 f.; 8.1–3 indicate, Gideon's authority extended not only over Manasseh, but also over Asher, Zebulon and Naphtali, north of the Valley of Jezreel,

[7] and even over Ephraim.[207] The procedure of these tribes in inviting Gideon to become their king after the termination, through his military prowess and leadership, of the Midianite danger, was almost exactly comparable to the invitation of the Northern tribes to David to become their king and military leader in the face of the great, common Philistine danger approximately a century later.[208] There is therefore no good reason to question the historical correctness of this record.

Obviously the ephod of Gideon, made out of the booty won in the Midianite victory and set up in Ophra, and undoubtedly in immediate proximity to Gideon's own house, was the symbol of his high authority over his own tribe and over the other tribes federated with or dependent upon him. It too played the same role as the ark, the *ḳubbe* and the *'oṭfe*. And, again like the ark, it was a cult-object of intertribal character, short-lived though this seems to have been.[209]

That Gideon's procedure in erecting this ephod at Ophra conformed to firmly established principles of primitive Semitic life is beyond all question. His victory over the Midianites had been decisive indeed, in that it effectually freed both his own and neighboring clans and tribes from a grave danger, which threatened to overwhelm them all. No doubt through these long pro-

[207] An authority over Ephraim, however, it is clear, which this proud and contentious tribe, always intensely jealous of its leadership in the federation of the tribes of Central Palestine (cf. Jud. 12.1–6), was inclined to dispute, and which Gideon was able to enforce only through the exercise of extreme tact and diplomacy.

[208] II Sam. 5.1–2.

[209] This seems to have endured only during the remainder of the life of Gideon (cf. Jud. 8.33). The murder of all the remaining sons of Gideon except Jotham by their half-brother, Abimelech (Jud. 9.5), the historicity of which there is not reason to doubt, and then the quickly ensuing fiasco and death of Abimelech obviously put a speedy end to the family of Gideon and its exercise of power and dominion. The tribe of Ephraim must have quickly regained the hegemony of the federated tribes of Central Palestine, which it had forfeited temporarily to Manasseh under Gideon. With this the importance of the ephod of Ophra must have gradually declined. What became of it eventually we do not know. Not impossibly it was one of the original tribal cult-objects which David brought up to Jerusalem and deposited there in his national sanctuary (see above, note 149).

tracted Midianite raids some of these Israelite clans and tribes [8]
on both sides of the Jordan had been more or less decimated and their further existence rendered precarious. One of the immediate and most significant effects of Gideon's great victory must have been the creation of a larger and stronger tribe of Manasseh, resulting from a fusion of the clans, and perhaps also of even some of the smaller tribes, which had been involved in the Midianite experience.[210] And whereas previously Gideon and his father's house had played, so it would seem, only an ordinary role in the affairs of his clan, now he was the recognized leader, not only of his own immediate clan, but also of the larger tribal organization of Manasseh, which he himself had actually called into being. This was the conventional occasion for the establishment of a *ḥaram* and the making and setting up therein of an ephod in ancient Israel or a *ḳubbe* among the later, pre-islamic Arabs.[211] Not only did it commemorate the great victory just gained, but also it served as the idol or cult-object of the new tribal organization and likewise as the symbol of Gideon's leadership and authority within the tribe. That the Israelite ephod was but an older form of the pre-islamic *ḳubbe* is now self-evident.

In I Sam. 14.3, 18, 20 we are introduced to another ephod, one quite different from that which Gideon set up at Ophra.[212] This ephod, it is clear, stood normally in the Benjaminite sanctu-

[210] Notice that in Jud. 5 only the name, Machir, occurs (v. 14), but that the name, Manasseh, is significantly missing. This suggests that at the time of the Battle of Ta'anach, some fifty years or so before Gideon, the tribe of Manasseh as such was not yet in existence, and that the then clan of Machir constituted the largest and strongest of the clans or small tribes, which were later incorporated by Gideon into the new tribe of Manasseh. This accords perfectly with the fact that in the genealogical tables Machir appears regularly as the first-born son of Manasseh (Gen. 50.23; Num. 26.29; 32.39 f.; Josh. 13.31; 17.1 [cf. also v. 2 for other Manassite clans]; I Chron. 7.14–19).

[211] Cf. Lammens, *op. cit.*, 162, and above, note 78.

[212] As has been said, Arnold's attempt to retain the reading, ארון האלהים, of 14.18, 20 and I Ki. 2.26 and to emend אפוד not only in 14.3 but also in I Sam. 23.9; 30.7 to ארון has very properly been generally rejected by biblical scholars. On the contrary, the reading of *G* in all these instances, supported by *MT* of I Sam. 23.9; 30.7, shows conclusively that, with Thenius and his successors (cf. Arnold, *op. cit.*, 18–23), האפוד must be read for ארון האלהים in I Sam. 14.18, 20; I Ki. 2.26.

[9] ary at Nob, and from there was carried by the chief priest of that sanctuary into the decisive Battle of Michmash, obviously both to function as oracle in that battle and also undoubtedly to give to the Benjaminites assurance of victory over the powerful and otherwise seemingly irresistible Philistines. In this respect, manifestly, it discharged precisely what was one of the major functions both of the ark of Ephraim and of the pre-islamic *ḳubbe.*[213] That the sanctuary at Nob was the tribal sanctuary of Benjamin, just as that at Shiloh was the tribal sanctuary of Ephraim, is evidenced by the role which this sanctuary played in the narrative recorded in I Sam. 21.1–10; 22.9–23, and especially by the unusually large number of priests who were stationed there. Unquestionably this ephod was the most important cult-object of this sanctuary, as is implied specifically in I Sam. 21.10. It must accordingly have been the particular cult-object of the tribe of Benjamin, and have borne to this tribe precisely the same relationship as did the ephod of Micah ultimately to the tribe of Dan or the ark to the tribe of Ephraim originally, and ultimately, as we have seen, likewise to all the federated tribes of Central Palestine. At Nob the ephod was housed in a permanent sanctuary, just as was the ark at Shiloh. Whether this sanctuary at Nob was a tent or a house is nowhere indicated. Quite obviously Ahimelech, the chief priest of this sanctuary, dwelt regularly either actually within the sanctuary structure itself or else in immediate proximity thereto. He was the *kohen moreh,*[214] the oracular priest, of the ephod, and so bore to it precisely the same relationship as did Eli to the ark or the pre-islamic *kahin* to the *ḳubbe.*

Likewise not without significance for our study is the fact, recorded in I Sam. 21.10, that the sword of Goliath was deposited in the sanctuary at Nob, obviously as a trophy of victory, and in particular was kept, wrapped in a piece of cloth, in a place immediately behind the ephod. This association of the sword of Goliath with the ephod parallels very closely the association of the sword of Jidua with the *Markab* of the Ruwala Bedouin,[215]

[213] Cf. Lammens, *op. cit.*, 106, 159 f.

[214] Cf. II Chron. 15.3.

[215] Above, note 53.

and so establishes another characteristic affinity of the ephod of Benjamin with the various cult-objects of the class which we are investigating. [10]

It is noteworthy that the verb which is regularly employed to describe the manner of transportation of the ephod is נשא,[215a] the very same word which we have found used regularly to describe the transportation of the ark, and the equivalent of the Arabic حمل, the verb which regularly describes the transportation of the *maḥmal* and its parallel cult-objects. Very significantly the ephod is carried or transported invariably by only one man, its functioning priest;[216] nor do we hear of its ever being transported in any other manner. This contrasts significantly with the manner of transportation of the ark, which, as we have seen, was normally carried either upon camel-back, upon a cart, or else by two priests.[217] Impliedly therefore the ephod, or at least this particular ephod of Benjamin, though of the same class of cult-objects as the ark and the *ḳubbe*, was of smaller size,[218] of a size and weight which would not constitute too heavy or awkward a burden for a single man to carry.[219]

[215a] In this connection and supplementing what has already been stated (above, p. 98 and note 166) attention may be called to Isa. 45.20; 46.1–7 as graphic illustrations of the use of the verb, נשא, as the technical term in biblical Hebrew for the carrying of sacred images or idols in ancient Semitic religious processions. In fact in Isa. 46.1 נשאתיכם, literally "your objects which are borne," seems to designate the images of Bel and Nebo, referred to earlier in the v.

[216] Therefore, with relationship to this particular tribal cult-object of Benjamin, the term, נשא אפוד, seems to have become a not uncommon term for "priest;" cf. I Sam. 14.3; 22.18, and above, note 193.

[217] Cf. II Sam. 15.24–29. Moreover, the ark, while in process of transportation, seems to have had normally two priestly attendants; I Sam. 4.4, Hofni and Phineas; II Sam. 6.3 ff., Uzza and Ahyo (Zadok?, cf. Arnold, *op. cit.*, 62, and above, note 143.); 15.24–29, Zadok and Ebyatar.

[218] So also Arnold, *op. cit.*, 95.

[219] It is quite possible, and even probable, that the small tent-shrine containing the betyl or the two betyls, typified by the ephod of Benjamin, was the oldest and most primitive form of this characteristic primitive Semitic cult-object, and that it goes back to the very earliest period of Semitic cultural evolution, perhaps even before the beginning of camel-culture, when the ass was the chief, if not the only, beast of burden, and when in consequence portable tent-shrines might not be too large or heavy to permit carrying

[11] In the case of the ephod of Micah, the Ephraimite, which later became the cult-object of the tribe of Dan, granting that the ephod itself was merely the tent-housing of the teraphim, it was actually the teraphim which constituted the oracle proper, or at least the source thereof, and so were consulted in the divinatory process. As Ezek. 21.26 and Zech. 10.2 indicate, consultation of the teraphim was an established process of divination or oracular decision in ancient Israel. We have suggested that the teraphim, the images normally housed in the ephod, corresponded exactly to the two betyls normally housed in the *ḳubbe*, to the two sacred stones or betyls of the ark, and to the two divine images which, we have inferred, were housed in the *sukkah* or tent-shrine of Amos 5.26. This conclusion is confirmed by the role of the teraphim of Laban, which Rachel stole.[220] For, as we have seen, not only were these transported in the *kar hagamal*, but also, as Gordon has shown conclusively,[221] possession of these teraphim, in theory at least, established Jacob's right to succeed Laban as head of the clan and to eventual possession of all of Laban's property. But, as we have learned, this was precisely one of the functions, or at least one of the implications, of possession of the *ḳubbe* and its contents, that its possessor was recognized almost automatically as the head of the clan. The teraphim of Jacob seem therefore to correspond exactly to the betyls within the *ḳubbe*, to the ephod, or the golden image therein, which Gideon set up at Ophra, and to the ark and its betyls in this, one of their most important functions,[222] as well as in their other dis-

either by human bearer or by ass (cf. the procedure of the Galli, described by Lucian, *The Enchanted Ass*, par. 37 Tooke's translation, II, 156 ff.). The advent of the camel as a beast of burden (cf. above, note 174) naturally permitted the development of tent-shrines of the same general type but of larger size and weight and perhaps of even more varied shape and general appearance, such as the ark of Ephraim or the still later *maḥmal* and *'oṭfe*.

[220] Gen. 31.19, 30 ff.

[221] Gordon, "The Story of Jacob and Laban in the Light of the Nuzi Tablets," *BASOR*, 66 (April, 1937), 25–27.

[222] Just what was the particular significance of the teraphim in the home of David at the time of his marriage to Michal, the daughter of Saul (I Sam. 19.13–16), is not plain. Despite the use of the seeming dual or plural, תרפים, it would appear that there was only one sacred image, and not two. It must

tinctive role as sources or instruments of divination. That the teraphim were therefore identical with the betyls or sacred images within the ephod, the *sukkah*, or the pre-islamic *ḳubbe*, seems reasonably certain. In fact it is quite probable that תרפים was the early Hebrew generic term for these sacred images,[223] just as, as we have concluded, אפוד was probably the generic term for the tent-shrine in which these teraphim were normally housed, at least in the earliest period of Israel's cultural life out in the desert and during the period of settlement in Palestine. This would then account adequately for the frequent, and seemingly normal, association of the teraphim with the ephod. [12]

The ephod of Benjamin too was employed regularly for consultation of the oracle.[224] But, quite significantly, neither in

have been of fair size, sufficient when covered by a garment and supplemented by the trappings mentioned in v. 13, to have in the darkness simulated fairly well the form of a man asleep in bed. On the other hand, it cannot have been too large and unwieldy to have been handled readily by a woman, and especially by a woman of high family, who presumably was not accustomed to acts requiring the exercise of undue strength. But just what was this teraphim doing in David's home at this time? And why was there only one sacred image and not at least two, as the form of the noun seems to imply? There is no good reason to identify this teraphim with the customary household deity or deities, which seem normally to have been associated with or even affixed to the doorposts of the house (cf. Ex. 21.6). This particular teraphim, obviously of far too great size to have been affixed to the doorpost, and manifestly standing within the house, was something quite different from the ordinary household deity. Can it be that it was a teraphim of Saul, which at marriage Michal had brought with her from her father's house, in order to establish the claim of her husband to the kingship after her father? For the Edomite custom of the succession of the son-in-law rather than the son to the kingship, and for the grounds for Saul's suspicion of and animosity towards David, and his fear that David's marriage with his daughter might constitute a potent claim on David's part to the right to succeed him as king, cf. "*Beena* Marriage (Matriarchat) in Ancient Israel and Its Historical Implication," 108 f. This explanation of the presence of the teraphim in David's home on what seems to have been the night of his marriage with Saul's daughter, purely hypothetical though it is, seems to have a considerable measure of probability.

[223] In fact תרפים seems to be used in precisely this sense in II Ki. 23.24.

[224] Sellin (*op. cit.*, 711) maintains that the ephod was employed only for oracles. But this is certainly an unjustifiable conclusion. The ephod of Gideon was no doubt used for oracular divination; but Jud. 8.27b clearly implies that it was an object of direct ritual worship, was, in other words, a god or the

[13] I Sam. 14 nor elsewhere do we hear of teraphim associated with it. Instead we hear only of the *'urim* and *tummim.*[225] Through them, though whether as the actual source or merely as the automatic instrument thereof is not altogether clear, the oracle was consulted and divination was practiced. The details thereof are scanty and the procedure is obscure. Apparently the questions through which the desired information was to be elicited from the oracle were couched in such simple and direct form that only three variations of answer might be given, affirmative, negative, and no answer.[226] Apparently too the divinatory procedure was a casting of something, since the verb, הִפִּיל, is used regularly to describe the act; but just what was cast, whether an arrow with a peculiar marking[227] or a lot of some other kind, is far from certain. Seemingly, from I Sam. 14.41, especially as reconstructed with the aid of *G*, *tummim* was the name of one lot or of one form of oracular answer to the question put to the oracle, and *'urim* was the name of the opposite lot or answer. But if so then it is strange that we have no name nor word which describes the third possibility in this oracular procedure, viz., no answer whatever.

Certain it is that the oracle emanated from the deity or deities

symbol of a god. Nor does Hos. 3.4 suggest that the ephod and teraphim were used only for oracular divination and no more.

[225] Cf. I Sam. 14.36–42, emended in accordance with *G*.

[226] Cf. I Sam. 14.36–42, 23.9–12; 30.7–8.

[227] So Sellin (*op. cit.*, 713), citing the *istiqsām*, the practice by the pre-islamic Arabs of divination by means of arrows (cf.Ezek. 21.26 and Wellhausen *Reste arabischen Heidentums*,[2] 207). In this type of divination there were likewise three alternative oracular responses, indicated by arrows with variant markings, (1) assent or command, (2) denial or forbidding, and (3) postponement or no answer (cf. Doutté, *Magie et Religion dans l'Afrique du Nord*, 127 f.) In this connection the close juxtaposition, in I Sam. 15.23; Zech. 10.2, of divination by means of teraphim and also by means of *ḳesem* (obviously closely related to the Arabic *istiqsām*) may be of significance. Also it may be noted that in Arabic الفذّ was the name of the first of the arrows used in the pre-islamic game of chance, *Meisir*, while افذّ seems also to have connoted an arrow with no feathers upon it, i. e. an arrow of peculiar appearance and not used for ordinary shooting (cf. Lane, *op. cit.*, 2355). These two Arabic words bear a suggestive resemblance to the Hebrew אפוד (notice the cognate אֲפֻדָּה, with doubling of the 'ד), although it is scarcely possible to establish with certainty any etymological relationship.

resident within or associated with the ephod; and there is no [14]
reason whatever to doubt that, at least by the time of Saul, if not from the very earliest times, this deity was Yahweh, the tribal Yahweh of Benjamin. In such case *'urim* and *tummim* could not have been the actual names of the sacred stones or cult objects, housed within the ephod. And yet we have seen that, despite the fact that the ark almost certainly contained two sacred stones, Yahweh was none the less the only deity associated with it, at least in the period from which all our historic records date.[228] So also it is not at all improbable that, notwith-

[228] Unquestionably Yahweh was likewise the deity of Gideon's ephod at Ophra, the tribal Yahweh of Manasseh, of course. Further indication that from quite early times Yahweh was conceived of likewise as the tribal deity of Benjamin, and also of the close association of the *'urim* and *tummim* with the ephod, may be found in a correlation of Deut. 33.8 with I Sam. 2.28. Unquestionably the priest of the *tummim* and *'urim* of Deut. 33.8 was Moses. But according to I Sam. 2.28 Moses was the ancestor of the levitical priestly family, which was charged with the task of bearing the ephod. Despite the implication of Mosaic ancestry for the family of Eli, in I Sam. 2.28, the function of bearing the ephod cannot be ascribed to this priestly family, for, as we have seen, their particular cult-object was, not an ephod, but the ark (unless, as we have established, the ark be regarded as actually an ephod of distinctive size and appearance and so having its own proper name). Actually, however, I Sam. 2.28, correlated with Deut. 33.8, seems to envisage the levitical priestly family at Nob, rather than that at Shiloh, and to ascribe Mosaic origin to it.

In truth it seems quite probable that both levitical priestly families, that of Eli at Shiloh and that of Ahimelech at Nob, were descended from Moses. On the one hand, the Egyptian names, Hofni and Phineas (cf. Meek, *Hebrew Origins*, 32) would point directly to Moses (in all likelihood also an Egyptian name; cf. *ibid.*) as the ancestor of the Elides. And the correlation of Deut. 33.8 with I Sam. 2.28 points to a parallel conclusion for the priests of Nob. It is not at all improbable that there is considerable historical validity to the tradition (I Sam. 14.3) that the priestly family at Nob was descended directly from Eli.

The entire matter is comparatively simple. According to Jud. 17.7 and 18.30 the young levite who came from Bethlehem, where he had been residing as a *ger*, or client, among the clans of Judah, to become, first the priest of Micah, the Ephraimite, and subsequently the priest of the tribe of Dan, was the grandson of Moses. This implies that after the conquest of Southern Palestine by the Judah, Simon, Levi and Kenite clans or tribes, under the leadership of Moses (Cf. "The Oldest Document of the Hexateuch," 48–50), the Judahites pushed as far north as Bethlehem. Moses himself, or at least his immediate family, settled there among the clans of Judah, in the role of

[15] standing that Yahweh was also the deity of the ephod of Benjamin, it may likewise have contained two sacred stones or two sacred images, one of which may well have conformed in some way to the *'urim* and the other to the *tummim*. The presence of these two names, and only these two names, even though there was the possibility of a third form of oracular response, viz., no answer, and their constant and almost inseparable association with it, offers some corroboration to this hypothesis of the presence of two sacred stones or images within the ephod of Benjamin. And, even though this is nowhere explicitly indicated, none the less we must conclude that these two sacred stones or images within this ephod, were teraphim.

Perhaps some further confirmation of our hypothesis that the ephod was the tent-shrine in which the teraphim were regularly housed may be found in Isa. 30.22, in the use of the obviously derivative term, אֲפֻדָּה. Seemingly the word is in parallelism with צפוי. If the parallelism be complete and absolute, אפדה would seem to be the gold envelope of the מסכה, the core of which, in turn, may have been made of some less costly metal, or even of

gerim, and contracted *beena* marriage relations with the Judahites (cf. "*Beena* Marriage [Matriarchat] in Ancient Israel and Its Historical Implications," 95, note 4). No doubt they functioned as the levitical oracular priests of these Judahite clans, since they must have inherited the technique of oracular divination from their ancestor, Moses. After a not too long period various levitical priests, all no doubt descendants of Moses (for the Mushite priestly family cf. Ex. 6.19; Num. 3.20, 33; 26.58; I Chron. 6.4, 32; 23.21, 23; 24.26, 30. Despite the fact that P, followed by the Chronicler, though with some confusion, makes these Mushites descendants of Levi in a younger and minor line, there can be no doubt that the name records the fact that from of old the descendants of Moses were recognized as functioning priests.), migrated in different directions in order to function professionally as oracular priests in different communities. In this way Jonathan, the grandson of Moses, came to Micah, the Ephraimite, and then to Dan. In the same way the young Levite of Jud. 19 came, also from Bethlehem of Judah, to become the professional oracular priest at a sanctuary somewhere near the southern border of Ephraim. I have long been of the opinion that this sanctuary was Shiloh, and that this young Levite was the ancestor of Eli and his family. Similarly some other descendant of Moses, whether through Eli, as I Sam. 14.3 has it, or through some other scion of Moses, became the founder of the family of levitical oracular priests at the Benjaminite tribal sanctuary at Nob.

wood. But it is not at all improbable that the entire מסכה was made of gold.[229] In such case the parallelism between אפדה and צפוי would be only relative; and אפדה would probably mean "cover," and even specifically "tent-cover." This would imply, in turn, that sacred molten images were regularly housed in tent-shrines, known either by the masculine name, אפוד, or the corresponding feminine, אפדה. But even if אפדה be used here as the complete and absolute parallel of צפוי, none the less it has the connotation of "covering," even though this be the close covering of a metal plating of the image; and this, in its turn, would seem to indicate that basically the אפוד or the אפדה was a covering[230] or, as we have suggested, a housing, for the sacred stones or images, the teraphim, of early Israelite religion, in other words, a tent-shrine, of the same nature as the ark, the *ḳubbe*, the *sukkah* of Amos 5.26, the *maḥmal*, and the *'oṭfe*. [16]

This exhausts the biblical evidence bearing upon the ancient ephod[231] and teraphim. This evidence is too scanty to be defini-

[229] Cf. Deut. 7.25; Isa. 40.18–20; 41.6–7; 44.9–20. In all these passages an idol, the core of which is of wood, i. e., it can be burned, and which is merely overlaid with precious metal, is called specifically פסל, just as in Isa. 30.22 the idol which has a metal plating (צפוי) is called פסיל, On the other hand, in all cases where the context is explicit (cf. Ex. 32.4, 8; 34.17 [cf. Lev. 19.4 and Ex. 20.23]; Hos. 13.2) the מסכה seems to be an image made entirely of molten metal, usually silver or gold, and formed by being poured into a mould (cf. Isa. 30.1). But if מסכה be an image of this kind, then in Isa. 30.22 זהב must be linked with מסכה, and not with אפדה; i. e., it must have been the image which was made entirely of gold. In such case אפדה could, of course, not be its overlay or plating. It seems therefore most probable that, just as we have proposed, אֲפֻדָּה is the feminine of אֵפוֹד and designated the tent-shrine in which the golden image was normally housed.

[230] Semantically then the much discussed אפוד בד would be merely "a covering of linen," i. e., as has been indicated (above, note 194), a simple piece of cloth, girt about the waist, which hung down and so "covered" the genitals.

[231] It is, of course, tempting to correlate אפדן of Dan. 11.45 with אפוד, particularly now that we have found good reason to believe that אפוד was itself the primitive Israelite tent-shrine; and this all the more so since Dan. 11–45 speaks of "the tents of the אפדן." But for cogent reasons this temptation must be resisted. It is also interesting to note that in Arabic (cf. Lane, *op. cit.*, 2353) فدن designates a kind of pavilion or lofty building, and also a red dye; but here too the resemblance must not be pressed.

[17] tive.[232] Yet it points unmistakably to the conclusion that אפוד was the generic term for the tent-shrine and תרפים the generic term for the betyls or idols within it. The ark of Ephraim would then have been a special ephod, unique in size and probably also in shape,[233] and so having its own distinguishing name, ארון יהוה, "the box of Yahweh."

We must now turn our consideration to another tent-shrine, likewise of peculiar character and probably also distinctive in size and perhaps in shape too, and which therefore also had its own distinguishing name, אהל מועד, the "tent of meeting."

viii. The "Tent of Meeting"

In an article written some twenty-five years ago[234] I showed that the so-called tent of meeting played an important role, not in the record of the E Code, as had been generally assumed by scholars up to that time, but rather in that of the J Code, that, in other words, it was an institution bound up with the Southern Kingdom and its historic traditions, and not with those of the Northern Kingdom.[235] I advanced two specific hypotheses, (1) that the tent of meeting was in large measure a replica, in tent-form, of the sacred cave upon the "mountain of Yahweh" out in the desert, which plays such an integral role in both the Moses- and the Elijah-traditions;[236] and (2) that this tent of

[232] I Sam. 15.23, in which teraphim are mentioned (Sellin, *op, cit.*, 716 would emend און to אפוד, which, though somewhat drastic, is by no means improbable. If accepted, it would constitute another instance of the conventional close association of ephod and teraphim.), sheds no additional light on the nature of either ephod or teraphim, other than to offer further confirmation of the association of teraphim with divination.

[233] May ("Ephod and Ariel," *AJSL*, LVI [1939], 44 ff.) too holds that the ark, the ephod and the sacred tent were closely related institutions, and that in particular *'aron* and *'efod* were synonymous terms.

[234] "The Tent of Meeting."

[235] So also Luther, in Meyer, *Die Israeliten und ihre Nachbarstämme*, 134 ff.

[236] Cf. also "The Oldest Document of the Hexateuch," 17 f., 29 f., 32–39, and below, note 289.

meeting had no connection at all with other sacred tents among [18]
the primitive Semites. The first hypothesis I would now modify in considerable measure; the second I would recall practically completely.

As is well known, in the P Code the tent of meeting plays a conspicuous role. It is the older name for the tabernacle in the wilderness. The younger name is *hamiškan*, "the dwelling-place." The two names are by no means synonymous. Rather the transition from the older to the younger name corresponds to, and is in fact the record of, a corresponding transition in the concept of Yahweh and of His particular dwelling-place. The idea underlying the term, אהל מועד, "tent of meeting," or, more literally, "tent of the meeting-place," is that Yahweh is a universal god, or better, the universal God, whose presence fills the entire universe, who dwells in heaven, as alone befits a universal God, who can be and is in all parts and places of the universe at all times, and who descends from His heavenly dwelling-place to confer with His particular people, Israel, through the medium of its properly accredited priest, at the door of this tent of meeting. The participants in this meeting are Yahweh, the universal God, and Israel, as represented by its highest ecclesiastical authority.

The universalistic tendency in Judaism reached what was probably its all-time extreme of formulation and expression in Deutero-Isaiah's concept of Israel as God's servant and witness unto all the nations and the agent of His purpose of salvation for all peoples; in Zechariah's formulation of a theory and program of proselytism to Judaism for both entire peoples and individuals;[237] and in Malachi's concept of Yahweh as the universal King, who, regardless of the local name under which He might be addressed, is actually worshiped in all sanctuaries throughout the entire world.[238] But, as Isa. 56.1–7 demonstrates clearly, ultimately a reaction against this extreme universalism, and

[237] Zech. 8.20–23. This theory was undoubtedly formulated and proclaimed in the high enthusiasm engendered by the dedication of the second Temple on Rosh Hashanah, 516 B. C. That this theory became a practical reality, and that there must have been many foreign proselytes to Judaism in the period, 516–500 B. C., or even for a few years after 500 B. C., is conclusively evidenced by I Ki. 8.41–43; Isa. 56.1–7 and Mich. 4.1–4 (= Isa. 2.1–4).

[238] Mal. 1.11 + 14b; cf. "Psalm 48," 44–47.

[19] particularly against the proselytizing movement, set in. Proselytes were looked upon askance, and a growing tendency began to manifest itself to relegate them to an inferior position in the worship of Yahweh, and eventually to debar them completely from admission to Judaism.[239] This tendency went hand in hand with a recrudescent, rapidly expanding and aggressive nationalism, which reached its climax in the ill-fated rebellion of the Jewish people against Persian dominion in 486 B. C.[240] The catastrophic

[239] It was against this reactionary tendency in Judaism in the period, 500–485 B. C., while the Temple was still standing in all its glory, that the prophetic author of Isa. 56.1–7 protested. He defended the proselytes valiantly, but to no avail. The anti-proselytizing reaction in the Judaism of the fifth century B. C. found concrete expression in the legislation in Deut. 23.2–4, which forbade specifically the admission into the Jewish community of eunuchs (cf. Isa. 56.1–7), Moabites, Ammonites and Edomites (Edomites were originally included in the provision of v. 4; vv. 8–9 record a later modification of the original law and provide for amelioration in the treatment of Edomite proselytes), and in Ezek. 44.6–14, which forbade absolutely admission of any foreigner whatever into the Jewish religious community, and which made the fact that the levitical priests of the second Temple, who had been its regular ministrants since its dedication in 516 B. C. (cf. Mal. 2.4–9), had countenanced the admission of these proselytes to Judaism and their active worship within the Temple (cf. again Isa. 56.1–7), the basis for its proposed demotion of these levitical priests to inferior ecclesiastical rank and function, and the restoration of the Zadokites, the pre-exilic Jerusalem priests, to their former office in the Temple and its cult. (This chapter, and in fact the greater part of Ezek. 40–48, must be dated to very shortly after 458 B. C., and be the work of Ezra and his associates, and must be regarded as an instrument in their program of extreme religious and cultural particularism and isolationism.) This anti-proselytizing tendency may be seen likewise in the attitude of indifference and complete disregard on the part of Johanan, the high-priest, and his associates, in 411–408 B. C., to the appeal of the Jews of Elephantine for aid in rebuilding their Yahweh-temple. Manifestly Johanan and his associates refused to regard these Egyptian Jews as true Jews, but chose rather to class them as foreigners who, in accordance with the provision of Ezek. 44.9, could not under any condition be admitted to Judaism. Obviously the legislation in Deut. 23.8–9 is later than 408 B. C. and represents a stage in the ultimate reaction away from the extreme, and even absolute, particularism and religious isolationism of Ezra, Nehemiah and Johanan; cf. "Supplementary Studies in the Calendars of Ancient Israel," 128–132.

[240] The evidence for this conclusion is so extensive and complex, and its implications are so far-reaching, that the treatment of this theme must be reserved for another occasion.

outcome of this rebellion left the little Jewish community of Jerusalem and its vicinity so decimated and crushed that, in 445 B. C., Nehemiah could describe it as "the remnant which is left from the captivity."[241] [20]

In 458 B. C. Ezra returned to Jerusalem at the head of a considerable body of Babylonian Jewish exiles, among whom was a comparatively large group of Zadokite priests, eager to regain the privileged position which they had held in the pre-exilic Temple, and so to oust the then functioning levitical priests from their high office. Ezra set to work diligently, not only to achieve this goal, but also to discharge the various other important tasks which had been entrusted to him by the Babylonian Jewish community. One of these tasks, and not the least in importance, was the introduction into the life and program of the Jewish community of Jerusalem of the principles and practices of Jewish exclusivism, particularism and isolationism, which had, during the preceding century and a quarter of exile, come to characterize the Jewish theory of self-perpetuation and way of life in Babylonia. In conformity with this program Ezra sought to inaugurate his marriage reforms.[242] Apparently, despite what must have seemed an auspicious beginning, Ezra's plans eventually miscarried in considerable degree. It was left therefore to Nehemiah to complete this program of marriage reforms. This he did with characteristic vigor, absolutism and ruthlessness.[243] He forced many Jews who had married foreign women, not only to send away these foreign wives, but also with them their children, born of these marriages. In accordance with the principle basic to the legislation in Deut. 23.4–7, even the offspring of marriages of Jews with foreign women could not be regarded as Jews.[244] This was, of course, the extreme of particularism and religious isolationism in Judaism. It represents a diametrical reversal of the principles and program which, as we have just seen, had been dominant in Judaism but sixty years earlier.

[241] Neh. 1.2–3.

[242] Ezra 9–10.

[243] Neh. 9.1–2; 13.23–28.

[244] Deut. 7.1–11 must be recognized for various reasons as coming from the period 458–444 B. C.

[21] In the catastrophe of 486–485 B. C. Jerusalem had been captured by the enemy and had been laid in ruins. The walls of the city had been breached, the gates burned, and the Temple likewise had been destroyed in considerable measure.[245] The basic task of Ezra, when he came to Jerusalem, for the accomplishment of which he, or better, no doubt, the Jewish community of Babylonia, had secured from the Persian government formal permission and likewise provision for material support,[246] was to rehabilitate the Temple, burned and laid in ruins some twenty-seven years previously. For this restoration of the Temple the architectural plan recorded in Ezek. 40–43 seems to have been the provisional pattern. If so, then it would follow that a quite drastic reconstruction of the Temple upon decidedly novel lines was contemplated. Ezra completed this task in due course of time. But it seems to have consisted of only a repair or rehabilitation of the destroyed Temple rather than a complete rebuilding, as at first projected.

However, shortly after 411 B. C. the occasion seems to have come for a rebuilding of the Temple upon almost radically new lines. In 411 B. C. Johanan, the son of Joyada and the grandson of Elyashib, became chief priest of the Jerusalem Temple through a coup, or at least something of that nature. Already some thirty-five or more years earlier, Johanan, then certainly a very young man, had departed from the traditional position of his priestly family, and become a supporter of Ezra and his program.[247] Apparently he had maintained this party-affiliation consistently and probably in defiance of his family. At the death of his father both he and his brother, Joshua or Jesus, were candidates for the succession. Joshua seemingly was supported by the native Palestinians, no doubt the numerically superior party. He enjoyed likewise the aggressive support of Bagoas, the then *peḥah*, or Persian military governor of the land. Obviously political considerations influenced Bagoas in his support of Joshua against his brother. Johanan, on the other hand, enjoyed the active support

[245] Cf. Isa. 63.18; 64.9–10; Obad. 11–14; Ps. 74.1–10; 79.1–6; Neh. 1.2–4.

[246] Cf. Ezra 7.11–26.

[247] Ezra 10.6; cf. "Supplementary Studies in the Calendars of Ancient Israel," 126 ff.

of the Zadokite priests and the other Babylonian exiles, who had returned under Ezra and Nehemiah. Their number at this time must have been considerable, and their social, economic and political influence, acquired during the governorship of Nehemiah, 444–432 B. C., must have been great. [22]

The issue was decided through an act of violence. Johanan slew his brother, Joshua, in the very Temple.[248] Angered by this defeat of his plans, and no doubt also seeing therein an opportunity for advantageous political action, Bagoas forced his way into the Temple, in open defiance of the Ezranic legislation of Ezek. 44.9, and subsequently imposed upon the Jewish people a heavy tax for every lamb sacrificed in the Temple. This oppressive condition continued for seven years, until 404 B. C., when Darius II was succeeded by Artaxerxes II. The harsh, restrictive measures of Bagoas in his treatment of the Jewish people, conforming no doubt to the general administrative policy of Darius II, were now repealed and a milder and more benignant administration of the Jews was inaugurated. Quite probably the influence of the Babylonian Jewish community had not a little to do with this change of policy.

The repeal of the taxes upon the sacrifices in the Temple offered a favorable opportunity for a thorough reorganization of the Temple itself and of its cult and ecclesiastical administration. The party of the returned Babylonian exiles, undoubtedly with the strong backing of the influential Jewish community still in Babylonia, and upholding the principles and program of legalism, ritualism, particularism and religious isolationism which the Babylonian Jewish community had always fostered, had now definitely gained the upper hand. The returned Zadokite priests had now to a very considerable extent replaced the native levitical priests,[249] who, in turn, were demoted to inferior priestly rank

[248] Probably upon Rosh Hashanah, when both men sought to perform the office of chief priest and to celebrate the unique and momentous rites of that day; cf. "A Chapter in the History of the High-Priesthood," 14–24.

[249] The story of the bitter struggle between these two priestly bodies for the ecclesiastical control and privileges of the post-exilic Temple is too long and complex to be dealt with here. Its treatment too must await some more suitable occasion.

[23] and function,[250] and were henceforth known professionally as the levites. The office of *kohen gadol*, "high priest," was now formulated and instituted.[251] The religious calendar was systematically reformed, largely in conformity with a pattern emanating from the Babylonian Jewish community,[252] and apparently the sacrificial cult too underwent far-reaching modification. All this reorganization is recorded in the Priestly Code, and especially in the main stratum thereof, Pg. This Code must have been in process of composition or compilation in Palestine during the last twenty years or so, and must have been formally promulgated in 404 B. C. or very soon thereafter. It provides the program and the enabling legislation for this drastic reorganization of the Temple structure, its ecclesiastical administration, its cult and ritual, the festival calendar, and the general religious practice of Judaism.

The universalistic spirit of native Palestinian Judaism was now definitely suppressed. Babylonian particularism and religious isolationism had triumphed completely. Bagoas' hostile and forceful penetration of the Temple, presumably into its innermost recess, had violated its inherent sanctity, had outraged the now dominant particularistic spirit of Judaism and had created a practical issue. This issue was met by a complete remodeling and eventual reconstruction of the Temple[253] in accordance with the Priestly Code's pattern of the tabernacle in the wilderness, represented as having been revealed to Moses by God Himself.[254] The basic consideration here, which dictated all the major details of this reconstruction of the Temple, was

[250] Yet apparently a rank and function not quite as menial and lacking in priestly authority and dignity as that previously contemplated for them in Ezek. 44.5–14.

[251] Cf. "A Chapter in the History of the High-Priesthood," 360–377.

[252] Cf. "Supplementary Studies in the Calendars of Ancient Israel," 132–148.

[253] Of course other equally important issues also contributed to the remodeling and reconstruction of the Temple, such as the propriety, and even the logical necessity, of making the Temple conform practically to the reorganization of its ecclesiastical administration, and also the very important consideration about to be presented.

[254] Ex. 25.8–9.

that it was henceforth to be looked upon as the actual abode of [24]
God.[255]

Although still regarded in P unqualifiedly as a universal deity, or rather as the universal Deity, Yahweh was also in large and real measure a particularistic deity, the particular God of Israel. With Israel He had His most immediate relations, and it was the object of His particular solicitude. Its worship of Him was alone in conformity with His wishes, as He had revealed them to Israel, and therefore was the only true worship of Him, and so far more pleasing to Him than the homage of all other nations.

In time, and probably not too long a time, the P writers evolved their peculiar and characteristic system of harmonization of the antithetical principles of universalism and particularism. It had decided affinities with, and yet was at the same time the very antithesis of, the doctrine of Deutero-Isaiah. The latter had conceived of Israel as the *'ebed Yahweh,* "the servant of God," in other words the prophet-people; for *'ebed,* or more specifically *'ebed Yahweh,* was a long established title for "prophet."[256] As His prophet-people its particular task was to bear testimony of Him and of His way of life for all men before the nations of the earth, that they, in turn, might learn His ways and come to walk in His paths, and that thereby His salvation might reach to the very ends of the earth and embrace all mankind.

The doctrine of the Priestly Code was that Israel was to be unto God a kingdom of priests and a holy nation,[257] i. e., holy to Him, His peculiar people, in other words, standing to Him in a closer, more intimate relationship than any other nation or people. Its role, according to divine program as conceived by Priestly theologians and writers, was to be, not that of a prophet-people, but that of a priest-people. Just as the priest, particularly according to the ecclesiastical scheme of P, was the indispensable

[255] That in the period with which we are dealing we should refer to the Deity as "God" rather than as "Yahweh," has been convincingly demonstrated by my colleague, Professor Blank, in his very significant article, "Studies in Deutero-Isaiah," *HUCA*, XV (1940), 1–46.

[256] Cf. Amos 3.7; cf. Blank, *op. cit.*, 18–27.

[257] Ex. 19.6a.

[25] mediator between God and ordinary men, mediated unto Him their worship, sacrifices and petitions, so Israel, the priest-people, was to be the mediator between God and all the other nations, the lay nations, as they might well be called. And just as the priest was the agent of atonement and reconciliation between layman and God, so Israel, the priest-people, was to be the agent of atonement and reconciliation between God and all the other more or less errant and sinful nations. Manifestly the Priestly Code "ecclesiasticized" Deutero-Isaiah's doctrine of Israel as the "servant" and of universal divine salvation to be achieved through his faithful service.

It is self-evident that these P theologians and writers still conceived of God in a strictly universalistic sense. Yet, as has been said, He was for them at the same time to an extreme degree, and probably in a very realistic sense, a particularistic deity. With Israel he had particular and intimate relations, such as He had with no other people. Israel was His own people, just as He was Israel's own God. What more fitting therefore than that the principle should now prevail that such a God, despite His acknowledged universalism, should be regarded as dwelling, not in heaven, where His particular relations to one people could have no adequate expression, but in the midst of that very people itself, and in the one, single Temple consecrated to His name, located not only in the very center of that people's land, but even in the very center of the entire earth?[258] This principle now became firmly established and found concrete expression in the Priestly Code.

The tabernacle in the wilderness, the pattern of which, so it was represented in P, emanated from God Himself, as was but proper, and which, in turn, was but the pattern for the now reconstructed Temple, was actually God's dwelling-place on earth. In it He abode in the very midst of His people and at the very center of His world. In it He was enthroned as King, prob-

[258] That the concept of Jerusalem, and especially of the Temple Mount, as the very center, the navel, of the earth, which played such an important role in later eschatological speculation and apocalyptic literature, was current in Palestinian Judaism already early in the fifth century B. C., I have demonstrated in "Psalm 48," 80–86.

ably as universal King,[259] in a special, innermost chamber, "the holy of holies," seated upon His throne, the ark, now called specifically "the ark of testimony,"[260] upon the golden "mercy-seat," and beneath the outspread wings of the two cherubim. There He dwelt eternally in august solitude. Into His austere presence only one mortal might come, the high priest, and that only once a year, upon the New Year's Day,[261] and that too only when enveloped in a thick cloud of incense, that he might not inadvertently gaze upon the actual face of God and so meet his death.[262] [26]

Thus it was that the tabernacle in the wilderness now came to be known as the *miškan*, the "dwelling-place," the dwelling-place of Yahweh in the midst of His people, Israel.[263] But this was not at all the name originally employed for the tabernacle in the Priestly Code. Originally in P the tabernacle was designated as the *'ohel mo'ed*, the place where God met with His people, or with their natural representative and mediator with the Deity, the high-priest. According to Ex. 25.22; 30.6, 36; Num. 17.19 the precise place where God would meet with the people was just before the veil which separated the holy of holies, the particular

[259] Rather than as merely King of Israel.

[260] ארון העדות. Is there in this name perhaps some evidence of Deutero-Isaiah's concept of Israel, the prophet-people, as God's witnesses, bearing unto all nations testimony of Him and His way of life? The "testimony" within the ark was undoubtedly believed to be the decalogue, inscribed according to ancient tradition, upon the two sacred stones, and especially the decalogue in its final, amplified P version, as recorded in Ex. 20.2–17 (note especially v. 11). In this form the decalogue was not particularistically Israelite or Jewish in character, but was decidedly universalistic, as if intended by God to constitute, in part at least, a way of life for all men. Note also that according to Gen. 1.1–2.4 (cf. "The Sources of the Creation Story") the Sabbath was instituted already at creation and long before the emergence of the Israelite people, quite as if God had intended it to be observed by all mankind. Note also the legislation in Gen. 9.1–6 and the late tradition based thereon of the seven so-called Noachidian laws, to be observed by all mankind.

[261] Later the Day of Atonement; cf. "The Three Calendars of Ancient Israel," 22–58.

[262] Lev. 16.2 ff. and cf. Lauterbach, "A Significant Controversy between the Sadducees and the Pharisees," *HUCA*, IV (1927), 173–205.

[263] Ex. 25.8 f.; 38.21 and *passim*.

[27] dwelling-place of God, from the so-called "holies," the main section of the interior of the tabernacle. But according to Ex. 29.42–43 the meeting-place of God with the people was at the door of the tent of meeting itself, and not at all at the veil. There seems to be a basic contradiction here; but it is easily resolved. Ex. 29.42–43 belongs unquestionably to one of the earliest strata of Pg, and was written undoubtedly before 411 B. C., before the architectural plan of the tabernacle, with the holy of holies as the innermost part of the sanctuary, was conceived of, and when the tabernacle was still looked upon merely as a large tent of sacred character, but not yet the permanent abiding-place of God. Ex. 25.22; 30.6, 36; Num. 17.19 belong to the later and main stratum of Pg, in which the original, simple tent-plan of the sanctuary has been redrawn, and provision has been made for the holy of holies. This later picture represents obviously a purposed and radical departure from what was undoubtedly the earlier concept, still well known to the first P writers, of the tent-sanctuary of Yahweh in the wilderness. It was this drastic reconstruction of the earlier picture which transformed this tent-sanctuary from the *'ohel mo'ed*, as it was known to the first P writers, to the *miškan* or dwelling-place of God in the midst of His people, as the sacred tent was conceived by the later P writers.[264]

[264] In developing their picture of the *miškan* these P writers revived with it the old figure of the ark. They remembered the old tradition of the ark lodged in the *debir* of the first Temple, a box-like structure containing the two tablets of the decalogue; and so they coined for it, in all likelihood, with a distinct dependence upon Deutero-Isaiah's doctrine of Israel's divinely appointed role as God's witnesses, the new title, ארון העדות, "the ark of testimony." But they remembered also another ancient and reliable historic tradition, viz., that in the *debir* of the first Temple, immediately after its erection, Yahweh's golden throne had once stood, with Yahweh Himself conceived as seated thereon (cf. "Amos Studies, III," 105 ff.). Accordingly and quite naturally they transformed the ark into something more than the mere box-like container of the two "tablets of testimony." They gave to it a heavy, golden lid, the *kapporet*, attached to which were the two cherubim with outspread wings, already present, though with different attachment, in the *debir* of Solomon's Temple (I Ki. 6.23–28; 8.6–7). Thus they made out of the ark the throne of Yahweh. In a way the circle of thought-evolution was now completed, and once again Yahweh, or God, was conceived as seated or dwelling enthroned, as the world-King, in the innermost section of His Temple.

But it is clear that neither the concept of the tent-sanctuary [28]
in the wilderness nor yet the name *'ohel mo'ed* nor the concept that it was at the door or entrance to this tent-shrine that the Deity met with the proper representative of His people were original with these earliest P writers. All this they had received from an older, pre-exilic tradition and literary record. This record we find in the J Code. Ex. 33.7–11 records Moses' established procedure with the *'ohel mo'ed.* These vv. have no actual connection with what immediately precedes.[265] The *'ohel mo'ed* appears suddenly and without any antecedent record of its fabrication or nature, as a well known and accepted cult-object, and only Moses' formal, ritual procedure with it is described.

Moses is the regular priest of the *'ohel mo'ed.* It is primarily an instrument for consultation with Yahweh, in other words for divination. Moses is therefore the oracular priest, the *kohen moreh* of II Chron. 15.3.[266] The origin of the *'ohel mo'ed* is here definitely assigned to the desert period and to Moses specifically. Moses, so the passage records, would regularly set up the *'ohel mo'ed*, at Israel's successive camping-places upon its journey through the wilderness, outside the camp, and even at some dis-

[265] So also Sellin (*op. cit.*, 168) and Gressmann (in *ZAW*, 40 [1922], 86). Ex. 33.4–6 describes the making of some object of primary religious import, though what it was is not stated, and is indicated only most loosely and vaguely. It was made out of the personal ornaments and jewels of the people. Certainly this was not the *'ohel mo'ed* (cf. below, note 290). It is difficult even to correlate this with the fabrication of the ark, as some scholars have interpreted it. The apparent parallelism with Ex. 32.2–4 would suggest that what was made from these personal ornaments and jewels was an idol, similar to the golden calf. Yet it is impossible to ascribe the fabrication of such an idol to Moses. Moreover, it is noteworthy that according to Ex. 32.2–4 the people had already divested themselves of their ornaments and jewels. Actually therefore Ex. 33.4–6 seems to offer, not a new narrative at all, but rather a parallel version of the golden calf episode recorded in detail in Ex. 32. In this, however, not Aaron, but Moses, was the chief actor. Apparently the narrative here, whatever its details may have been, has been suppressed almost completely in favor of the parallel golden calf narrative in Ex. 32.

[266] That II Chron. 15.3 is distinctly reminiscent of, and probably is even patterned after, Hos. 3.4 is self-evident. It is noteworthy therefore that ללא כהן מורה וללא תורה of II Chron. 15.3 corresponds closely in form and even more closely in thought to ואין אפוד ותרפים of Hos. 3.4.

[29] tance therefrom.[267] Moses himself, in his capacity of oracular priest, would go out from the camp to the *'ohel mo'ed* in order to consult Yahweh. Likewise whoever desired a revelation from Yahweh would accompany Moses thither, while the rest of the people, remaining in their tents, could follow Moses with their gaze and, impliedly, observe his entire procedure. When Moses had entered the sacred tent, the Deity would descend, in the form of the pillar of cloud, to the door of the tent, and there would converse with Moses, standing within the tent, face to face, just as one man speaks to another. And when Moses, having received the divine revelation, would leave the sacred tent in order to return to the camp, his youthful apprentice,[268] who was presumably learning the technique of the oracular priest, would remain within the *'ohel mo'ed*, obviously so that there might always be some properly trained oracular priest present to receive the divine revelation, whenever Yahweh would choose to speak. The role of this young apprentice within the sacred tent is, of course, identical with that of the youthful Samuel before the ark in the sanctuary at Shiloh.

This is practically all that we know of the *'ohel mo'ed* as it appears in the J Code; for subsequent J narratives merely confirm what is here stated, of the location of the sacred tent outside the camp, of Yahweh descending in the form of the pillar of cloud, and of the door of the tent as the place of meeting between Moses and the Deity.[269]

That this picture of the *'ohel mo'ed* and of the manner of functioning with it, at least in its present form, is none too old, certainly not older than the middle of the eighth century B. C., is evidenced by its universalistic background. The immediate

[267] In precisely the same manner as, as we have seen (above, note 180a), the Bedouin marriage-tent is regularly pitched at some distance from the camp.

[268] In Ex. 33.11 specifically designated as Joshua b. Nun; but this is probably here, just as it is certainly in Num. 11.28, a harmonistic gloss.

[269] That Ex. 34.29–35 is but loosely related to the account of the *'ohel mo'ed* in Ex. 33.7–11, and is at the most only a quite late legendary and theological outgrowth of this account, cf. "Moses with the Shining Face," *HUCA*, II (1925), 1–27. However, for a possible modification of this general conclusion so far as vv. 34–35 are concerned cf. below, note 290.

implication of the constantly recurring motif, that Yahweh descends to the door of the sanctuary, in the form of the pillar of cloud, in order to confer with Moses, is that normally He dwells somewhere aloft, presumably in heaven. But, as we have already indicated, the concept of Yahweh dwelling in heaven, rather than in the Temple at Jerusalem which, as we have seen, prevailed in the younger stratum of Pg, or of Yahweh dwelling upon a sacred mountain out in the desert, as the older and more primitive concept, current at least as late as the time of Elijah, i. e., about 860 B. C.,[270] ran, implies a positive universalism, which could, at the very best, not be much older than the time of Amos.[271] [30]

Moreover, it is certain that the J writers did not invent the institution of the *'ohel mo'ed*, but that, precisely as with the P writers, with them also both the specific name and also their account of Moses' procedure with this tent-shrine were based upon a definite knowledge of a still older institution in Israel, a tent-shrine, of which Moses was the oracular priest, and which was both the place and the instrument of Yahweh's revelation of His will and purpose to His people. In this connection we naturally think immediately of the tent-shrine erected in Jerusalem by David[272] as the sanctuary of the national Yahweh,

[270] Cf. "The Oldest Document of the Hexateuch," 32–39 and "Amos Studies, III," 187–190.

[271] Corroboration of this conclusion may be seen in the narrative of Num. 11.29, in which the *'ohel mo'ed* plays an integral part; for the pious wish there put into Moses' mouth, "Would that all of Yahweh's people were prophets, that Yahweh would put His spirit upon them," implies a concept of the nature, function and manner of divine call of the prophet altogether different from those of the professional prophet, which apparently found its first positive expression in Amos 3.3–8; cf. "Amos Studies, I," 29–67.

[272] II Sam. 6.17; I Ki. 2.28, 29, 30; I Chron. 15.1; II Chron. 1.4; 2.13; Ps. 15.1; 27.5, 6; 61.5; also Ezek. 41.1; I Chron. 9.23; also the import of the terms, אהל and אהלי in the symbolic names, אהלה and אהליבה (Ezek. 23.4 ff.), אהליבמה (Gen. 36.2 f.) and אהליאב (Ex. 31.6; 35.34; 36.1, 2; 38.23); also the Phoenician name, אהלבעל, and the Sabaean names, אהלעתתר and אהלאל, cited by May, "Ephod and Ariel," *AJSL*, LVI (1939), 54, note 53. May calls attention likewise (*ibid.*, 59, note 81) to the fact that in the Ras Shamra legend of Dan'el (No. II, Col. V, 11.32 f.). אהל and משכנת are employed in synonymous parallelism for the habitation of the god, Kšr = Hyn. Likewise in Dan'el, No. I, 11.212, 222 אהלם is used in a passage which deals with divination

[31] whom his creation of the united Israelite nation had called into being. Unquestionably this national tent-sanctuary in Jerusalem was erected by David because, with his pastoral background, this seemed the normal and proper kind of a sanctuary to erect in honor of Yahweh, Yahweh being to David, because of the pastoral background of David's childhood, not a native Palestinian deity but primarily a pastoral deity, whose origin and quite probably whose true home were still to be found out in the desert.[273] For David, with his shepherd point of view, the natural and proper sanctuary of Yahweh was, not a magnificent temple, built of wood and stone and magnificently decorated, but a simple tent-shrine, such as his ancestors must have known in their pastoral life, and still earlier in the nomadic and semi-nomadic periods of their cultural evolution. The supplanting of David's tent-sanctuary by Solomon's magnificent temple marked the beginning of an altogether new economic and cultural epoch in Israel's history, an epoch of which this temple, of new and revolutionary style, was the actual symbol.[274]

Yet while there were undoubtedly close affinities between David's tent-sanctuary at Jerusalem and the original *'ohel mo'ed*, still they were by no means identical. The name, *'ohel mo'ed*, was apparently never applied to David's tent-sanctuary; nor was that an *'ohel mo'ed* in the strict meaning of the term. Rather that was primarily a sanctuary, even a temple, though still in tent-shape. It was a sanctuary in the larger sense, like the sanctuary at Shiloh, in which the ark was deposited, or, with even greater and more significant similarity, like the Kaaba at Mekka, in which too the betyls or images of many pre-islamic deities were collected

procedure. All these references confirm our major hypothesis, viz. that the sacred tent, conceived both as the housing of the gods and also as an instrument of oracular divination was current, not only among the Sabaeans but also among the Phoenicians of the 15th century B. C., and undoubtedly also among their primitive, nomadic, Semitic ancestors.

[273] In fact, as we have just pointed out, even one hundred and fifty years after David, Elijah, likewise a shepherd, and probably a Kenite as well, feeling the need of immediate, personal communion with Yahweh, fled into the desert, to the "mountain of Yahweh," where obviously he still conceived of Yahweh as actually dwelling; cf. "Amos Studies, III," 186 ff.

[274] *Ibid.*, 59–81; 100–134.

and deposited,[275] in order thus to give concrete expression to the [32]
principle of the all-inclusiveness and absolute unity of Allah, and to establish likewise that these particular deities had themselves ceased to exist, were all either absorbed in or supplanted by Allah. David's tent-sanctuary at Jerusalem, precisely like the Kaaba, had much of the nature of a national pantheon. And, again like the Kaaba, it too implied that all the old, tribal Yahwehs, and particularly those whose ancient cult-objects, such as the ark, the ephod of Benjamin, and the brazen serpent, were now deposited in the national shrine, had been absorbed in, identified with and supplanted by the national Yahweh of united Israel.

On the other hand, the original *'ohel mo'ed* was, strictly speaking, not so much a tent-sanctuary as a simple tent-shrine, one in which, undoubtedly, a deity, Yahweh, was thought to reside, which was used for purposes of divination and oracular decision, whose oracular priest Moses was, and the origin of which was to be found, not in Palestine, but out in the desert, in the period of tribal sojourn there before entrance into Palestine. But these considerations all point to the unmistakable conclusion that this original *'ohel mo'ed* was but another *ḳubbe*, and actually a very early form thereof, and that the name, *'ohel mo'ed*, was, again, not a generic term, but rather the proper name of this particular *ḳubbe* or ephod, just as we have seen that *'ᵃron Yahweh* was the proper name of another particular object of that same class in ancient Israel and as *al-Markab* is the name of the *ḳubbe* or *'oṭfe* of the Ruwala Bedouin today. Just why this particular *ḳubbe* was called *'ohel mo'ed*, is not clear, for certainly in the original concept, it was not Yahweh who met with Moses at the door of the tent-shrine, but rather Moses who met with Yahweh, and not at the door merely, but within the tent.[276]

[275] Cf. Lammens, *op. cit.*, 142–145.

[276] For certainly, if Yahweh was thought to dwell permanently within this sacred tent, just as Al-Lat, Al'Uzza and other deities were thought to dwell within their respective *ḳubbes*, then the tradition that Moses would meet with Yahweh at the door of the *'ohel mo'ed*, with the implication that this was the reason for this specific name for this sacred tent, must have been the invention of the J writers, growing out of their theological doctrine that Yahweh actually dwelt, not within the tent, but in heaven. In connection

33] One consideration in particular points directly and convincingly to the identification of the *'ohel mo'ed* with the later, preislamic *ḳubbe*. Despite its relatively late date and the very long interval which therefore separated it from the original and historic *'ohel mo'ed*, the Priestly Code preserved the tradition that its *'ohel mo'ed*, even in the elaborate form in which it conceived of this sacred tent, was to be made of leather and dyed red.[277] But, as we have learned, these were two of the constant and unfailing characteristics of the *ḳubbe*. That the *'ohel mo'ed* was a *ḳubbe*, or at least an early forerunner thereof, can no longer be doubted.

Despite the implication of I Sam. 2.27–28 and also of Deut. 33.8, Moses himself had no immediate association with the ark, nor yet with the ephod of Benjamin, nor with any ephod or *ḳubbe* other than the *'ohel mo'ed*. With it his association is inseparable. The *'ohel mo'ed* cannot be interpreted correctly without correlating it with Moses as its oracular priest, its *kohen moreh*. Moreover, as we have seen, all the biblical evidence points unmistakably to the conclusion that the *'ohel mo'ed* was of specifically desert origin.

And still one other circumstance of historical significance do we note in connection with the *'ohel mo'ed*, viz., that never[278] do we hear of betyls or images associated with it. From the very

with the question of the original implication of the name, *'ohel mo'ed*, a passage from Ibn Doraid (*Kitāb al Ishtiqāq* [ed. Wüstenfeld], 215), to which my attention was first called by my good friend, Dr. Joshua Finkel, and which I subsequently found cited by Lammens (*op. cit.*, 135), is of great interest, to say the very least; وهم اشراف فى الجاهلية لهم قبة وهى التى يقال لها قبة المعاذة من لجا اليها اعاذوه. "And these nobles in the 'Days of Ignorance' had a *ḳubbe*, which was called 'the *Ḳubbe* of Refuge,' because to whoever entered it they granted asylum." The similarity between the names, אהל מועד or אהל המועד and قبة المعاذة is more than striking. Can it be that early Arabic tradition had some vague reminiscence of the name, אהל מועד, and interpreted מועד as from a stem, עוד — عاذ, "to seek refuge?" If so, regardless of whether this etymology be correct, it follows that these early Arabs must have identified the *'ohel mo'ed* with their *ḳubbe*.

277 Ex. 26.14; 36.19; 39.34.

278 Unless we except the possible implication of Ex. 33.4–6, suggested in note 265.

beginning the cult of Yahweh connected with the *'ohel mo'ed,* [34]
and therefore with Moses, appears to have been imageless. This is a matter of deep historic import; for the question of the origin of the imageless worship of Yahweh, so characteristic of the official worship of Him, at least in Judah, from the time of the first reformation, that in the fifteenth year of Asa, in 899 B. C.,[279] has as yet not found a satisfactory answer. The command in Ex. 34.17, "Gods of molten metal thou shalt not make for thyself," the second command in the Kenite Code,[280] obviously represents no innovation, but merely reduces to formal legislation, in the name of Yahweh, what had long been regarded as a basic institution of His true worship, at least in the Southern Kingdom. As I have indicated elsewhere,[281] this particular command was directed immediately against the presence of the golden image of the enthroned Yahweh in the Jerusalem Temple. One of the major results of this successful reformation was the destruction of this image and the substitution for it of the ancient ark of Ephraim as the chief cult-object within the Temple. It follows therefore that the antipathy to the use of images in the worship of Yahweh within the Southern Kingdom is older than the erection of Solomon's Temple. Undoubtedly David conformed strictly to this principle,[282] and the origin of this deep-rooted antipathy, which exerted such a distinctive and compelling influence upon

[279] Cf. "The Oldest Document of the Hexateuch," 98–119.

[280] *Ibid.*, 57, 71–73.

[281] "Amos Studies, III," 100–134.

[282] The presence of the teraphim in David's house at the time of his marriage with Michal (I Sam. 19.13 ff.) may not be regarded as disproving this statement; cf. above, note 222. Neither may we regard the presence in the tent-sanctuary of David at Jerusalem of various originally tribal cult-objects, such as the ark of Ephraim, the ephod of Benjamin, or even the brazen serpent (cf. II Ki. 18.4) as further disproof of this statement, any more than the reputed presence of the three hundred and sixty idols in the Kaaba at Mekka qualifies in any way Islam's absolute prohibition of the cult of idols. As has been pointed out (above, note 149), these various tribal cult-objects were collected by David and deposited in his national sanctuary at Jerusalem primarily, if not solely, for political reasons and not at all for purposes of actual worship. There is not the slightest reason to doubt that the official cult of the national Yahweh in David's tent-sanctuary at Jerusalem was imageless.

[35] the subsequent development of the religion of Israel and upon later Judaism, must be sought in the pre-Davidic period. But, as we have learned, an imageless worship of Yahweh was not at all the rule among the various tribes of Israel in the pre-Davidic period. We have investigated the tribal cult-objects of Ephraim, Manasseh, Benjamin and Dan and found them in every case to have been primarily either images or betyls, in other words teraphim housed within ephods. We have also had reason to assume that other tribes too had ephods as their tribal cult-objects and instruments of divination, and this, in turn, implies that each tribe had its image or betyl, its teraphim, as the concrete representation of its tribal Yahweh.

Only in the tribe of Judah, the dominant tribe in the Southern federation of tribes which was called into existence by David,[283] and which became, after the division of the Kingdom, the nucleus of the Southern Kingdom, was the representation of Yahweh by an image or a betyl forbidden so absolutely by tradition and established custom and doctrine, that we hear of no image whatever in its tribal cult. And while there is no direct proof which associates the original *’ohel mo‘ed* with Judah, there is sufficient indirect evidence to warrant the assumption that it was actually the cult-object, the *ḳubbe* or ephod, but imageless, of that tribe.

Of particular significance in this connection is the fact that, on the one hand, as we have noted, Moses is inseparably associated with the original *’ohel mo‘ed*, and, on the other hand, that, also, as we have already noted, Jud. 18.30 indicates unmistakably that the grandson of Moses had been living at Bethlehem of Judah, among the clans of Judah; and this, in turn, suggests very strongly that Moses himself had actually dwelt there, and so had enjoyed relations of utmost intimacy and undoubtedly also of priestly authority with these same clans of Judah. Moses was unquestionably the leader of that federation of Israelite clans which, very soon after the exodus from Egypt and the solemnization of the covenant with Yahweh at the "mountain of Yahweh" in the Sinaitic wilderness, effected an entrance into Canaan from the south.[284]

[283] Cf. I Sam. 25; 30.26–31.

[284] "The Oldest Document of the Hexateuch," 49–51.

This federation included a small group of Levites, still obviously in a tribal, or at least a clan, state, and not yet dispersed as priestly officiants among the various tribes of Israel, and also Kenites, Judahites, Simeonites and Calebites.[285] Apparently Moses himself had succeeded in bringing this federation of clans, or at least the Judahite clans of this federation, as far north as Bethlehem. There they had established themselves in permanent residence; and there, it is clear, Moses and his Levite fellow-clansmen had settled down among these Judahites and found security for themselves; and from there, as we have pointed out, in the course of the next two generations various individual Levites had migrated in order to seek for themselves opportunities to function among the other tribes of Israel in a priestly capacity, since they had speedily come to be regarded as particularly expert in the techniques of divination and consultation of the oracle of Yahweh. This technique they must have acquired as an inheritance from their great ancestor, Moses, the *kohen moreh* of the original *'ohel mo'ed.* That this original *'ohel mo'ed* was associated with Judah from the very moment of its entrance into Palestine from the south, and that in it Moses functioned as the oracular priest of the clans of Judah, we need no longer doubt. This office of Moses as the *kohen* of the *'ohel mo'ed* will account completely for his role as the leader of the federated clans, which invaded and gradually conquered southern Palestine, for, as we have seen, the *kahin*, or the *rabb el-ḳubbe*, was regarded as the head of his clan or tribe by the pre-islamic Arabs; and Moses is here functioning in precisely the same capacity. In a very literal sense it could be said that it was through the favor and active support of Yahweh, whose will was communicated to these federated clans through Moses, His oracular priest, with the *'ohel mo'ed* as his oracular instrument, that these clans had [36]

[285] Cf. Jud. 1.4–21. These vv. constitute a unified narrative, as the mention of Judah in v. 19 indicates. The paragraph, as it obviously is, records, though not at all in strictly chronological order, the manner in which Southern Palestine, as far north as Jerusalem, was gradually wrested from its earlier Canaanite inhabitants by Judah. The passage affirms that in this conquest Calebites, Simeonites and Kenites, the latter the kinsmen of Moses through his marriage with the sister of Hobab, their *kahin*, were federated with Judah.

[37] successfully invaded southern Palestine and established their permanent residence there.

But here the pressing question arises, how shall we account for an imageless ephod or *ḳubbe*, such as the *'ohel mo'ed* undoubtedly was? We have learned that the ephod or the *ḳubbe* was merely the tent-housing of the teraphim, of the betyls or images, which were themselves, or else were the visible representations of, the tribal Yahwehs or other deities. The very idea of an imageless tent-shrine seems therefore altogether anomalous. However, this imageless tent-shrine, such as the *'ohel mo'ed* was, has one significant and illuminating parallel; for, as we have learned, the rise of Islam did not immediately terminate the employment of the *ḳubbe*. Manifestly it was not so much the *ḳubbe* itself to which Islam objected, as the images or betyls which had been regularly housed therein. Accordingly, as we have seen, at the critical Battle of Siffin, Moawiyya did not hesitate to take a *ḳubbe* with him into battle in order to ensure victory for himself and his army; but this *ḳubbe* was empty. Also, as we have likewise learned the institution of the *ḳubbe* has never died out completely in Islamic practice. It survives still today in the *maḥmal* and the *'oṭfe*; but within these two modern forms of the primitive Semitic sacred tent in place of the ancient images or betyls we find either a woman of exalted rank or else a copy, or even two copies, of the Koran or of some other book of high religious authority among the Moslems. The discontinuance of the use of images or betyls in connection with the *ḳubbe* was the result of an iconoclastic religious reformation, such as, in one sense, Islam actually was.

Inasmuch as the ancient Israelite tent-shrine seems to have been likewise associated with images or betyls, we must conclude that the complete absence of images from the *'ohel mo'ed* of Judah was likewise the result of an iconoclastic reformation, probably the very first such reformation in the history of religion. This reformation must, of course, be associated with Moses, and must be regarded as one of his greatest actual historical achievements, perhaps the very greatest, which established for the subsequent religion of Israel and for Judaism eventually one of its most distinctive basic principles. In this sense Moses was truly the founder

of the characteristic worship of Yahweh and of the religion of [38]
Israel. From this historical nucleus it was a simple and natural procedure for evolving tradition and eventual literary records to ascribe to Moses all the significant innovations and distinctive religious institutions, principles and practices which Israel gradually developed in its religious unfolding; and particularly from his role as *kohen moreh*, oracular priest of Yahweh, with the *'ohel mo'ed* as the instrument of divination, to conceive of Moses and to represent him in literary records as the great lawgiver of Israel, as the medium of revelation by Yahweh to Israel of His divine law. And if it seem to some too venturesome to ascribe to Moses, in the second half of the thirteenth century B. C., the leadership in an actual iconoclastic reformation, we must remind them that actually in 899 B. C., but a little more than three hundred years after Moses, we actually have precisely such a reformation, and that too with all the implications that this was by no means the first such iconoclastic reformation in Israel's history.

And if it be asked, how could Moses possibly have come at the idea of an imageless tent-shrine and the principle that Yahweh must be represented by no image nor betyl, we can answer only by conjecture; for obviously our sources are most meager. Yet conjecture is not difficult. Certainly Moses could not have become acquainted with the tent-shrine in Egypt, for, as is now completely apparent, it is not only a distinctively primitive Semitic religious institution, but is also definitely the creation of a desert environment. It follows therefore that Moses could have become acquainted with the tent-shrine only in a desert milieu; and this, in turn, points to the period of his contact with the Kenites and of his marriage with the sister of Hobab, their priest-chieftain.

That Yahweh, or rather the Yahweh of Moses, who was adopted as their deity by the clans or tribes which emerged from Egypt, was originally the particular clan or tribal deity of the Kenites, I have endeavored to establish in an earlier study.[286] That this Yahweh was the deity whose priest, *kohen*, Hobab was, is self-evident. And equally self-evident is it that it was from Hobab that Moses must have learned of Yahweh and of the

[286] "The Oldest Document of the Hexateuch;" cf. also Budde, *Die Religion des Volkes Israel bis zur Verbannung*, 1–31.

[39] manner of His worship.[287] That as chieftain and *kohen* of his clan or tribe Hobab must have possessed a tent-shrine, must have been, in other words, and to use the later Arabic term, a *rabb ḳubbe* or *rabb bait*, is an altogether reasonable conjecture. And that it was from Hobab that Moses borrowed the institution of the tent-shrine and also learned the technique of divination as *kohen* in connection with this tent-shrine is an equally reasonable inference.[288] That the tent-shrine or ephod of Hobab contained a betyl, or two betyls, or even an image or two images, of Yahweh is a further reasonable inference; for there is no ground whatever for believing that the abolition of the betyls or images from the tent-shrine had been achieved already by the Kenites. Rather there is every reason to believe that it was Moses himelf who, in borrowing from the Kenites Yahweh and His worship and the particular institution of the tent-shrine, removed from the latter all betyls or images, and so instituted the principle, which later became basic, first for Judah, and then, in course of time, for all Israel, that Yahweh, eventually the national god of Israel, must under no condition be represented by betyl or image of any kind.

If this chain of argument be correct, and it seems altogether natural and reasonable, then the formulation and successful inauguration of this principle would be one of the actual and distinctive achievements of Moses, which would in a very real sense justify the role, which tradition has ascribed to him, of founder of the religion of Israel and its first and great priestly interpreter of the oracle of Yahweh and lawgiver in His name.[289]

[287] This is the particular implication of Ex. 18.9–11; cf. *ibid.*, 127–135.

[288] Whether האהלה of Ex. 18.7 refers to the tent of Moses or to the tent-shrine of Yahweh, the *'ohel mo'ed*, is, of course, not at all certain. More probably it refers to the *'ohel mo'ed*; cf. below, note 290.

[289] Some further, though, it must be admitted, inconsequential, substantiation of our hypothesis that the *'ohel mo'ed* was in origin a primitive Semitic tent-shrine of the ephod or *ḳubbe* type, just as were the ark and the ephods of Benjamin, Dan and Manasseh, may be seen perhaps in the manifest confusion between the *'ohel mo'ed*, here located in Shiloh, and the ark, which was regularly deposited there, in Josh. 18.1; 19.51 (both passages late P writings).

Dr. Joshua Finkel has directed my attention to another possible point of contact between the *'ohel mo'ed*, the ark and the Arabic *ḳubbe*. That the "holy of holies" within the tabernacle in the wilderness and in the later

The occasion for the making and setting-up of the *'ohel mo'ed* [40]
is easily imagined. It must have been after the exodus from

Temple at Jerusalem was actually regarded basically as a tent or tent-shrine, is suggested by the two veils, or *p̣arokot*, which covered its opening towards the main portion of the sanctuary. *Tosefta Sheḳalim* (ed. Zuckermandel), 178, bottom, (cf. *Yalkut Shim'oni*, 375; these references I owe to the kindness of my colleague, Professor Alexander Guttmann) records the fact that, assuming that it had become ritually defiled during the course of the year just ended, the outer one of these two veils was removed every Yom Kippur, the second veil was unfolded in its stead, and a new veil was provided to replace this latter veil. Dr. Finkel has correlated this ceremony with the annual change of the covering of the Kaaba (cf. Snouck Hurgronje, *Mekka*, I, 5). Certainly the covering of the Kaaba gives to it too, and probably this was purposed originally, the semblance of a tent-sanctuary (so also Wellhausen, *Reste arabischen Heidentums*[2], 73). Similarly, in the first century of Islam the tent or *ḳubbe* of Moḫtār, when it accompanied the army into battle, was mounted upon a mule and was covered with rich cloths of silk and brocade (Lammens, *op. cit.*, 125). In this connection we think too of the ark, as conceived by P, when on the march, protected by a covering of leather, over which was spread a blue robe (Num. 4.6; cf. also Ginzberg, *Legends of the Jews*, III, 157). As these P writers thus represented it, the ark thus arrayed upon the march, must have been strikingly similar in appearance to the *maḥmal* in its gala attire.

A word may be said here in conclusion concerning my earlier hypothesis that the "tent of meeting" was patterned after the sacred cave upon the "mountain of Yahweh" in the desert ("The Tent of Meeting"). That this "mountain of Yahweh," with the cave upon it, was known to and revered by the Kenites, I have endeavored to show ("The Oldest Document of the Hexateuch," 32–39; "Amos Studies, III," 167–194). That the Yahweh of the mountain was the Yahweh of the Kenites is self-understood (cf. Ex. 3.1), as is also the fact that this mountain was regarded as His permanent abode and the cave perhaps, in the earliest form of the tradition, as the particular spot where He was always to be found. Certainly the primitive Semitic tent-shrine was regarded as the housing or abiding-place of the god or gods associated with it. Undoubtedly too it was patterned after the tent in which the nomad Semite himself normally dwelt. The tent was, of course, the type of dwelling best suited to the desert wanderings or migrations characteristic of the nomadic life. But it is not at all improbable that the tent, with its single entrance or opening, was itself in origin but a man-made replica of the cave, undoubtedly a much earlier type of human residence, the use of which in the most primitive Semitic world and its cultural antecedents is well authenticated. It is therefore a hypothesis not at all improbable, that the primitive Semitic tent-shrine, the Israelite ephod, was patterned, even though somewhat remotely, after the sacred cave; and the ephod of the Kenites in particular after the sacred cave upon the mountain in the desert so intimately linked with the cult of the Kenite Yahweh.

[41] Egypt, but so soon thereafter that the memory of that great deliverance and the consciousness that it was Yahweh, or more specifically the particular Yahweh of the Kenites, a deity hitherto unknown to those clans which had emerged from Egypt, who had wrought this deliverance in their behalf, were still strong upon the people. With this to them new Deity they had entered into covenant at His sacred mountain out in the desert, whereby He had undertaken to become their god, and they, in turn, had agreed to become His people and to worship Him and Him alone. With this moment a new clan or tribal federation had come into existence, which, in considerable measure, superseded all earlier clan or tribal organization of the constituents of this federation; and for them as a federation the worship of a new deity had begun. This was the logical moment for the creation and inauguration of the proper symbol of this new deity and this new tribal federation, a new ephod, in other words. It must have been upon just this occasion, precisely as the biblical tradition records, and at just this place that Moses, the leader and oracular priest of this tribal federation, made and set up this new ephod, the *'ohel mo'ed.*[290] Almost immediately thereafter, in accordance with the

[290] It is clear that in all essential respects this occasion for the making and setting-up of the new ephod parallels exactly the occasion for Gideon's making and setting up his new ephod and of David's setting up his new tent-sanctuary at Jerusalem. In all three cases we have a wondrous deliverance, through the aid of a powerful deity, from a grave danger, which threatened the very existence of the Israelite clans or tribes involved therein; and in all three cases apparently this deliverance was followed by a definite inter-clan or inter-tribe reorganization and fusion, which brought into existence a new tribal or national unit, larger and more powerful than had existed previously, and with this, in turn, a somewhat new and decidely larger concept of deity, with much greater power and wider range of authority.

Returning to the *'ohel mo'ed,* it is indeed a tempting hypothesis to regard the narrative in Ex. 18 in its very earliest form (cf. "The Oldest Document of the Hexateuch," 134 f.) as the record, or at least as a modified form of the record, of the actual setting-up and consecration of the *'ohel mo'ed.* The narrative in its present form records a number of details which smack decidely of a dedication ceremony. In the ceremony apparently Hobab, the Kenite priest, the original priest of Yahweh (cf. "The Oldest Document of the Hexateuch," 39–47), consecrates the *'ohel mo'ed* and inducts Moses into his sacred office as *kohen* of this particular ephod, and with this as the formally recognized leader of this new clan and tribal organization. He even advises Moses

promise of their new Deity, the migration of this federation of [42]
clans and tribes away from the sacred mountain in the desert to their new abode in southern Palestine and their conquest of this

as to the most effective manner of administering the laws and institutions essential to the unified living of such a group of people, laws and institutions which were, however, of oracular origin, emanating directly from Yahweh, with Moses as the *kohen moreh*, the active agent of this oracular revelation, and the *'ohel mo'ed* as the instrument thereof.

But if this be so, then it follows necessarily that this present narrative in Ex. 18, in its original form, must have been preceded by an account of Moses' fabrication of the *'ohel mo'ed*, undoubtedly at the command of Yahweh; for in Ex. 18 the *'ohel mo'ed* seems already present and merely awaiting dedication in order for its use to be inaugurated, while the latter half of the narrative of Ex. 18 implies that the technique of oracular revelation through Moses had already been formulated.

But granting this, then it follows that an account of the making of the *'ohel mo'ed* by Moses, undoubtedly at the bidding of Yahweh, must have preceded this narrative. Actually nowhere in the Bible do we find the record thereof, but this is perfectly comprehensible; for the Priestly redactors of the Pentateuch quite naturally suppressed this record in favor of their own detailed account of the making of their *'ohel mo'ed*. However, one small fragment of what must have been the original account of the making of the *'ohel mo'ed* has survived, viz. the basic stratum of Ex. 33.7–11, which recounts Moses' naming of and formal procedure with the *'ohel mo'ed*, after it had been made. Actually this fragment cannot have been the immediate continuation of the missing record of the fabrication of the *'ohel mo'ed*. Rather this must have immediately preceded the narrative in Ex. 18, while the record of Ex. 33.7–11 must, in turn, have followed immediately upon Ex. 18.

We would then have, with proper consecution of details, the full narrative of the making of the *'ohel mo'ed*, of its dedication, with Hobab, the original priest of the Yahweh of the mountain, playing the principal role of officiating ministrant, of the inauguration of oracular procedure, with Moses as oracular priest, acting largely in conformity with the organized system suggested to him by Hobab, of the installation by Moses of a body of judicial officials charged with the task of administering justice for the people in accordance with the gradually developing body of legal precedents growing out of the revelation of divine judgments mediated by Moses, and finally of Moses' procedure with the *'ohel mo'ed* in carrying out the oracular process.

This becomes all the clearer when the text of Ex. 33.7–11 is carefully analyzed. A moment's thought shows that v. 10b repeats what has already been adequately stated in v. 8 and indicates the hand of the redactor. Vv. 9–10 are manifestly the interpolation of a J redactor animated by a definite theological motive. With the omission of these two vv. and the possible emendation of וקרא in v. 7 to ויקרא, and also the omission of יהושע בן־נון in v. 7 (cf. above,

[43] country and their settlement there must have taken place. Undoubtedly upon this migration these federated clans and tribes

note 268), the passage reads quite smoothly: "And Moses would take the tent and would pitch it outside the camp at some distance from the camp — now he had dubbed it *'ohel mo'ed* (i. e. "tent of meeting") — and everyone who would 'seek' Yahweh would come out to *'ohel mo'ed*, which was outside the camp. And whenever Moses would go out to the tent, all the people would rise and stand, each one at the entrance of his tent, and they would watch Moses, until he had entered the tent. And Yahweh would speak to Moses face to face, just as one man speaks to another; and then he would return to the camp; but his apprentice, a lad, would never depart from within the tent."

It should be noted that in v. 7bβ אהל מועד is used without the article, quite as a proper name, just as we have claimed. The transition from v. 8 to v. 11 seems to be somewhat abrupt, as if the present vv. 9–10 have replaced something which stood here originally and recorded Moses' procedure immediately after he had entered the tent and preparatory to his face to face conversation with Yahweh. It is tempting indeed to regard Ex. 34.34–35 as the missing section of this narrative, with v. 34a following immediately upon 33.8, and 34.34b and 35 following, in turn, between 33.11a and 11b. Were this reconstruction correct it would follow that ordinarily Moses wore something over his face, a veil or mask (cf. Hoffmann-Gressmann, "Teraphim," *ZAW*, [40] 1922, 75–137), which he would remove during his face to face conversation with Yahweh and his immediately ensuing oracular communication to his people, and which he would redon when he left the *'ohel mo'ed* to return to the camp and to normal association with the people.

It is noteworthy that, in significant contrast to Ex. 34.29–33, which records the details of a single incident, vv. 34–35 record customary procedure, precisely as does Ex. 33.7–11. This is the basic reason for dissociating these two vv. from 29–33 and hypothetically interpolating them into Ex. 33.7–11 in the manner just indicated. If this interpolation be accepted, then it records a peculiar ritual procedure on the part of Moses in connection with his functioning as oracular priest of the *'ohel mo'ed*, viz. the wearing of a face-covering of some kind ordinarily and the removal of this both during the process of oracular revelation to him within the *'ohel mo'ed* and also during the communication of this revelation to the people at large. If only we had some well authenticated parallel to this procedure on the part of some other primitive Semitic *kahin* in connection with his oracular ministration, we would not hesitate to accept this interpolation as justified and illuminating of Moses' oracular technique. But having no parallel whatever to this procedure, it must suffice to have indicated the possibility of this interpolation, with its far-reaching implication, and to leave the matter rest here. (This interpretation of Ex. 34.34–35 modifies somewhat the interpretation of Ex. 34.29–35, which I proposed some twenty years ago; cf. "Moses with the Shining Face," 1–12.)

But even without this interpolation Ex. 33.7–11, as we have emended

must have been led by the *'ohel mo'ed*, in the manner characteristic of the *kubbe* or the still earlier ark.[291] [44]

the passage, throws some light upon Moses' technique as oracular priest of the *'ohel mo'ed*, viz. upon the manner in which he received the revelation from Yahweh, through face to face conversation, within the *'ohel mo'ed* and, in turn, communicated this to the people, and likewise upon the reverent attitude of the people while the oracular procedure was in process, and, finally, upon the necessity of the constant presence in the *'ohel mo'ed* of a person understanding the proper technique of revelation, in order to be present and receive the divine communication, whenever Yahweh might, of His own volition, and not merely in response to Moses' oracular query, choose to speak. One thing in particular is patent, viz. that Yahweh is conceived as dwelling, or at least as being constantly present, within the *'ohel mo'ed*, But, as we have seen, nowhere in the entire narrative is there the slightest suggestion of an image or teraphim therein. That Ex. 33.7–11, as emended, and either with or without the interpolation of 34.34–35, is a unit with Ex. 18 is now almost beyond question.

But whether this entire passage may be regarded as a part of the larger K document, as I contended in 1927 (cf. "The Oldest Document of the Hexateuch," 127–135) is by no means certain; for a basic contradiction seems to exist between them. The K document (Ex. 33.20–23) says explicitly that no mortal being, not even Moses, might look upon the face of Yahweh with impunity, whereas 33.11 records explicitly that Moses received the oracular revelation from Yahweh through face to face conversation, just as one man speaks to another. This contradiction is too basic and of too far-reaching theological import to be reconciled, unless we assume, what is by no means improbable, that through his consecration as *kohen* of Yahweh Moses' nature was thought to have been changed completely, so that what was absolutely forbidden to him as an ordinary man, now became permitted to him as a regular part of his priestly functioning.

If this hypothesis be acceptable, then we may continue to regard the narrative of Ex. 18 in the form in which we have just expanded it, as a part of the K document. Otherwise we must regard it as a fragment of some other document which paralleled in considerable measure the K document and dealt with a closely related theme, and which was of equal or almost equal antiquity. Between these two hypotheses, the first, completely unsupported by direct evidence though it is, appears the more reasonable. And if we bear in mind that at the very best we have the K document in only exceedingly fragmentary form, and that many, if not even most, of its essential details have been lost for one reason or another, this hypothesis may not seem quite as extreme and as difficult of acceptance as at first thought.

[291] In the later narrative of the Book of the Covenant, the Northern origin of which I have established (cf. "The Oldest Document of the Hexateuch," 91–95; "Amos Studies, III," 225–240), as is but natural, the ark,

[45] It is clear from all this discussion that, precisely like that of the ark, the history of the *'ohel mo'ed* falls into three distinct periods. The first period was that immediately following its fabrication by Moses, the period of the brief desert migration[292] and of the settlement in southern Palestine. No doubt along with Moses, its *kohen*, after the conquest of southern Palestine the *'ohel mo'ed* was established at or in the immediate vicinity of Bethlehem in Judah, and there it survived long enough at least to evolve a clear and persistent tradition, which, as we have seen, left a significant impress upon the development of the subsequent religion of Israel and even upon later Judaism. During this first period the *'ohel mo'ed* was apparently naught but a normal ephod, perhaps of slightly unusual size and shape, although of this we cannot be certain. What distinguished it chiefly from other ephods was the fact that it was imageless. None the less that Yahweh, the Yahweh of the federation of southern clans and tribes, was thought to dwell within the *'ohel mo'ed* seems quite certain. At any rate the oracular procedure must have been carried on by Moses and his successors, during this first period, in the conventional manner within the shrine, and not at all at the door thereof.

The second period in the history of the *'ohel mo'ed* is really the record of a tradition rather than of actual, historical circumstance. It is the tradition recorded in the J Code. This tradition could scarcely have taken shape until some time after Amos and

itself a primitive ephod, as we have learned, took the place of the *'ohel mo'ed* as the guide of the people through the desert. But that in the original and historically more correct narrative the *'ohel mo'ed* must have played this role for this particular tribal federation is almost self-evident. As I have shown elsewhere ("The Oldest Document of the Hexateuch," 39–51), the K document represents Hobab as the guide of these federated tribes through the desert. Undoubtedly there is a large measure of historic truth in this statement, for, as priest-chieftain of the Kenites, Hobab must have been thoroughly familiar with the desert, at least within a reasonable radius of the sacred "mountain of Yahweh," while in his role as *kohen* of Yahweh he may well have had some direct connection with the *'ohel mo'ed* as well as with the particular ephod of his own Kenite clan or tribe.

[292] For the brevity of the migration of this Southern federation of clans or tribes from the "mountain of Yahweh" to Southern Palestine, cf. "The Oldest Document of the Hexateuch," 49–51.

the beginning of the development of the concept of Yahweh as a universal god, who, by reason of the very quality of universality, was no longer regarded as dwelling in any one, particular spot upon the earth's surface nor in any one particular shrine or sanctuary, but rather, as befits a true universal deity, in heaven. By this time undoubtedly the actual *'ohel mo'ed* of Moses had disappeared completely,[293] and only a vague reminiscence thereof had survived. And so this tradition, recorded in J, evolved a new picture of the *'ohel mo'ed*, no longer as the dwelling-place af Yahweh, but merely as the place of divine revelation. But now, as a necessary corollary of the belief that Yahweh dwelt in heaven the precise place of revelation is no longer within the tent-shrine, but at the door thereof, whither Yahweh can conveniently descend from heaven in the traditional form of the pillar of cloud in order to confer with Moses.[294] [46]

The third period in the history of the *'ohel mo'ed* is, of course, that of the Priestly Code. As we have seen, the P writers began

[293] Presumably it had disappeared completely even quite some time before David; for otherwise, in the light of his Bethlehemite origin, in his organization of the national religion of the united Israel which he had called into being the *'ohel mo'ed* would certainly have played a conspicuous role, and, like the ark of Ephraim, it would undoubtedly have been brought up to Jerusalem with proper ceremony and would have been deposited in his national sanctuary there. However, we may infer that at Bethlehem the memory had persisted of the ancient tent-shrine of Yahweh, with its own peculiar name. And so when David, the Bethlehemite, with his pastoral background and his pronounced pastoral sympathies, came to erect a national sanctuary for Yahweh at Jerusalem, he made it a tent-sanctuary, although, of course, of relatively large size, patterned after what had by now become the traditional picture of the old tent-shrine of Moses; and very quickly to this national tent-sanctuary the old, traditional name came to be attached, *'ohel mo'ed.*

[294] It is not without significance that even though this J tradition of the *'ohel mo'ed* could have developed only some two centuries or more after the erection of Solomon's Temple, and at least a century and a half after the reformation of 899 B. C. had established the ark within the *d^ebir* of the Temple as the most important cult-object there, it never makes the slightest reference to the ark or suggests any connection of the *'ohel mɔ'ed* therewith. Obviously to the J writers the *'ohel mo'ed* was still merely the ancient oracular tent-shrine and nothing more, and was in no sense regarded by them, as it was by later P writers, as the forerunner or pattern of Solomon's Temple. As conceived by the J writers the *'ohel mo'ed* must have been still a comparatively simple oracular tent-shrine and naught else.

[47] their record of the *'ohel mo'ed* with direct dependence upon the older J tradition. To them it was at first not yet the dwelling-place of Yahweh, but merely the place where He would meet with His people, represented by the chief priest; and the door of the tent-shrine was still the place of meeting. Quite speedily, however, because of rapidly changing theological principles, this initial P concept of the *'ohel mo'ed* was modified and the place of meeting between Deity and priest was transferred to within the sanctuary. Hand in hand with this change went a change in the concept of the nature of the tent-sanctuary. Undoubtedly without clear realization thereof and influenced only by compelling theological considerations, the P writers returned in considerable measure to the primitive concept, and now came to represent the entire tent-sanctuary as the dwelling place of Yahweh, the *miškan*, in the midst of the people. The term, *'ohel mo'ed*, did not disappear from use completely, but more and more it was relegated to a secondary position, and *miškan* became the customary term to designate the wilderness tent-sanctuary of P. The tent-sanctuary was still the place of oracular revelation by Yahweh through the mediation of the chief priest. But the primary role of the tent-sanctuary now was as the earthly residence of Yahweh. There, within the holy of holies, He sat enthroned in invisible, eternal solitude, above the ark, between the two cherubim. It was these P writers who, for the first time, brought the ark into relationship with the *'ohel mo'ed*. For them this process was inevitable, for to them this traditional tent-shrine of the wilderness had become the pattern for the late post-exilic Temple, and but little more.

Such seems to have been the origin and the history of the *'ohel mo'ed*.

ix. Historical Survey

We have traced the evolution of the *ḳubbe* backwards from the pre-islamic period of Arab culture and religious practice through Nabataean and Syrian antecedents,[295] to the religious practice

[295] And we have even found indication of Sabaean and Ugaritic antecedents also; above, note 272.

of ancient Israel. There, in the earliest period of Israel's cultural evolution, the period of desert sojourn and of the settlement of the Israelite tribes in Palestine, we found the ephod, the historical antecedent of the *ḳubbe*, in active use. [48]

It was a simple tent-shrine, which housed the clan or tribal deities. During the desert period these were probably represented by rude betyls or sacred stones, in which the deities were thought to be embodied. Occasionally, if not regularly, an ephod housed two such betyls. It served normally as the source or instrument of oracular revelation, through the mediation of the *kohen*, the oracular priest. But in addition thereto the ephod, with the betyl or betyls therein, was regularly carried into battles of critical character in order to give promise of divine aid as well as to ensure the utmost personal heroism on the part of the clan warriors, and thus provide a maximum guarantee of victory. Furthermore, so it seems, the ephod led the clan upon its migrations in search of pasturage, or even of new territorial homes, and designated the places for the nightly encampment and for eventual permanent settlement.

The generic name, ephod, seems to have meant basically "covering," i. e., "housing." The betyls or divine symbols within the ephod seem to have been known as teraphim. Possession of the clan teraphim, or still better of the ephod which housed the teraphim, established the social position of the holder as the recognized head of the clan, while their transmission in any way from one person to another determined the right of succession to clan authority and leadership.

Apparently every Israelite ephod, precisely like the later Arabic *ḳubbe*, was made of red leather. As Lammens has shown,[296] the practice of making utensils for both sacred and profane use out of leather was among the pre-islamic Arabs of great antiquity and undoubtedly reflected the very earliest Semitic practice. The import of the red color of both ephod and *ḳubbe* is not at all clear.[297]

Each clan, and eventually each tribe, had its own ephod, so it seems. Some significant occasion in the life of the clan or tribe,

[296] *Op. cit.* 128–130.
[297] Cf. above, p. 67.

[49] and particularly, in the case of a tribe, its being called into being, because of some momentous experience, such as a great victory and a great deliverance, and especially when this resulted in a fusion of smaller clan elements and the emergence of a larger ethnic unit therefrom, justified the fabrication of an ephod, with its betyls housed within it. Each ephod, and accordingly therefore each clan or tribe, had its own *kohen*.

Apparently in the very earliest stages of the cultural evolution of the primitive Semites, the ephod, together with the teraphim within it, were of no great size and weight, not too great to be carried conveniently either by a man, or else by two men, or else upon the back of an ass. The development of camel-culture among the early Semites, whenever that may have begun, provided, of course, a new manner of transportation, and so permitted the development of ephods, and of the teraphim within them, of larger size and weight. This, in turn, allowed some minor variation in external form and appearance of individual ephods, although the general tent-form seems to have been scrupulously adhered to. With this different ephods came to have individuality and to acquire distinctive names, such as *'^{a}ron Yahweh* and *'ohel mo'ed*.

The settlement of the Israelite tribes in Palestine naturally effected a gradual modification of the tent-shrine and its cult. Speedily, of course, the clans and tribes ceased to wander and settled down in fixed dwelling-places. More and more they abandoned their former pastoral life, especially in central and northern Palestine, and adapted themselves to agricultural civilization. Steadily their native, pastoral deity, Yahweh, was syncretized with the Canaanite *b^{e}'alim*, and, particularly after the decisive Battle of Taanach, old, established Canaanite shrines became centers of Yahweh-worship. This worship was still nominally Yahweh-worship; but inasmuch as the blessings of nature which were now needed above all else, and which the deity was expected to provide, were of agricultural character, actually this nominal Yahweh-worship became increasingly Baal-worship in performance. The name was still the name of Yahweh, but the rites were in steadily expanding measure the rites of Baal. More and more the pre-Palestinian, pastoral character of Israelite worship sank into the background, and the institutions and cult-objects thereof tended to fall into disregard and constantly diminishing use. [50]

Now, as was quite natural, the ephod, together with the teraphim which it housed, became less and less a shrine in itself. Rather it tended to become merely another cult-object, a cult-object which, like all other cult-objects, was itself housed in a fixed sanctuary. Thus we find the ark housed in the sanctuary at Shiloh, the ephod of Benjamin housed in the sanctuary at Nob, and as, as is clearly implied, the ephod of Micah, the Ephraimite, eventually housed in the sanctuary at Dan.

More and more too the teraphim within the ephod ceased to be rude, unformed betyls and came to be instead images, usually no doubt in human form, carved out of wood or stone (*peśel*) or made of, or at least overlaid with, silver or gold (*maś-śekah*).

Gradually too the functions of the ephod declined in frequency and scope. With the permanent settlement in Palestine the role of the tent-shrine as the guide upon clan or tribal migrations naturally ceased immediately. The function of the tent-shrine in battle, as the guarantee of victory, persisted longer; but we hear of it in this role for the last time during the reign of David,[298] and never again thereafter. By this time, so it would seem, the ephod and teraphim had become a fixed, immovable cult-object in the various major sanctuaries of the land and had lost completely its primary character as a transportable shrine. Apparently the oracular function of the ephod and of the teraphim within it persisted longest, even down to the time of Hosea;[299] but with the Deuteronomic reformation, as was but natural, despite their pastoral origin the teraphim fell into disrepute even as oracular instruments, and came to be regarded as ordinary idols and nothing more.[300] Perhaps the last direct effect of the old tent-shrine as the basic cult-institution in the earliest worship of Yahweh may be seen in David's erection of his national sanctuary, under the persistent influence of the

[298] II Sam. 11.11.

[299] Hos. 3.4.

[300] II Ki. 23.24; Zech. 10.2; notice that in both these passages the teraphim appear merely as instruments of divination and nothing more.

[51] pastoral background of his boyhood, as a tent-sanctuary, a tent-shrine; however, no longer of the old, simple type, but rather a temple, which, as we have seen, became the permanent repository of various old tribal ephods and cult-objects. Yet it was in a sense an ephod too, the last and, physically, the greatest of the ephods, a tent-shrine erected on the memorable occasion of the fusion of all the tribes into one, unified nation, and as the symbol of the calling into existence of the deity of that nation, the national Yahweh of Israel.

As has been said, the erection of the Temple of Solomon marked the beginning of a new era in the life of Israel in all its aspects, political, cultural, economic, social and religious. The period of purposed and aggressive religious syncretism in Israel had begun. The period of pastoral religion and desert culture was now definitely ended. The consciousness of desert, pastoral origins and antecedents persisted only in the minds of the prophets and of the shepherd population in the extreme South. It persisted as a memory, growing steadily vaguer with each passing generation, as an ideal of the true Yahweh-life and worship and as a hope for its eventual revival; a hope never to be realized, yet the dream of which, with all its implications of true democracy and social justice, could never be uprooted completely from the spirit of the people of Israel, even down to the present day. In this new era, and almost at its very beginning, the old Ephraimite "box of Yahweh" was transformed into the most important cult-object in the Temple at Jerusalem, and thereafter continued to play a significant role in Israelite religious tradition.[301] The "tent of meeting" had, so it would seem, disappeared completely even long before this; but its memory persisted, no doubt with gradual transformation of many of its essential details; and, as we have learned, the tradition of it exerted a potent influence upon the religious program of the post-exilic Priestly reformers. All other ancient tent-shrines disappeared completely.[302] The ephod in Israel had practically ceased

[301] Cf. "Amos Studies, III," 100–134.

[302] According to Jud. 18.30 the ephod and teraphim continued to function actively as one of the chief cult-objects of the important Northern sanctuary at Dan until the Assyrian conquest in 732 B. C.

to be, ceased to be because culturally by the time of Solomon [52]
it had become completely outgrown.

It is our hope that this study may have revealed somewhat of the nature of the original Yahweh, as a desert, pastoral deity, of the character and manner of His earliest worship, of its evolution and that of its cult-objects and institutions during the earliest period of Israel's sojourn in Palestine, and of its gradual transformation during subsequent periods.

www.ingramcontent.com/pod-product-compliance
Lightning Source LLC
Chambersburg PA
CBHW050814160426
43192CB00010B/1762
* 9 7 8 1 7 2 5 2 9 3 1 0 6 *